T0304121

The Development of Economics in Japan

This book covers the development of economics in Japan from the inter-war period to the 2000s, focusing on the international theoretical contributions of Japanese economists. The first focal point is the international contributions of Japanese economists before and after World War II. The second focal point is the controversies concerning macroeconomic policies in Japan in the period of the 'Great Depressions' in the 1930s and the period of Japanese 'Great Stagnation' in the 1990s and the early 2000s.

In short, economics in Japan is considered from both a theoretical and a policy-oriented point of view. The intimate relationship between economic theory, thought and policy is also fully examined, as well as the development of both academic and non-academic (practical) Japanese economics and the influence of Marx, Walras, Keynes, Fisher and Cassell.

Toichiro Asada is Professor of Economics at Chuo University, Japan.

Routledge studies in the history of economics

The Development of Economics in Japan

From the inter-war period to the 2000s

Edited by Toichiro Asada

Routledge
Taylor & Francis Group

LONDON AND NEW YORK

First published 2014
by Routledge
2 Park Square, Milton Park, Abingdon, Oxon OX14 4RN

and by Routledge
711 Third Avenue, New York, NY 10017

Routledge is an imprint of the Taylor & Francis Group, an informa business

British Library Cataloguing in Publication Data
A catalogue record for this book is available from the British Library

Library of Congress Cataloging in Publication Data
The development of economics in Japan : from the inter-war period to the 2000s / edited by Toichiro Asada.
pages cm
   1. Economics–Japan–History–20th century. 2. Economics–Japan–History–21st century. I. Asada, Toichiro, 1954–
   HB126.J2D47 2013
   330.952–dc23   2013020590

ISBN: 978-0-415-66429-5 (hbk)
ISBN: 978-1-315-86692-5 (ebk)

Typeset in Times
by Wearset Ltd, Boldon, Tyne and Wear

Contents

Figures

Tables

Contributors

Toichiro Asada is Professor of Economics at the Faculty of Economics, Chuo University, Tokyo, Japan. After he received his BA in Economics from the School of Economics and Political Sciences of Waseda University in Tokyo, he studied Economic Theory at the Graduate School of Economics at Hitotsubashi University in Tokyo, and received his MA in Economics from Hitotsubashi University. He received a PhD in Economics from Chuo University. Before he became a Professor of Economics at Chuo University, he was Associate Professor of Economics at Komazawa University in Tokyo. He was a Visiting Scholar of Economics at the New School for Social Research in New York during April 1989–March 1991, and the University of Bielefeld in Germany during April 2001–March 2003. He was a Visiting Professor of Economics at University of Technology Sydney from September 2009 to March 2010. He has published many papers in economic theory in academic journals such as the *Journal of Economics*, *Journal of Macroeconomics*, *Journal of Economic Behavior and Organization*, and *Structural Change and Economic Dynamics*. His books include *Open Economy Macrodynamics* (Springer, 2003) and *Monetary Macrodynamics* (Routledge, 2010), both of which are joint books with C. Chiarella, P. Flaschel and R. Franke.

Toshiaki Hirai is Emeritus Professor at Sophia University, Tokyo, Japan. He graduated from The Graduate School of Economics, The University of Tokyo. He is a former Professor of Economics, Sophia University, Tokyo, Japan. He works mainly on the history of economic doctrines (e.g. Keynes's economics, the Cambridge economists and the Wicksell Connection). His books include *Keynes's Theoretical Development* (Routledge, 2008), *The Return to Keynes* (co-editor, The Belknap Press of Harvard University Press, 2010) and *Keynesian Reflections* (co-editor, Oxford University Press, 2013). He is a contributor to the *Journal of the History of Economic Thought, European Journal of the History of Economic Thought, History of Economics* and *History of Economic Ideas*. Recently he has been studying globalization in relation to social philosophy.

Asahi Noguchi is Professor of the School of Economics at Senshu University in Kawasaki, Japan. He studied at the Graduate School of Economics, University of Tokyo. His research topics cover a variety of areas related to international economics, history of economic theory and economic policy. He has written numerous Japanese books and published articles in both Japanese and English on these topics. Recent articles include 'Shifting Domestic and International Perceptions of Japan's Economy' (*Japanese Journal of Political Science*, Volume 13, Part 2, June 2012) and 'The State of Macroeconomics in View of the Global Economic Crisis', in *Keynesian Reflections: Effective Demand, Money, Finance, and Policies in the Crisis* (edited by Toshiaki Hirai, Maria Cristina Marcuzzo and Perry Mehrling; Oxford University Press, 2013). He also edited a book titled *Studies in Economic Policymaking: Preconceived Ideas versus Economics* (in Japanese) (Nakanishiya, 2007).

Masazumi Wakatabe is Professor of Economics, Faculty of Political Science and Economics, Waseda University, Tokyo, Japan. He graduated from Waseda University, and studied at the University of Toronto. He works mainly on the relationship between economics and policy during economic crises. His books, all in Japanese, include *Economists' Battles* (Toyo Keizai Shimpo sha, 2003), *The Showa Depression* (edited by Kikuo Iwata, Toyo Kezai Shimpo sha, 2004; awarded the Nikkei Prize for Excellent Books in Economics), *The Economics of Reform* (Diamond sya, 2005) and *Economic Crises and Policy Responses* (Nihon Hyoron Sya, 2009; awarded the Ishibashi Tanzan Prize). Recently he published *The Anatomy of Abenomics* (Nihon Keizai Shimbun sha, 2013).

Preface

This book consists of six essays on the development of economics in Japan from the inter-war period to the 2000s. In this sense, the book covers some topics on the history of economic thought in Japan. However, we do not intend to provide an exhaustive survey on the development of economic thought in Japan. Instead, we focus on the controversies surrounding the practical macroeconomic policy in Japan, as well as the international contributions of Japanese economists before and after World War II. Our approach is historical as well as theoretical.

For the convenience of readers who are not accustomed to the related topics, we provide a General Introduction, which explains the detailed background of the essays. We hope that this book helps shed some light on the academic research of the development of economic thought in Japan.

October 2013
Toichiro Asada, Tokyo, Japan

General introduction

Toichiro Asada

The distinctive feature of this book

This book covers the development of economics in Japan from the inter-war period to the 2000s, focusing on the international theoretical contributions of Japanese economists as well as the practical macroeconomic policy controversies before World War II and the 1990s–2000s in Japan, which were largely influenced by western economic thought and theories.

In this book, we focus on two topics. The first focal point is the international contributions of Japanese economists before and after World War II (Chapters 1, 2 and 3). The second focal point is the controversies concerning macroeconomic policies in Japan in the period of the 'Great Depressions' in the 1930s and the period of Japanese 'Great Stagnation' in the 1990s and the 2000s (Chapters 1, 4, 5 and 6). In other words, we consider economics in Japan from both theoretical and policy-oriented views, and we study how economic theory, economic thought and economic policy are intimately related to each other in Japan. We also consider how the development of both academic and non-academic (practical) Japanese economics was influenced by the economic theory and economic thought which originated in western countries—for example, the economics of Marx, Walras, Keynes, Fisher, Cassel, etc. Our study will shed some light on the general understanding of the dynamic interaction between economic thought, economic theory and practical economics showing up the experiences in Japan. This means that the range of our study is beyond the mere examination of economics in Japan.[1]

Part I: From the inter-war period to the 1970s

Part I consists of three chapters that study the theoretical development of Japanese economics from the inter-war period to the 1970s.

Chapter 1, 'The lost thirteen years: the return to the gold standard controversy in Japan, 1919–1932' (by M. Wakatabe), explores the relationships between economic ideas and economic policies during the period up to, and including, the Showa Depression, the Japanese equivalent of the Great Depression, paying particular attention to the gold standard controversy. The controversy over the return to the gold standard was one of the most vigorous debates in the history of Japanese economic policy making. The controversy was quite significant, and even epoch-making, in two senses. First, it was a major 'macroeconomic' debate in prewar Japan, before the term 'macroeconomics' was even coined. Second, the significance of the gold standard has recently been stressed as a pretext of the Great Depression in the literature. The chapter also emphasizes the intricate role of non-academic economists, such as Tanzan Ishibashi and Kamekichi Taka-hashi. Those economic journalists, though remaining in minority positions, followed the arguments of contemporary economists such as Cassel, Fisher, Hawtrey and Keynes carefully, arguing strongly against the return at the old parity, which required deflationary policy. Also with the crisis deepening and prices falling, they advocated the re-suspension of the gold standard, and reflation policy to restore the pre-crisis level. This chapter shows that Japanese economists, broadly defined, could apply theory to the policy discussions skillfully.

Chapter 2, 'Prof. Aoyama's study on Robertson and Keynes in interwar Japan in comparison with my interpretation: "with or without" Dynamic General Equilibrium Theory (DGET)' (by T. Hirai), concentrates on the theoretical contributions of Hideo Aoyama (1910–1992), who was one of the leading theoretical economists during the inter-war period in Japan on Walrasian general equilibrium (WGE) and Keynes's economics (KE). Aoyama, Professor at Kyoto University, has some claim to a creditable place in the history of economic thought as a Japanese scholar who studied the Cambridge School and the Stockholm School at the highest level during the inter-war period. His ingenious argument on Robertson's theory and Keynes's theory in relation to the theories of the Wicksell Connection and WGE is impressive from a historical as well as a theoretical point of view. This chapter has two objectives. One is to examine the study of Robertson and Keynes conducted by Aoyama concentrating on his activities in the inter-war period, and the other is to present the author's own study in the same sphere for the sake of comparison. In this chapter, Hirai juxtaposes Aoyama's interpretation together with his own interpretation of Robertson's trade cycle theory, Walrasian general equilibrium theory and the Wicksell Connection, and Keynes's theory, including the *Treatise* (1930) and the *General Theory* (1936).

Chapter 3, 'Japanese contributions to dynamic economic theories from the 1940s to the 1970s: a historical survey' (by T. Asada), focuses on the international theoretical contributions of the Japanese economists to the development of the dynamic economic theories after World War II up to the 1970s. Until the end of World War II, Japan was purely an importer of economic theory and had very little to export, except a few important exceptional contributions, such as Kei Shibata's contribution to Marxian economics and Walrasian/Casselian general equilibrium analysis, and Masazo Sono's contribution to mathematical consumer theory. However, the situation dramatically changed soon after World War II, especially in the research area of mathematical economics. In this chapter, the author surveys the international contributions of some distinguished Japanese theoretical/mathematical economists of the first generation after World War II, especially focusing on the development of dynamic economic theories from the 1940s to the 1970s. The author takes up the theoretical contributions by Takuma Yasui, Michio Morishima, Hirofumi Uzawa, Takashi Negishi, Nobuo Okishio and Hukukane Nikaido.

Part II: Economics of the lost twenty years in Japan from the 1990s to the 2000s

Part II consists of three historical and theoretical chapters that are related to the 'deflationary depression' of the Japanese economy from the 1990s to the 2000s, which is called the 'lost twenty years'.

Chapter 4, 'Controversies regarding monetary policy and deflation in Japan from the 1990s to the early 2000s' (by A. Noguchi), discusses the monetary policy controversies in the period of the Japanese deflationary depression. Japan's economy went through an unprecedented long period of stagnation during the 1990s. After the burst of the bubble at the beginning of the 1990s, asset prices started to decline rapidly, as well as the economy itself. Partly due to the appreciation of the yen, the CPI increase rate dropped to the negative range in the middle of the 1990s. Although the inflation rate did recover slightly for a short period of time from 1996 to 1997, the economic downswing in late 1997 put Japan's economy almost in a continuous state of deflation. This downslide in the consumer price became so serious that the Bank of Japan (BOJ) decided to reduce the overnight call rate, the operational target of monetary policy, close to zero, which was called the zero interest rate policy. CPI declines and asset-price declines continued despite the zero interest rate policy, and in particular after the suspension of the zero interest policy in August 2000, which was decided after heated debates. Eventually, BOJ was forced into an unprecedented policy of monetary expansion called 'quantitative easing' in May 2001. Japan's deepening price deflation was accompanied by the stagnation of the real economy, such as declines in the real growth rate as well as nominal growth rate and increase in the rate of unemployment. The phrase 'Japan's lost decade', which was later called 'Japan's lost twenty years', depicts the situation quite accurately. This situation caused serious debate among numerous Japanese scholars and economists on monetary policy and deflation in Japan during the period from the 1990s to the 2000s. In this chapter, the author surveys the 'money supply controversy' in the early 1990s, the 'deflation controversy', which argued whether deflation was good or bad, and the controversy relating to the 'liquidity trap', and provides an appraisal of actual monetary policy taken by the BOJ, as well as addressing some lessons for similar situations in the near future.

Chapter 5, 'Is there any cultural difference in economics?: Keynesianism and monetarism in Japan' (by M. Wakatabe), studies the cultural background of the improper macroeconomic policy in Japan, which caused the 'lost twenty years' of the Japanese economy that accompanied the deflationary depression. The author argues that there are some cultural components to the reception of economic ideas. He focuses on economic ideas which influence economic policy. In particular, he concentrates on Keynesianism and monetarism in Japan. Needless to say, both ideas were created outside Japan. He emphasizes that the cultural difference between Japan and the western countries caused different interpretations of economic ideas such as Keynesianism and monetarism. He argues that Keynesian economics in Japan was strongly influenced by Marxism and developmentalism, and monetarism was not only the minority but was also vilified in the academic circle of economics in Japan. He argues that such a particular cultural background can explain why the majority of Japanese economists have the following biases irrespective of their ideological differences: (1) no widespread support for expansionary macroeconomic policy (austerity bias); (2) neglect of the monetary factor's influence on the nominal economic variables, such as the rate of inflation, as well as real economic variables, such as the real growth rate and the rate of unemployment, and the resulting neglect of the usefulness of the monetary policy (non-monetary bias); (3) adherence to the so-called 'structural reform', which is not a well-defined concept (structuralist bias).

Chapter 6, 'Macrodynamics of deflationary depression: a Japanese perspective' (by T. Asada), tries to develop an original mathematical macrodynamic model that can interpret deflationary depression in Japan during the 1990s and 2000s. This chapter is a supplement to Chapter 4 by A. Noguchi, which surveys the debate on monetary policy and deflation in Japan since the 1990s among Japanese economists. The first part of this chapter presents the following five 'stylized facts' that characterize the 'lost twenty years' with deflationary depression in Japan (1990s–2000s). (1) The ratio of the gross nominal balance of the national debt to the nominal GDP (B_N / Y_N) increased sharply. (2) The nominal government investment expenditure (G_N^K) decreased rapidly and the nominal government consumption expenditure (G_N^C) had the tendency to increase, but the nominal total government expenditure $(G_N = G_N^K + G_N^C)$ had the tendency to decrease. (3) The nominal GDP (Y_N) was stagnant. (4) The growth rate of nominal money supply (μ) was quite low—that is, only about 2 percent per year in this period in contrast to about 10 percent per year in the 1980s. (5) The traditional negatively sloped Phillips curve, which shows the negative correlation between the rate of unemployment and the rate of price inflation, is quite well suited to the Japanese economy in this period. Then, the author presents a formal dynamic model that is consistent with the above 'stylized facts', which can interpret why the monetary and fiscal authorities in Japan failed to stabilize the Japanese economy at the normal growth path with normal employment. The author constructs a mathematical model that is called 'high-dimensional Keynesian nonlinear macrodynamic model' with capital accumulation, variable prices, variable rate of employment and variable inflation expectations to study what is the appropriate fiscal and monetary policy mix. Incidentally, 'high-dimensional' dynamic model implies the dynamic model with many variables. It is concluded that the Japanese monetary and fiscal policy mix by Japanese monetary and fiscal authorities in this period was so inappropriate that the deflationary depression was caused. In the final part of the chapter, the author presents an analytical critique of the 'New Keynesian' dynamic theory in contrast to the traditional 'Old Keynesian' dynamic theory that is adopted in this chapter.

Historical background to Part II: Japan's lost twenty years

Next, let us summarize the historical background of Part II of this book for the convenience of readers.[2]

Figure I.1 shows Japan's Phillips curve for the 28-year period from 1980 until immediately before the subprime mortgage crisis in 2007, which began in the United States. A Phillips curve represents the relationship between the unemployment rate and the rate of inflation (rate of increase in consumer price index). As shown in the figure, the 'completely unemployment rate' was at the 2 percent level during the 1980s, a period with a continued mild annual inflation rate of about 2 percent. Conversely, the 'completely unemployment rate' was around 5 percent during the 2000s, a period when the rate of inflation fell to a mild annual deflation rate of approximately −1 percent. Compared to the indices in Europe and the United States, Japan's 'completely unemployment rate' index is biased towards showing an extremely low unemployment rate. Differences aside, it is important to note that Japan's unemployment rate in the 2000s was nearly double the unemployment rate in the 1980s when measured using the same index. Furthermore, the rate of inflation increased by approximately 2 percent in the one-year period from 1996 to 1997. This increase reflected the fact that consumption tax was raised by 2 percent (from 3 percent to 5 percent) by the administration of Prime Minister Ryutaro Hashimoto. In effect, this furthered the worsening of the subsequent deflationary depression.

As shown, the Japanese economy during the 2000s fell into long-term stagnation, associated with a mild and sustained decrease in prices (deflation) of around 1 percent annually. The increase in the unemployment rate was not the only index

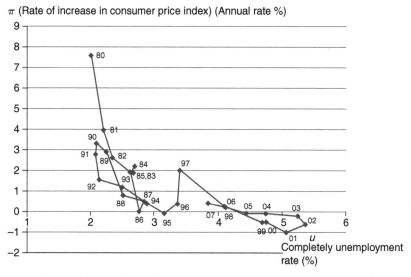

Figure I.1 Japan's Phillips curve (1980–2007) (source: Asada 2013; original data source is the Cabinet Office of the Japanese Government).

which changed during this process of deflation. Figure I.2 shows the growth rate of nominal GDP (nominal growth rate), an index which shows the gross income of citizens as measured in money, and the growth rate of real GDP (real growth rate), an index for the real economic affluence of citizens. It can be seen that both of these rates decreased while moving closely in conjunction. As shown, even mild annual deflation around 1 percent has a serious impact on the nominal income of citizens, the real income of citizens and the unemployment rate.

What is the main cause of the deflationary depression which continued in Japan for twenty years? The answer is the extremely inactive monetary policy of the BOJ, which continued during these twenty years. This conclusion cannot be refuted so long as we recognize the following fact: in the mid-to-long term, the growth rate of money stock existing in a certain country has the greatest impact on the inflation rate in that country. The only institution with the ability and authority to control the growth rate of money stock is the central bank of that country.

As shown by Yoichi Takahashi (Professor of Kaetsu University, Tokyo), there is a close statistical relationship between the inflation rate and the growth rate of the money stock in each country. In the 2000s, both the inflation rate and the money stock growth rate of Japan were extremely low when compared to other countries in the same period. The same fact can be confirmed by looking at Figure I.2. The figure shows that during the past thirty years, in the Japanese economy, the nominal growth rate (g) and the real growth rate (gR) have moved in extremely close conjunction with the growth rate (gM) of the money stock ($M2$). Additionally, the difference between g and gR ($g-gR$) in this figure shows the rate of increase in the GDP deflator (the inflation rate measured by a certain type of index). In other words, g is greater than gR during periods of inflation,

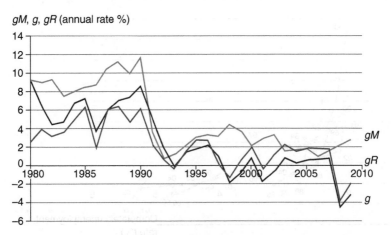

Figure I.2 Growth rate (gM) of money stock ($M2$), nominal growth rate (g) and real growth rate (gR) (source: Asada 2013; original data source is the Cabinet Office of the Japanese Government).

while *g* is less than *gR* during periods of deflation. This figure shows that, in the 1980s, an average annual money stock growth rate of approximately 10 percent supported an average annual nominal growth rate of approximately 6 percent, an average annual real growth rate of approximately 4 percent and an average annual inflation rate of approximately 2 percent. Conversely, from 1990 to 1993, it can be seen that there was a rapid decrease in the nominal growth rate and the real growth rate, which was triggered by a rapid decrease in the money stock growth rate due to monetary tightening that was implemented by the Bank of Japan with the intention of suppressing the economic bubble. Furthermore, as shown in Figure I.1, the inflation rate fell and the unemployment rate increased during this process. For about a twenty-year period beginning from the 1990s, the Bank of Japan suppressed the money stock growth rate to an annual rate of around 2 percent. This was only one-fifth of the growth rate during the 1980s. As a result, the average nominal growth rate was an annual rate of about −0.7 percent, the average real growth rate was an annual rate of about 0.6 percent and the average inflation rate was an annual rate of about −1.3 percent.

In other words, the extremely inactive monetary policy by the Bank of Japan established the 'lost twenty years' with deflationary depression. In Figure I.2, the falling economy in 1997 was due to the increase in consumption tax, while the rapid decline in 2008 was due to the global financial crisis triggered by the sub-prime mortgage crisis, which started in the United States. Excluding these declines which were caused by factors other than the Bank of Japan's monetary policy, changes in the growth rate of money stock show a time lag of about one to two years, following changes in the nominal growth rate and real growth rate.

The highest nominal GDP ever recorded by Japan was 521 trillion yen in 1997. Even in 2010, a year in which the Japanese economy had yet to be affected by the 2011 Great East Japan Earthquake, the nominal GDP had declined to 480 trillion yen, a decrease of 41 trillion yen when compared to 1997. If Japan's nominal GDP had continued to grow from 1997 at the annual rate of 4 percent, which is the average for OECD countries, Japan's nominal GDP in 2010 would be about 870 trillion yen.[3] In such a case, Japan would be free from currently developing problems such as the shortage of tax revenue, the rapid increase in the ratio of government debt to GDP and shortages of financial resources for social insurance and social security. The Ministry of Finance would then have no pretense for raising consumption tax.

Misunderstandings of the cause of deflation in Japan

During the period of deflationary depression in Japan, some parties (including the Bank of Japan, a directly interested party) insisted that the Bank of Japan's monetary policy was not responsible for deflation. They tended to assert that the inflation rate is mainly decided by something other than money; in other words, something other than the monetary policy of a central bank. Most influential is the 'declining population deflation hypothesis' that was disseminated by Kosuke Motani (Senior Counselor to the Development Bank of Japan).

This hypothesis states that deflation is caused by the decreased birthrate and aging population due to a declining population. This hypothesis was even used in a lecture given by the Bank of Japan Governor Masaaki Shirakawa. However, there is actually no relationship between the inflation rate and population growth rate of countries. This has been indicated based on statistical data by Kikuo Iwata (Professor of Gakushuin University in Tokyo until March 2013) and Yoichi Takahashi.

Next, let us consider the theory that deflation is caused by a rising yen. It is true that a rising yen causes a decrease in domestic prices for imported goods, which in turn encourages deflation. However, as pointed out by Koichi Hamada (Professor Emeritus, Yale University), according to the monetary approach of international macroeconomics, mid-to-long-term fluctuations in the exchange rate are caused by the relative ratio of the money stock existing in countries. In other words, the currency of a country which has increased (decreased) its money stock relative to another currency will fall (rise) relatively when compared to the currency of other countries. There is empirical support for this theory. That is, the cause of a rapidly rising yen following the 2008 subprime mortgage crisis is that the Bank of Japan's monetary easing was extremely insufficient when compared to the central banks of other countries (particularly the United States). Ultimately, the cause of deflation and the cause of a rising yen is the same.

Regime change of Japanese monetary policy in 2013

Now we are in a position to refer to the drastic regime change of Japanese monetary policy just before the completion of this book, which is due to the change of government.

In the Japanese Lower House general election, which was held on December 16, 2012, the LDP (Liberal Democratic Party), led by President Shinzo Abe, increased its number of seats by 2.5 times compared with prior to the election, thus capturing more than half the seats in the Lower House. The LDP formed a coalition government with the New Komeito Party, which gave the two parties more than two-thirds of the seats in the Lower House. This ensured that Abe became the Prime Minister and led the Japanese Government for a second time in January 2013. Prior to the election, the DPJ (Democratic Party of Japan) was the ruling party. However, in a crushing defeat, the seats held by the DPJ fell to one-fourth of the number prior to the election. Ultimately, the elimination of nuclear power and amendment of the Japanese constitution failed to become major issues in the election. Instead, attention was given to economic measures, especially monetary policy.

The manifesto of President Abe's LDP for this election declared the following goals: 'Clearly set an annual price escalation target (inflation target) of 2 percent, create a mechanism for strengthening the partnership between the government and the Bank of Japan while considering amendment of the Bank of Japan Act, and seek to break away from deflation and a rising yen through bold monetary easing.' Although similar measures have previously been proposed by Your Party, it was the first time in Japan that such measures had been directly released as a manifesto by a major political party which had a good chance of becoming the ruling party. As a result, monetary policy arose as a major issue for the first time in the history of Japan's general elections. This is worthy of being noted as a revolutionary development.[4] Although the Bank of Japan has made absolutely no attempt to implement such a monetary policy, in fact it is nothing more than global standard monetary policy which is normally implemented by America's Federal Reserve Board and the central banks of advanced countries other than Japan. Soon after the establishment of the Abe administration, the word 'Abenomics', which describes the economic policy of the new government, became internationally well known.

Koichi Hamada, Haruhiko Kuroda and Kikuo Iwata are three key persons for the monetary policy of 'Abenomics'. Hamada was appointed as Special Adviser to the Cabinet (Economic Adviser) in December 2012 in order to advise the new Cabinet on economic measures, especially monetary policy. Kuroda was appointed as the Governor of the Bank of Japan, and Iwata was appointed as one of two Deputy Governors of the Bank of Japan in March 2013. All of them were quite active during the period of the 'lost twenty years' in Japan, as the eager proponents of the 'reflation policy', which aims at recovery from the deflationary depression by means of the central bank's inflation targeting of about 2 or 3 percent annual rate of inflation, although their proposal was totally neglected by both the Japanese government and the Bank of Japan during such a long period of fifteen years up to 2012. In other words, the core part of 'Abenomics' is the drastic regime change of the Bank of Japan's monetary policy that is based on reflation. This bold economic experimentation in Japan is in process at the time of writing in 2013. In the near future, probably in two or three years' time, the researchers of modern economic history and modern economic thought will be able to evaluate the result of this quite exciting ongoing experimentation in Japan objectively.

Acknowledgment

Publication of this book was financially supported by JSHET (Japanese Society for the History of Economic Thought) and the Japan Society for the Promotion of Science (Grant-in Aid (C) 25380238).

Notes

1 This does not mean that the treatment of economics in Japan in this book is exhaustive. For example, Ikeo (ed.) (2000) and Kurz, Nishizawa and Tribe (eds.) (2011) contain the topics of economics in Japan which are not examined in this book.
2 This section and the next two sections are based on Asada (2013). I am grateful to the public relations office of Chuo University for permitting me to utilize the materials that are contained in Asada (2013).
3 $(521)(1.04)^{13} \cong 870$.

4 Although I do not personally support the LDP's nuclear power policy and proposal to
   amend the Japanese constitution, I think that the monetary policy declared before the
   general election by President Abe's administration is fundamentally correct and reasonable. It is ironic that the LDP, which is considered to be a conservative party,
   adopted the active monetary policy that is usually the policy of the liberal or left-wing
   parties in western countries, while the Japanese left-wing parties strongly opposed the
   active monetary policy, in line with American conservative camps. This fact was
   pointed out by Tadasu Matsuo (Professor of Ritsumeikan University, Japan), a
   mathematical-oriented Marxian economist who supports the reflation policy.

References

Asada, T. (2013) 'Economic basis for the monetary policy of the new administration of
   President Abe', *Chuo Online*, January 10, 2013 (www.yomiuri.co.jp/adv/chuo/dy/
   research/20130110.htm).
Ikeo, I. (ed.) (2000) *Japanese Economics and Economists since 1945*, London:
   Routledge.
Kurz, H., T. Nishizawa and K. Tribe (eds.) (2011) *The Dissemination of Economic Ideas*,
   Cheltenham: Edward Elgar.

Part I

From the inter-war period to the 1970s

1 The lost thirteen years

The return to the gold standard controversy in Japan, 1919–1932

Masazumi Wakatabe

1 Introduction: economic ideas and policy

1.1 Issue and perspective

This chapter explores the relationship between economic ideas and economic policy during the period up to, and including, the Showa Depression in Japan, paying particular attention to the return to the gold standard controversy. There has been a growing interest in the way in which a certain economic policy is determined, in a newly emerging field of positive political economy in particular, according to which policy is determined in a choice-theoretic manner in that policy makers maximize their objective functions subject to constraints.[1]

One major issue of this approach is how to specify constraints, especially information set. Though the rational expectation would presume that economic agent, policy maker for that matter, knows a 'true' theory about the economy, it cannot be applied in a straightforward manner to a real policy-making process, since, as the history of economic thought abundantly shows, theory itself evolves. This paper will concentrate on information set regarding economic policy making. From a history of economic thought perspective, one should explore what kind of theory, model, vision, or beliefs policy makers have had in various time and places.[2] It is only through the exploration that one can evaluate the validity of any policy, since a proper evaluation of any policy requires the examination of not only the effects but also the available policy alternatives.

1.2 The gold standard and its controversy

The gold standard controversy was probably the most significant economic controversy in modern Japanese history. Japan suspended the gold standard from September 12, 1917 to January 11, 1930, spanning almost thirteen years. But the controversy began on June 9, 1919 when the United States returned to the gold standard at prewar parity as the first country to return to it. Since then, the controversy continued with its focus changing, but the decision to return to it by the Hamaguchi cabinet did not end the controversy: rather it became more fiercely debated among the protagonists until the suspension by the Inukai cabinet on

December 13, 1931, and it continued even after that, with its relation to the depression and its possible remedies. The thirteen years in this chapter refer to those from 1919 to 1932.

The controversy was quite significant, even epoch-making, in two senses. First, it was a major 'macroeconomic' debate in prewar Japan, before the term 'macroeconomic' was coined; second, the significance of the gold standard has been recently stressed as a pretext of the Great Depression in the literature.

After the stalemate due to the Keynesian–Monetarist debate during the 1970s, there has been great progress in research on the Great Depression with the rise of the International View on the Great Depression, which is now a consensus.[3] The core of that consensus is the reexamination of the role of the gold standard. The gold standard requires a fixed linkage between gold and a currency of a particular country, which requires a fixed exchange rate between countries on the gold standard. There is, however, a well-known trilemma, 'irreconcilable trinity,' among three objectives of free international capital movement, stable exchange rate, and stable domestic price level: a country can maintain two objectives at once, but not all of them simultaneously. A country on the gold standard must sacrifice the stability of the domestic price level. The problem had been inherent in the system, but the restored gold standard system after World War I displayed a severe defect: the asymmetry between a country with a balance of trade surplus and one with a balance of trade deficit. A country with trade deficit was penalized by the outflow of gold from that country, but one with trade surplus was not penalized when the country sterilized the inflow of gold. A country with trade deficit had to sacrifice the domestic price level stability.

This problem was exacerbated after World War I, mainly due to the conduct of US monetary policy. Notwithstanding the major inflow of gold, the US did not pursue an expansionary policy, which required other countries, in turn, to act accordingly, since they had to maintain fixed exchange rates with the US dollar. Deflationary pressures had been accumulated through the gold standard, which contributed to a worldwide severe downturn, known as the Great Depression. More importantly, this feature of the gold standard, known as 'Golden Fetters' (Eichengreen 1992), worked as a policy framework which restricted macroeconomic policies: no country could continue an expansionary monetary policy since such a policy would be eventually restricted by the amount of gold reserves. Using the distinction between policy framework, 'policy regime,' and 'policy action,' the restored gold standard became a 'deflationary regime.'

Other features are in order. First, as Bordo and Kydland (1995) point out, the so-called classical gold standard period from the 1880s to 1914 was a kind of contingent rule, contingent in the sense that a country was allowed to leave the standard temporarily in the case of economic crises or war, assuring a certain degree of flexibility to the system. Second, during the classical period, the participation to the gold standard was considered as a 'Seal of Good Housekeeping' regarding macroeconomic performance (Bordo and Rockoff 1996; Sussman and Yafeh 2000; and Schiltz 2011). A country on the gold standard could have easier access to capital from capital-exporting countries such as Great Britain.

Along with the 'contingent' nature of the standard, it prevented any country from leaving the standard opportunistically. Therefore, it is quite understandable that, after World War I, the major contingency, most countries that went off the gold standard wanted to return to it as soon as they could. Third, the restoration of the gold standard was promoted by close cooperation by powerful central bankers, Governor Montagu Norman of the Bank of England and Governor Benjamin Strong of the New York Federal Reserve Bank in particular. It required careful cooperation and coordination among central banks to manage the prewar 'age of globalization' (James 2001). Fourth, like all institutions, there was an ideological dimension attached to the gold standard. As the system which had worked as the main pillar of the international economy for several decades, it represented something 'stable,' 'sound,' and 'good.' If such an idea is called the 'Gold Standard Ideology' (Temin 1989) or the 'Gold Standard Mentality' (Fukai 1938, 2), it would become another kind of 'fetters' which restricted the conduct of policy makers, when the maintenance of the gold standard became increasingly difficult. Fifth, there were several influential economists who pointed out the severe limitations and defects of the gold standard. In particular, the best economists of the inter-war period, Gustav Cassel of Sweden, Irving Fisher of the US, and Ralph G. Hawtrey and John Maynard Keynes of Great Britain, all recognized the defects of the gold standard, and the controversy erupted as to the desirability and possible alternatives. Indeed, what would later be called macroeconomics emerged from this controversy.[4] Therefore, the 'orthodoxy' of the gold standard was increasingly questioned in economic knowledge, and a term such as 'orthodoxy' could be quite misleading in this regard. Indeed, as Laidler (1999) shows, the inter-war period was marked by the lack of a single, dominant orthodoxy, several theories competing against each other. It was no coincidence that what was regarded most orthodox at the time was called the 'Treasury view.'

Furthermore, there were several ideas which 'fettered' the conduct of policy makers and economists alike. One notable example was liquidationism: viewing business cycles as an autonomous adjustment process, it held that any intervention to the economy was undesirable and counterproductive. There was a clear and close connection between these two sets of ideas: the gold standard presupposed an automatic adjustment mechanism, while liquidationism embodied a confidence, perhaps overconfidence, on such an adjustment mechanism.[5]

The literature on the return to the gold standard and the Showa Depression is quite extensive, most of which comments on the economic policy and thought of the day (Nakamura and Odaka 1989; Teranishi 1989; Nakamura 1989, 1997). The relationship between economic thought and policy has been discussed in detail in Takahashi (1954–5), Nakamura (1994), Cho (2001), Kanamori (1999), and Miwa (2003). Takahashi's detailed account stands out as a testimony by one of the most active participants of the controversy, but as such, caution is required. Nakamura (1994), whose first edition published in 1967, is a pioneering work on the controversy and still worth reading, while Cho (2001) provides a good account of the reactions of Marxian economists and the influence of

economic thought abroad on the controversy. Kanamori (1999) chronicles contributions of *Toyo Keizai Shimpo* (*The Oriental Economist*), the central organ of
the advocates of the new parity return. Miwa (2003), a collection of papers on
the history of economic policy of the inter-war Japan, analyzes the policy-
making process of the return to the gold standard from the viewpoint of interests.
Almost all relevant documents are collected in Nihon Ginko Chosa-kyoku
(1968). This chapter focuses on the role of two sets of ideas, the gold standard
mentality and liquidationism, in the controversy.

This chapter is organized as follows. The next section turns to the controversy
up to the decision to return in 1929. Section 3 discusses the controversy during
the Showa Depression. The end of the depression is taken up in Section 4. The
last section provides a conclusion.

2   Toward the return

2.1   The background

This section follows the controversy up to the decision to return in November,
1929. Inter-war Japan must be understood from both political and economic
aspects. From the political aspect, it was a turbulent, yet burgeoning period of
party politics in which political parties competed with each other ferociously,
and from this competition emerged two dominant parties, Seiyukai and Minseito,
toward the end of the 1920s. The electorate was still quite limited to the property
class, and corruption was rampant, but a parliamentary democracy was growing
to the extent that it became customary that the leader of the winning party at the
general election was appointed as Prime Minister by the Emperor. It is against
this background that a controversy could exert a real influence on the course of
economic policy.[6]

On the other hand, the Japanese economy had experienced a long slump and
stagnation after a boom due to World War I in which heavy industries had a
chance to develop.[7] Japan went off the gold standard in September 1917 when
the US also did so. As all other major countries returned to the gold standard,
Japanese policy makers, economists, and the general public became frustrated,
contemplating a prompt return. The frustration stemmed from the fact that the
Japanese economy had long stagnated during the 1920s, despite the fact that
there had been expansionary fiscal and monetary policies: the Seiyukai government relied on government expenditure, and the Bank of Japan lent to rescue
failed corporations. A resultant fiscal deficit and the 'abuse' of the power of the
Bank of Japan were very much criticized in the media.

2.2   Dramatis personae

The overall majority of the participants—policy makers, academic economists,
business economists, and media people—supported the return at the old parity,
which was above the ongoing exchange rate throughout the late 1920s. The most

eloquent advocate was Junnosuke Inoue, the Minister of Finance, who eventually decided on the return.[8] His acceptance of the post in the Hamaguchi cabinet was taken as a surprise, since he did not seem to support the return. But after his appointment, he wrote several pamphlets to urge a prompt return at the prewar parity. Though he was the most eloquent, other politicians also endorsed the return at the old parity. Indeed, throughout the 1920s, the necessity of the return on principle was rarely questioned, independent of party line, and the return usually meant that at the old parity. Nonetheless, the Seiyukai committed less to the restoration of the gold standard than Minseito, a difference which would matter at a critical moment of the crisis.

At the center of the decision making was the Ministry of Finance, but its government officials kept silent during the controversy, playing only a supportive role in the controversy. Though Jyuichi Tsushima, a high-ranking official who was sent to the US to negotiate loans for the preparation of the return, thought a 'little devaluation' was necessary, such an opinion did not go public. The Bank of Japan attracted more attention than the Ministry of Finance due mainly to the presence of Eigo Fukai, then Vice Governor, later to become the Governor.[9] He was an extremely intelligent person who could read several foreign languages, respecting Norman and Strong, and paying close attention to central bank cooperation. Though he had a firm belief in the gold standard, he was not unaware of severity of the downturn associated with the return at the old parity. No doubt he believed in the eventual recovery, but he nonetheless was concerned with the situation that the return was sold by politicians as a remedy for stagnation to the general public. Later he would recollect that 'misunderstanding' on the side of the general public was one of the reasons why the return failed (Fukai 1938, 322–4, 1941, 251).

The majority of the business community also supported the return at the old parity. To understand the economic thought of the business community, it is useful to examine those of Baron Seinosuke Go, Shigeaki Ikeda, and Toyotaro Yuki, the core member of Zaikai Sewa-nin (caretakers of the business community), rather than those of associations of business people, individual business firms, or conglomerates known as the Zaibatsu. As Matsuura (2002) suggests, during the 1920s, they were the key people who dealt with the problems occasioned by successive economic and financial crises. Zaikai Sewa-nin is a personal network of politically influential business people with a clear economic vision of maintaining, or reforming, the economics system. While several business associations could not reach a conclusion as to the desirability of the return, and even Zaibatsu corporations could not do so (Miwa 2003, chap. 7), those Zaikai Sewa-nin were staunch advocates of the return at the old parity.

In academia, there certainly were economists, such as Senjiro Takagi (Professor at Keio University), who received his PhD in economics at Yale under the supervision of Irving Fisher, or Sa-ichiro Takashima (Nagoya College of Commerce), who argued for the return at the new, devalued parity. But the overall majority was again in favor of the return at the prewar, old parity. For example, Seibi Hijikata (Imperial University of Tokyo) wrote *Kin Kaikin* (Hijikata 1929), in which he pointed out the deflationary effects of the return at the old parity, and he urged the government to plan for a probable increase in unemployment. In the upshot, he demanded remedies for the effect, but at the same time his proposed policy would bring about precisely that effect.

More significant were the reactions of two representative economists of the 1920s, Tokuzo Fukuda (Tokyo College of Commerce) and Hajime Kawakami (Imperial University of Kyoto).[10] Though he used to be very cautious about the return, Fukuda changed his mind around 1925, supporting the return at the old parity. The main reason, according to him, was the existence of huge 'nonperforming loans' which, he believed, made monetary policy of the Bank of Japan ineffective. A necessary policy was to promote Zaikai Seiri (liquidation of the economy). No wonder he became very critical of the advocates of the return at a new parity. They:

> want to return to the standard, without having pains which the Japanese economy should feel in due course. These pains should be felt one way or another. To avoid such pains would only prolong the solution. The important task at hand is to ease, diffuse and lessen the pains to the extent we could bear upon. The contractionary policy [of the Hamaguchi cabinet] is the most appropriate way for that purpose.
>
> (Fukuda 1930, 242)

Also he made pithy remarks on those advocates of the return at a new parity who learned much from Keynes and Cassel: 'The unemployment problem in Great Britain only applies to Great Britain, not to the rest of the world, and not to Japan at all.' The root cause of the stagnation of the Japanese economy was its *Strukturwandle* (structural change). But:

> in this country there are many of those who have a blind faith in Keynes and Cassel. As for the current problem of the return, there are those who advocate the return at the new parity, relying on Keynes' pamphlet or Professor Cassel's purchasing power parity over and over again, like the same old tune.
>
> (222–3)[11]

A more interesting case is that of Kawakami. He was one of the earliest economists who introduced Fisher into Japan during the so-called money and prices controversy in 1913–14. But he transformed himself greatly when he began devoting himself to study Marxian economics. As is revealed in his encounter with Tanzan Ishibashi, Kawakami the Marxist regarded depressions as inevitable and necessary in capitalism; therefore, 'remedies' for depressions were meaningless. Furthermore, he considered that the gold standard was essential to capitalism and its abolition was impossible within capitalism. All other Marxists, such as Shintaro Ryu, also emphasized the 'cleansing effect' of recessions and depressions.

The same is true of the media in general, and economic media in particular. In particular, major newspapers with the highest readership—*Osaka Mainichi, Tokyo Nichinichi, Osaka Asahi,* and *Tokyo Asahi*—were decidedly in favor of the return at the old parity. Most representative was the following remark by Dr. Terutomo Makino,[12] Chief of the Economic Division of *Tokyo Asahi* newspaper: 'the return to the gold standard would temporarily make the ongoing recession worse. It will be severe, but we could do nothing about it.'

2.3 Advocates of a new parity

There were, however, several people who did not think the return at the old parity 'inevitable.' They were the minority. True, there were several academicians and influential business people, such as Sanji Muto of Kanebo, Kenkichi Kagami of the Tokyo Marine Insurance, and Kota Yano of the Daiichi Life Insurance, who supported the return at the new parity. But in terms of quantity and quality, the central figures were economic journalists and commentators, called—somewhat derogatorily—the 'economists on the street' or *Toyo Keizai Shimpo* group.

The center of the group was Tanzan Ishibashi, proprietor and editor-in-chief of the weekly magazine *Toyo Keizai Shimpo* (*The Oriental Economist*) from 1924 to 1946.[13] As the editor-in-chief throughout the controversy, Ishibashi fought against two main sets of dominant economic 'ideas': the gold standard mentality and liquidationism. First, he did not think there were reasons to believe the gold standard as inherently desirable (Ishibashi 1970–2, 6, 10–11). The managed currency system was much more desirable than the gold standard. Though there were some concerns about losing discipline under the managed currency system, this problem could be dealt with by 'organizing a money controlling agency in an appropriate manner' (367). If such a 'controlling agency is not under control of the government, the value of money would be stabilized, even without the gold standard.' It also required fiscal discipline on the government's side: 'when the government is pursuing a loose fiscal policy, it is difficult to set up a controlling agency.' Second, he criticized liquidationism. In his understanding, the economic policy of the Hamaguchi cabinet was based upon the idea that boom was considered as 'empty,' 'false.' They wrongly believed that 'a sound economy and finance is created out of recessions' (7, 517–19). But recession is the 'worst sin in the human society' since the sole source of wealth, labor, was not utilized efficiently during recession. But how is the 'human society able to maintain booms'? To this question, he answered with its emphasis on the stability of the value of money: 'it is possible to maintain booms or prevent recessions, just to minimize the fluctuations of the value of money' (519).

Although Ishibashi was concerned with what would be called macroeconomic stability, he did not neglect or ignore other institutional problems. On the contrary, Ishibashi, the well-known advocate for the democratization movement throughout the period, made clear the need for reforms in a wide variety of fields. He would advocate 'further fundamental rationalization of the economy soon after the monetary system is reformed by the suspension of the gold standard' (366). The reforms should include those of 'education, local government, and industrial organization,' but 'it was essential to make stringent laws to punish irresponsible firms and banks.'

Ishibashi fought the controversy in another way. As the proprietor of the Toyo Keizai Shimpo company, Ishibashi was in a unique position to fully utilize his company for the campaign against the return at the old parity. He did not reject the opposing opinions; on the contrary, he always welcomed them, even asking people such as Kawakami to contribute to the magazine *The Oriental Economist*. But the stance of the magazine was no doubt that of anti-old parity return, as was clearly shown in 'Op-Ed' columns of the magazine, most of which Ishibashi wrote. Also with a view to disseminate the accurate information of the current status of economic knowledge abroad, the magazine frequently published translations of relevant documents by notable economists and others.[14] Also he gathered economists and journalists around him, organizing lecture tours all over Japan and holding debate conferences in many places.

The second most important figure was Kamekichi Takahashi. After having worked as a staff writer and editor of *The Oriental Economist*, he retired from the Toyo Keizai Shimpo to become a freelance economic commentator. He wrote prolifically, on almost all economic issues of the day, which in part explains inconsistencies in his work. For example, he once attributed the cause of ongoing deflation to a worldwide increase in productive capacity made possible by the re-entrance to the world market of Europe after World War I, the Soviet Union after a brief interruption due to the Russian revolution, and China, predicting the ongoing deflation to be 'permanent' (Takahashi 1931).[15] Thus, went the argument, it required 'Zaikai Seiri' to adjust the Japanese economy to bear upon deflation.

These inconsistencies notwithstanding, he nevertheless was concerned with macroeconomic stability, advocating the return at a new parity. It was Takahashi who, introducing Cassel's argument of the purchasing power parity, persuaded Ishibashi to change his mind to support the return at a new parity in 1924. In the aforementioned same book, he criticized contractionary policy of the Hamaguchi cabinet and proposed a new parity (devaluation) as a remedy for the ongoing depression.

Other notable figures were Toshie Obama and Yasuzumi Yamazaki. Obama was chief of the economic division of the *Chugai Shogyo Shimpo* (later to become *Nihon Keizai Shinbun, Japan Economic Newspaper*), then a small financial newspaper, and was known for his popular economic commentary. He changed his mind around spring 1929 after Eigo Fukai's lecture at Osaka. He became aware of 'pains,' the deflationary effects associated with the old parity return, doubtful of the validity of the old parity return as a remedy for 'stagnation' (Ogura 1955, 516). Another journalist, Yamazaki, was chief of the economic division of the *Yomiuri Shinbun*, a rapidly growing, yet small newspaper.[16]

2.4 *Focus of the controversy*

The controversy spanned a long period, with its focus shifting around. In essence, the return to the gold standard had been considered as 'the' remedy for a contemporary major economic issue, such as wide fluctuations of the exchange rate and inflation, and after the eruption of the Showa Banking Panic of 1927, it was expected as the 'fundamental remedy of stagnation.' Also there loomed large a practical consideration: many people, policy makers and economists alike, thought the return was inevitable. The issues were now the timing and the level of parity.

2.4.1 *The case for the old parity*

Why was the return at the old parity thought to be desirable? Though the reasons had shifted during the long controversy, there were mainly four reasons. First, the desirability of the exchange rate stability was rarely contested. Before the restoration, the idea of the managed currency had been floating around, but after the restoration in most countries, the possibility disappeared, and the gold standard was left as the only choice for Japan.

Second, deflation was considered desirable. The return at the old parity involved an appreciation of the yen, which necessitated contractionary fiscal and monetary policies to decrease the costs of domestic production and the general price level. The deflation was also considered as the convergence of the 'high' Japanese price level to the 'international price level' (Tokyo Shoko Kaigi Sho 1927, 2). In the background, there was a wide held concern over losing 'international competitiveness.' The deflation was thought to be desirable to regain the 'international competitiveness.' Moreover, it should be noted that memory of inflationary episodes was quite recent and vivid: Japan had experienced high inflation after World War I, and Germany and other Central European countries hyperinflation. Such a memory would play a significant role in economic policy debate.

Third, what Fukai called 'sentiment and national pride' played a significant role in the entire controversy.[17] The return to the gold standard was considered as the 'major trend all over the world': Great Britain and other pound sterling countries had already returned to it by 1925, Germany in 1924, and France in 1928. Also Japan fought World War I on the winning side, even though the Japanese war effort was quite limited. People thought that France, whose economy was devastated, could devalue, while Japan could not. Together with the gold standard mentality, the return to the standard had symbolized Japan's formal and 'proud' entrance to the international community.

Fourth, recessionary effects of the old parity return were accurately recognized among policy makers and academicians alike (e.g., Eigo Fukai and Tokuzo Fukuda). One strand of thought emphasized the necessary 'ease' for 'pains' in the form of remedy for unemployment (Hijikata 1929).[18] But as Yamazaki, a noted critic of the old parity return policy, perceptively commented, there were those who demanded recessionary measures to punish those who did well in the previous boom: 'the business community should feel pain. It has been insincere since the war time. Therefore, only through great pain, it will be rationalized' (Yamazaki 1929b, 95). Here we can discern moralistic appeal of liquidationism.

Another version of liquidationism stressed cleansing effects of not only recessions, but also financial panics. Sadatsugu Katsuta, business economist, insisted the need for a panic to liquidate the business community, maintaining the old parity at the same time. He would later declare the following during the Showa Crisis: 'I want to accelerate the great depression' (Nihon Ginko Chosa-kyoku 1968, 23, 621).

2.4.2 The case for a new parity

The new parity group argued otherwise. First, the stability of the exchange rate was quite important, and the new parity was desirable precisely for that purpose, since the return at the devalued rate which accorded the purchasing power parity was more stable than the old parity, which required an extra effort to deflate the economy.

Second, deflation was as much undesirable as inflation. This insight was most clearly expressed in Ishibashi. The longing for deflation is 'wrongheaded,' he declared (Ishibashi 1970–2, 6, 3–11). Adjustments with deflation would take a long time, dampening the profit rate and thus employment and income. As for the 'international competitiveness,' it is essential to distinguish between the internal value of a currency and the external value. It is possible to recover the so-called 'international competitiveness' by devaluation rather than deflation. Clearly, Ishibashi, often dubbed as a John Maynard Keynes in Japan, owed a great deal to contemporary economic discussions, especially those of Cassel, Fisher, Hawtrey and Keynes (Keynes 1971/1923).

Third, Yamazaki considered 'sentiment and pride' to be the 'only, most powerful argument,' perhaps because he thought that there was no economic argument for the old parity. He of course rejected it as 'unnecessary' preoccupation (Yamazaki 1929a, 148). As the case of France and other countries such as Italy and Belgium showed, the return to the gold standard with devaluation was legitimate. Japan was not devastated by the war as France was, but after almost a decade-long stagnation, and a major financial panic called the Showa Financial Panic, Yamazaki thought it advisable to return to the standard through devaluation.

Fourth, liquidationism did not hold at all: 'if the return at the old parity were leading to further industrial development, it would follow that occasional appreciation leads to industrial development. Of course, no one would believe such an absurd argument' (151–2).

Those who suffered most were industry and business people. 'It may appear to be a justice to incur sufferings to business people by the old parity return, but it is indeed an injustice' (148). Also as Ishibashi and Kamekichi Takahashi did, one could argue that there was no inconsistency between the return at the new parity and Zaikai Seiri. On the contrary, for them, it was through devaluation which would facilitate liquidation and reorganization of the economy.[19]

3 In the midst of the crisis

3.1 The onset of the depression

The Hamaguchi cabinet decided to return to the gold standard at the old parity in November 1929, and the decision was put into action in January 1930. At first, people enthusiastically welcomed the decision, and the stock market price soared. But it did not last long: the real GNP growth rate plummeted to almost 0 percent in 1931, and the unemployment rate went up.[20] It was the beginning of the Showa Depression, the Japanese counterpart of the Great Depression.

There has been an argument that the timing was not suited to the return, since it was implemented when the Great Depression began. This line of argument was precisely that of Inoue, Minister of Finance (Inoue 1930), but it was inconsistent with his original argument. For, from the liquidationist point of view, the Great Depression should have been welcomed since it would further accelerate deflation and the liquidation of the economy. Moreover, Inoue could have left the gold standard or devalued yen, if he thought the Great Depression was the major factor in recession in Japan, but he did not. In fact, Kazuo Aoki, Inoue's secretary and one of his most trusted subordinates, suggested that the opposite was the case: Inoue appeared to consider the ongoing depression as a sign of his policy having been smoothly implemented (Ando 1965, 1, 76–7).

3.2 The so-called 'remedies'

Nevertheless, the government and the business community initiated several 'remedies' for the depression. First, Zaikai Sewa-nin arranged consolidation and merger and acquisitions. At the same time, government-sponsored banks played an active part in lending loans to rescue failing firms. Shimakichi Suzuki, Governor of the Nihon Kogyo Ginko (Industrial Bank of Japan), who resisted Inoue's instructions, was replaced with Toyotaro Yuki, one of Sewa-nin and a close friend of Inoue's (Matsuura 2002, chap. 3).

In the government, the Ministry of Commerce and Industry (Shoko-sho, later to become the Ministry of Trade and Industry) gained power and importance. From 1929 to 1930, nineteen cartels were set up. Since there was no effective mechanism to punish cartel-breaking outsiders, the business community demanded the government restrict competition. Thus, the Important Industries Control Law (Juyo Sangyo Tosei Ho), a landmark law of the industrial policy of Japan, was passed in April 1931 (Hashimoto 1989, 117). The interest of the business community and that of the bureaucrats coincided at the time, though the business community was opposed to any further step toward control over it.

In this process, new ideas gained popularity, one of which was 'rationalization.' Originally a German idea, proposed by Walther Rathenau and Wichard von Moellendorff in the 1920s, it had not been noticed until the depression. Rationalization, however, in the new context was now accepted as allowing mergers and acquisitions or cartelization. The Tokyo Chamber of Commerce (Tokyo Shoko Kaigi Sho) started publishing *Industrial Rationalization Data Series* in November 1930, while Japan's Chamber of Commerce (Nihon Shoko Kaigi Sho) created a journal entitled *Industrial Rationalization* (*Sangyo Gorika*) in December 1930.

3.3 The turning point

The year 1931 marked the turning point from a recession to the worldwide depression. The major cause of the deterioration was a chain of financial and currency crises in 1931 (James 1986): as the fixed exchange rate regime, the gold standard was likely to invite currency crisis. The bankruptcy of Kredit Anstalt in May 1931 in Austria ignited the series of crises, destabilizing the German financial system, and a speculative attack began mounting on Great Britain. After a struggle lasting for a couple of months, Britain gave up defending the pound sterling, leaving the gold standard on September 21, 1931. In the United States, the Federal Reserve Board (FRB) raised its discount rate to defend the dollar, chilling the already damaged economy further.

After Great Britain, Japan became the next target of speculative attack. Inoue was determined to defend the yen, but such an act merely resulted in the rapid depletion of gold specie reserves. He morally denounced major Zaibatsu corporations for the speculative act of buying dollars in anticipation of the falling yen, and the mass media followed suit. Ironically, this denunciation would lead to terrorism against the Zaibatsu leader: Takuma Dan of the Mitsui Corporation was assassinated in 1932. The real issue was, however, not a speculative act but the fixed exchange regime. Kamekichi Takahashi rightly pointed out that a speculative attack showed a shaken confidence in the gold standard.

As was the case in Great Britain, the currency crisis left Japan with no choice but to leave the gold standard. A major difference from other countries was, however, that the controversy over the standard had not yet ended in Japan, while it had already ended in Great Britain. Also, the reaction of policy makers was quite different: Inoue refused to throw in the towel. At the same time, a group in the army led by Lt. Col. Kanji Ishihara, with a view to a radical restructuring of Japan, staged the Manchurian Incident on September 18, 1931, which many—in and outside of the government—regarded as a chance to change the policy stance. The aforementioned Aoki, close subordinate of Inoue, advised him to change the policy stance on the grounds that the irregularity of the turn of events would justify the change without any implication of the responsibility of Inoue's, urging him to abandon the gold standard, but Inoue did not take the advice (Nihon Ginko Chosa-kyoku 1968, 22, 5).

3.4 The continued controversy

The media opinion shifted drastically as the depression progressed. Those who praised the return now demanded 'remedies' for the crisis, though they did not yet endorse the devaluation, or the leaving of the gold standard. The argument for new parity did not gain wide support among the media.

The controversy over the return was ended, but it continued as one over the desirability of the suspension and devaluation. However, a liquidationist argument did not disappear even during the depression. The representative example was the debate meeting organized by *Toyo Keizai Shimpo* on September 1 and 8, 1930. The debate was published in two issues of *The Oriental Economist* (Nihon Ginko Chosa-kyoku 1968, 23, 613–31). Eight people were gathered to attend the meeting: all four advocates of the new parity return were called for, which gives an interesting impression that the new parity argument had the same weight in the controversy as others. Other participants were Katsumaro Akamatsu, secretary of the working people party Social People's Party (Syakai Taishu To), Yoshiro Yasuda, editor-in-chief of the weekly magazine *Diamond*, Katsuta, and Hisashi Morita, chief of the economic division of the daily newspaper *Jiji Shimpo*. Except Akamatsu, those people were in support of the old parity.[21]

The debate began with the assessment of a newly published pamphlet entitled *Inoue Zosho no Sakkaku* (*The Illusion of Finance Minister Inoue*) written by Sanji Muto, famous businessman turned politician and staunch advocate of the suspension and devaluation.[22] Then the discussion turned to the reliability of the Bank of Japan to conduct a proper monetary policy. Yamazaki questioned it, displaying his deep distrust of Vice Governor Fukai, who refused to accept any arguments for the new parity, while Obama and Ishibashi believed in Fukai's economic knowledge, insisting that the policy of the Bank of Japan would change as soon as the Finance Minister was replaced.[23] Then they discussed a wide variety of problems, such as the validity of devaluation as a countermeasure against deflation, the effectiveness of devaluation as a cure for depression, the relationship between inflation and liquidation, the degree and timing of implementing devaluation, and so on.

Clearly, the argument for the new parity was considered as a version of the price level stabilization policy at this moment. However, the liquidationist argument was quite persistent. Indeed Katsuta, Yasuda, and Morita insisted the necessity of liquidation during the depression, arguing against any measures or remedies. They did not necessarily oppose devaluation on principle. Katsuta in particular was quite willing to admit theoretical effects of the devaluation, while he questioned its practicality.[24] His main objection to it was, however, his belief that devaluation would jeopardize the ongoing liquidation. Therefore, according to him, even though the government had to intervene, such an intervention should be taken *after* the liquidation process. Thus he declared, 'I want to accelerate the great depression' (Nihon Ginko Chosa-kyoku 1968, 23, 621).

As several opinion polls revealed, the interest in, and support for, the suspension and devaluation increased considerably, but did not form a majority. There is the distinct possibility that the suspension and devaluation would have never gained a majority.[25]

4 Ending the crisis

4.1 Policy change

Ending the depression required a drastic policy change, which comprised of two stages, the suspension of the gold standard and the initiation of reflationary policies.[26] What made this policy change possible in Japan was ultimately the change of government. The major opposition party, Seiyukai, had a meeting of MPs, adopting a resolution advocating the suspension on November 11, 1931. The same day, however, Finance Minister Inoue declared his firm intention to maintain the gold standard.

The change of government was initiated by the resignation of the governing Wakatsuki cabinet due to inconsistencies of opinions among the ministers.[27] Kenzo Adachi, influential and skilled politician and Minister of Internal Affairs, dissented, believing the necessity of forming a coalition government with the opposition party to deal with emergencies. Adachi was a supporter of the suspension.

The opposition party formed a new government, with Tsuyoshi Inukai as Prime Minister. Korekiyo Takahashi,[28] the new Finance Minister, decided to suspend the gold standard on the same night of his appointment, December 13, 1931, taking advice from none other than Eigo Fukai (Fukai 1941, 257–64). Thus Japan left the gold standard, as most other countries had already done. However, the perception of Takahashi and Fukai was rather too optimistic, doing nothing further to stimulate the economy: while Takahashi did allow the yen to fall, he nonetheless declared that the suspension was not a countermeasure against the depression, and not a reflationary, expansionary monetary policy altogether. It took a while for him to complete the policy change.

As a result, the stock price plummeted, and the unemployment rate soared from mid-1931. The most shocking event was the assassination of Prime Minister Inukai by the military on May 15 (the 5.15 Incident). Facing such an urgent situation, the government finally decided to turn to reflation policy.

In order to make a decisive policy change, the government—the Ministry of Finance and the Bank of Japan in particular—looked for cooperation. The result was the Bank of Japan's policy of purchasing newly issued government bonds, initiated on November 16, 1932.[29] It had been about a year since the suspension of the gold standard and about six months since the 5.15 Incident.

4.2 The rise of reflationists

In this period, the controversy continued, advocates of the new parity transforming to reflationists. Now with all major countries off gold, the maintenance of the gold standard became outmoded, and the urgent issue was how to escape the depression. Reflationists demanded decisive government action in the form of further expansionary monetary and fiscal policies.

Ishibashi wrote several of his masterpieces during this period, 'The Suspension of the Gold Standard and the Increase of the Purchasing Power,' and 'The Meaning, Method and Effects of Inflation.' In the latter, he explained the necessity of certain inflation, first to rescue the current devastated money and banking situation caused by the 'lost balance between loan and debt,' and second to rescue 'useless unemployment of people and equipment' caused by stagnant production. Certain inflation was required to achieve the 'normal development of economic activities'; therefore, inflation here should not mean 'supplying more money than is required to sustain development of economic activities' (Ishibashi 1970–2, 8, 441–2). Reflation was equivalent to 'stabilizaion of prices, or inflation to offset damages caused by deflation in the past' (463).

He referred to three methods of reflation policies: first, lowering of the interest rate; second, open market operation; and third, promotion of public works. Among them, the third method was ruled out on the grounds of difficulties in establishing the proper amount and timing of public works, leaving monetary policy as the only option. Moreover, Ishibashi was aware that fiscal policy alone could not sustain inflation. An increase in government bonds, unless bought by the Bank of Japan, would not lead to an increase in money supply, which would not lead to inflation. Thus he had high hopes of using both as reflationary measures, though he considered open market operations more direct than manipulation of the interest rate.

The essence of his argument was the generation of inflationary expectation by a determined policy stance of increasing money supply. At first, it might not be easy for the effects of reflation to be felt. But a change in expectation and the effect of inflation would 'work as cause and effect to each other, in a cumulative manner' (Ishibashi 1970–2, 8, 457). For, if the expansion of money supply was continued 'in a determined manner,' no 'bank would sit idle with money indefinitely.' At first, money flew into the call market, lowering its rate, then into stocks already issued and newly issued. The purchasing power would be realized in the form of the purchase of stocks already issued, that of stocks newly issued, then that of other assets such as real estates. Seeing this process from interest rates, through lowered short-term and long-term rates, investment would be increased, which in turn would generate demand for goods and labor. Reflationists argued that 'we should continue inflation persistently until those effects are materialized' (458). Ishibashi concluded in an optimistic tone: 'it is quite logical that an increase in money supply would lead to inflation faster than one might feel in the beginning; there is no doubt about it.'[30]

In the same article, he answered criticisms of reflationary policy, one of which concerned the controllability of inflation: 'once inflation is set in motion, it should be continued forever,' which had led to hyperinflation in post-World War I Germany. Ishibashi pointed out that hyperinflation was caused only by the 'fiscal need of government in emergencies,' while there was a clear limit to the inflation he called for. This reflation is different from hyperinflation:

which was inevitable out of external causes such as war, and reflation is under the control of the government or central bank. What kind of danger is there? Those who maintain that once inflation is started it cannot stop should think harder.

(463)

4.3 Economic performance after reflation

Performance after the policy change was remarkable, to say the least. Under the so-called Takahashi fiscal policy—in fact, this should be called Takahashi Fukai monetary and fiscal policies—the economy recovered dramatically: it changed from big deflation to mild inflation, stock prices soared, and production rose at an unprecedented rate. The average inflation rate was around 2 percent per annum from 1932 to 1935, while the average annual rate of real GNP growth during the Takahashi era reached a record high of about 7 percent, which would not be broken until Japan experienced the era of rapid economic growth during the 1960s. Reflationary policy brought depreciation of the yen, which gave stimulus to stagnant heavy industries, and the industrial structure changed rapidly thereafter. Moreover, with soaring stock prices, corporate financial structure also began changing, relying more on equity finance than on bank loans. A structural change of the economy was facilitated by ending deflation.[31]

5 Concluding remarks

5.1 The Showa Depression and its aftermath: a decisive turning point

What was attempted in order to escape the Great Depression was 'socialism in many countries' (Temin 1989). State regulation, control, and intervention increased in many countries, notwithstanding Nazi Germany, the New Deal policy in the United States, and the rationalization movement in Great Britain.

Japan seemed to have escaped the depression under the leadership of Finance Minister Korekiyo Takahashi, but during the crisis, in which people sought out 'remedies,' several initiatives gained attractiveness and support among policy makers and the general public alike, the most notable one being that of the military. The invasion of Manchuria and the subsequent establishment of the puppet state there were enthusiastically welcomed by the people as the fundamental remedy of the current depression (Young 1998). Takahashi resisted such movement as much as he could, but after his assassination on February 26, 1936 by an attempted coup, the military had a free hand, initiating a movement toward a militaristic regime. Though Tanzan Ishibashi continued criticizing the military, a truly brave act under the circumstances, his efforts ended in vain.

With the demise of parliamentary politics, the bureaucracy as well as the military gained more power. Ministry of Finance officials gained more authority over the budget, while Ministry of Commerce and Industry officials gained more authority and control over industry through industrial policy. As Chalmers Johnson puts it, 'economic crisis gave birth to industrial policy' (Johnson 1982, 114).

Through the controversy over the return to the standard and the ensuing Showa Depression, the gold standard mentality and liquidationism receded, while another set of ideas, or rather 'ideologies,' emerged, among which were rationalization, state intervention of the national socialism sort, and developmentalism.[32]

5.2 Summary of the controversy

The arguments here are summarized as follows. First, the thirteen years in which the controversy was fought was, for contemporaries, the 'lost thirteen years.' During the 'stagnation' after World War I, people thought that fiscal policy became too 'loose,' fiscal deficits ballooning, and the Bank of Japan becoming a bank for rescuing already bankrupt corporations. It was mainly due to people's expectations that the return to the gold standard became *the* remedy for a long stagnation.

Second, as is usually the case with policy controversy, it had less to do with economics than it had to do with moral and 'good' values embodied in the gold standard. It is precisely because of moral appeal that Zaikai Seiri (liquidation) became a buzzword. Related to this point is the issue of 'justice': the advocates for a new parity had to fight against the popular misunderstanding that a new parity return was to rescue those who became rich during the war.

Third, past memories played an important role in the controversy. Devaluation, and later reflation policy, did not gain much popularity when high inflation home and abroad was still remembered.

Fourth, the overall majority of the political and business community, the media, and academia supported the return at the old parity. The majority of economists were preoccupied with the gold standard mentality and liquidationism. The Marxians either distanced themselves from the controversy or were preoccupied with the same sets of ideas as other more orthodox economists.

It was the advocates of a new parity return, the minority, who made the controversy worthy of its name. Though they did remain a minority to the last stage of the controversy, their influence grew as the depression worsened. This is not to say that they did not make mistakes. On the contrary: many advocates—Sanji Muto, Toshie Obama, and Yasuzumi Yamazaki—once believed in the return at the old parity. Ishibashi, the central figure, was no exception, converting to a new parity return upon the advice of Kamekichi Takahashi. More important was how they changed their mind. Though they were economic journalists, rather than academic economists, they argued as theoretically as they could: indeed they were accused by their critics of being 'too abstract, too theoretical.' They, Ishibashi in particular, did try to learn from contemporary economic arguments such as Cassel, Fisher, and Keynes.[33] Related to this, an exact understanding of the available information was crucial. The Genoa conference upheld the resolution of the return to the gold standard, but it also allowed the return at a new parity, which Japan could have adopted.[34] What prevented Japan from adopting devaluation was a preoccupation with 'sentiment and national pride,' and liquidationism.

Lastly, it is difficult to assess the extent of influence of the advocates of a new parity on the actual course of events. Though their influence should not be exaggerated, it was true that Korekiyo Takahashi had contacts with the advocates of a new parity, and learned from contemporary economic arguments such as Fisher and Keynes. In his speech on 'The International Economic Situation and Emergency Policy of our Country,' delivered on April 21, 1933, he referred to 'Mr. Fisher and the Academic Meeting held at the University of Chicago [probably the Harris Foundation Conference of 1931–2],' Keynes, Hawtrey, and the report of the Macmillan committee (Takahashi 1936, 559, 567–8, 570).

5.3 The evaluation

The evaluation depends on criteria, the content of information set. One could argue that, for example, a new trend of economic thinking, which would later be called macroeconomics, had already begun in the 1910s, in the works of Fisher, which was absorbed in Japanese academia immediately. Also economists who represented the inter-war period—Cassel, Fisher, Keynes, and Hawtrey—expressed serious doubts as to the desirability of the gold standard, pointing out the danger of pursuing the return at the cost of price instability, namely deflation. Against this background, advocates of the new parity made a better case than those of the old parity.

However, one could argue that such an understanding was not permeated: after all, the new trend was still 'new.' Moreover, there were economists who supported the return to the gold standard at the old parity in Great Britain, such as Edwin Cannan and T. E. Gregory (e.g., Gregory 1925). However, the arguments for the old parity return were confused and flawed. If the purpose of the return was stability of the exchange rate or that of price level, the new parity return would have served better. Also, since the distinction between internal and external values of a currency did not require a 'new' thinking, advocates of the old parity return made quite a basic mistake in confusing the issue in this respect.[35]

Thus one is left with 'sentiment and grace' and Zaikai Seiri (liquidation of the economy), corresponding to the gold standard mentality and liquidationism, respectively. Though both were problematic, liquidationism was particularly so, since it had a serious flaw as a prescription for policy. Liquidationism maintains that an economy should go through a 'painful' restructuring process in the short run, while it will recover and prosper 'after a while.' The problem is that it is quite unclear as to how long the restructuring process takes. Therefore, the only logical policy is no policy at all. But this could not be maintained in reality: indeed, even Inoue had to take 'remedies' to rescue selected corporations.

As DeLong (1990) argues, liquidationism might have been valid until the late nineteenth century, when business cycles had been characterized as sharp V-shape-like fluctuations.[36] The same could have been true of the gold standard, though one should bear in mind that it was managed more flexibly before World War I. The gold standard mentality and liquidationism became 'ideologies' when they were held, and even they became obsolete.

Appendix

Table 1.1 Chronology of events

Dates	World	Japan
1917	September 7: US suspended the gold standard	September 12: Suspended the gold standard, setting the embargo on gold exports
1919	June 9: US returned to the gold standard at the old parity	
1920	September: The Brussels conference	
1922	April–May: The Genoa conference	
1923		September 1: The Great Kanto Earthquake
1925	April 28: British Finance Minister Churchill gave a budget speech outlining the return to the gold standard at the old parity	
1927		March: The Showa Banking Panic
1928	June 25: France returned to the gold standard at a devalued new parity	
1929	October 24: The stock market clash of Wall Street	July 2: The Hamaguchi cabinet November 21: Cabinet decision to lift the embargo at the old parity; return to the gold standard
1930		January 11: Implementation of the decision November 14: Prime Minister Hamaguchi was shot at Tokyo Station
1931	September 21: Great Britain suspended the gold standard	September 18: The Manchurian Incident December 13: The Inukai cabinet; Finance Minister Takahashi suspended the gold standard
1932		February 8: The former Finance Minister Inoue was assassinated March 8: Takahashi announced the Bank of Japan purchase of newly issued government bonds May 15: The so-called 5.15 Incident: attempted coup by Navy officials, Prime Minister Inukai assassinated November 25: The Bank of Japan began purchasing newly issued government bonds

Acknowledgment

A preliminary version of this chapter has been presented on various occasions. I would like to thank participants at the Seminar of the Economic and Social Research Institute of the Cabinet Office of the Japanese Government, Annual Meeting of the History of Economics Society (Japan), and the Study Group on the Showa Crisis. This is part of a broader project on Economic Policy and the Economists in Economic Crises of the 1930s. Financial assistance from the Japanese Society for the Promotion of Science (No. 15530127) and the Foundation for the Encouragement of Society of the Japanese Economy, Waseda University (Research Grant for Special Research Projects, No. 2003B–002) is gratefully appreciated.

Notes

1 About the burgeoning literature, see Dixit (1996). Also see Hamada and Noguchi (2005) and the literature cited there.

2 This perspective is drawn from Laidler (2001). For a useful study on the relationship between policy makers' beliefs and policy reactions regarding post-World War II American stabilization policy, see Romer and Romer (2002).

3 For the literature, see the classic account of Eichengreen (1992). Also see Temin (1989), Bernanke (2000), James (2001), Mouré (2002), and Bordo and Filardo (2004). For a popular version of the story, see Ahamed (2009).

4 For the return to the gold standard controversy in Great Britain, see Moggridge (1972) and Pollard (1970). For Keynes's views on the gold standard, see Barkai (1993). For the development of macroeconomics in the period in general, see Laidler (1991, 1999) and Wakatabe (2005).

5 On liquidationism during the Great Depression era, see DeLong (1990), which lists Joseph A. Schumpeter, Lionel Robbins, Friedrich A. von Hayek, and Seymour Harris among the proponents. The common feature is the business cycle model in which misplaced overconfidence of the rate of return by an entrepreneur leads to investment boom, which turns into depression, as the true rate of return is revealed. With the advancement of real business cycle theory or dynamic macroeconomics, there has been a revival in liquidationism of this sort. For a critical review of the 'modern' version, see Aghion and Howitt (1998, 239–43). DeLong evaluates the 'old' version higher than the 'modern' counterpart, since the 'old' one does not depend on real, technological shocks to explain the cause of cycles. As for the empirical evidence, or lack thereof, see Cabarello and Hammour (2000). For the contrary view regarding Hayek and Robbins, see White (2008).

6 The era from 1918 to 1932 is characterized politically as a 'developing democracy' phase by Takenaka (2002).

7 The basic figures from 1915 to 1919 are as follows: the nominal growth rate per annum was 27.3 percent, the real growth rate was 7.3 percent, and the change in prices (CPI) was 14.7 percent. On the other hand, from 1920 to 1929, the nominal growth rate per annum dropped to 0.6 percent, real growth rate to 1.8 percent, and CPI to −1.6 percent. See Okada, Seiji, and Kikuo (2002). Also see Patrick's classic 1971 article. A cause for persistent deflation during the 1920s might be due to a constant deflationary pressure by the anticipated return to the gold standard at the prewar parity. See Faini and Toniolo (1992).

8 Inoue was Governor of the Bank of Japan from March 1919 to September 1923 and was also Minister of Finance for a brief period from September 1923 to January 1924.

9 Fukai served as Vice-Governor from June 1928 to June 1935, and was then promoted to Governor and remained as such until February 1937.

10 For their contributions in general, see Inoue and Yagi (1998).

11 In September 1925, Fukuda was invited to visit Moscow by the Soviet government, debating with Keynes there. Keynes, also invited, criticized the return at the old parity in a similar vein, which he espoused in *The Economic Consequences of Mr. Churchill*. Although Eli F. Hecksher of Sweden completely agreed with Keynes, Fukuda dissented, emphasizing the structural change (*Strukturwandel*) of the economy. See Fukuda (1930, Book II, Chapter 3). As is seen from his usage of a German word, Fukuda's argument is also a copy of German discussions. On German economic discussions of the day, see James (1986, Chapter IX).

12 Makino was one of a very few newspaper writers who received a Doctorate in economics from the Imperial University of Tokyo.

13 For the place of Ishibashi's thought in modern Japan, see Nolte (1987).

14 For example, the special issue on the 'Study of the Gold Standard' of the *Oriental Economist* (February 13, 1932) published translations of Fisher, Cassel, Keynes, Hawtrey, MacKenna, Kitchen, and the Macmillan committee report.

15 He referred to the deflation in late nineteenth century Europe and the US as a historical example (Takahashi 1931, 110–1).

16 In 1927, both *Chugai Shogyo Shimpo* and *Yomiuri Shinbun* sold roughly 100,000 copies each. This should be contrasted with other major newspapers: *Osaka Asahi*, 1.26 million; *Tokyo Asahi*, 400,000; *Osaka Mainichi*, 1.16 million; *Tokyo Nichinichi*, 450,000. See Yamamoto (1981, Supplementary Figure 6).

17 Fukai used the expression in his speech at the meeting of Osaka Keizai-kai, a business association located in Osaka, in November 1928.

18 To be fair to Hijikata's proposal, it should be evaluated against the fact that there was no formal unemployment insurance system in Japan at that time.

19 Takahashi (1930b), though with a sensational title, addressed corporate governance issues which had appeared with the rise of large corporations in Japan.

20 The unemployment rate was 5.3 percent in January 1931, and peaked to 7.2 percent in July 1932. These figures, though they seem to be low compared to the American figure of about 25 percent or the German one, which was even more than that, should be considered in the context of the prewar Japanese economy in which the agricultural sector was still large and the potential growth rate was high. It should also be noted that there were no consistent official data on the unemployment rate. I use the ones that Adachi (2003) reports.

21 Akamatsu spoke only twice in the debate, and did not attend the second meeting. As a left-wing socialist politician, he hoped that the deflationary crisis would give an opportunity for working people to draw concessions from the government and business people. Takahashi, who used to be a left-leaning activist-theorist, criticized Akamatsu, maintaining that the crisis only weakened the position of the working people.

22 It was no coincidence that the pamphlet was published by Toyo Keizai Shimpo Sha.

23 Fukai wrote a foreword to the Japanese translation of Irving Fisher's *Money Illusion* (Fisher 1928), whose translator was working for the Bank of Japan.

24 For Katsuta, devaluation in a deflationary economy was quite unprecedented: 'I have never heard of any country which devalued its currency in the midst of deflation.'

25 See the results of opinion polls reprinted in Nihon Ginko Chosa Kyoku (1968, Vol. 23).

26 This perspective, which accords with the recent consensus of the Great Depression literature, is drawn from Okada *et al.* (2002).

27 Former Prime Minister Hamaguchi was shot by a terrorist on November 14, 1930. He recovered for a while, but as his health deteriorated, was eventually replaced by Baron Reijiro Wakatsuki. Inoue remained as Finance Minister. Hamaguchi died in August 1931, and Inoue was assassinated in February 1932, shortly after he was ousted from the post.

28 For the life and achievements of Korekiyo Takahashi, see Smethurst (2007). This Takahashi had no relation to Kamekichi Takahashi.
29 This policy remains to this date particularly notorious, since it was abused by the government to finance military spending, especially after Takahashi's assassination. However, the policy itself was not Takahashi's invention: it had been already contemplated during the Russo-Japanese war and was again discussed in 1930 (Ide 2001). Moreover, the essence of the abuse was the seizure of power by the military: in 1934 and 1935, Takahashi resisted demands from the military.
30 Ishibashi referred to Keynes's *Treatise on Money* (1930), but his argument resembled those of Hawtrey (Hawtrey 1931). See Wakatabe (2005).
31 Some attribute the cause of recovery to the deflationary economic policy of Inoue, in that belt-tightening and crisis 'prepared' the later success of Takahashi's reflationary policy (Banno 2001, 241). Though it is not quite clear that this version of liquidationism is falsifiable, one could examine the degree of liquidation of nonperforming loans during the depression. Adachi (2004) shows the following: first, the estimated amount of 'bad loans' during the depression was about the same as that during the Showa Banking Panic; second, the causes of bad loans during the depression were more likely to be different from those during the panic; and third, bad loans during the depression were more likely to be caused by deflation. Notwithstanding difficulties of such an econometric study, it is likely that liquidation did not progress during the depression.
32 For a history of developmentalism, see Johnson (1982) and Gao (1997).
33 Their works were translated into Japanese. Ishibashi read extensively, as the list of books he read during this period abundantly testifies. See Ishibashi (1970–2, Vol. 15).
34 Cassel interpreted the resolution in that it aimed for price stabilization by returning to the gold standard, and price stabilization should not be sacrificed to the return (Cassel 1924, 174). The same is true of Hawtrey, who made it clear that 'further deflation is out of the question' (Hawtrey 1922, 303).
35 It is likely, however, that this confusion is also a part of the gold standard mentality.
36 Kamekichi Takahashi, along with Yasuzumi Yamazaki, recognized structural change of the twentieth century economy, believing that liquidational function of business cycles—what Takahashi called 'effects of boom and recession'—was considerably weakened due to the increased price and wage rigidities associated with a widespread use of large-scale production. See Takahashi (1930b, 510–14).

References

Adachi, S. (2003) 'Seisaku Tenkan no Timing (The Timing of Policy Change),' *Nihon Keizai Weekly* (*Economic Research Japan*), Tokyo Branch, CSFB, No. 129 (in Japanese).

Adachi, S. (2004) 'Bad Loan Problem and the Transformation of the Financial System in the Showa Crisis,' in K. Iwata (ed.) *Showa Kyoko no Kenkyu* (*Studies on the Showa Depression*), Tokyo: Toyo Keizai Shimpo Sha, pp. 219–48 (in Japanese).

Aghion, P. and P. Howitt (1998) *Endogenous Growth Theory*, Cambridge, Mass.: MIT Press.

Ahamed, L. (2009) *Lords of Finance: The Bankers Who Broke the World*, New York: The Penguin Press.

Ando, Y. (ed.) (1965) *Showa Keizaishi he no Syogen* (*Testimony to the Economic History of the Showa Era*), 3 vols., Tokyo: Mainichi Shinbun Sya (in Japanese).

Banno, J. (2001) *Nihon Seiji Sippai no Kenkyu* (*Studies of Failures in Japanese Political History*), Tokyo: Kobosya (in Japanese).

Barkai, H. (1993) 'Productivity Patterns, Exchange Rates, and the Gold Standard Restoration Debate of the 1920s,' *History of Political Economy*, 25: 1–37.

Bernanke, B. S. (2000) *Essays on the Great Depression*, Princeton: Princeton University Press.

Bordo, M. D. and A. Filardo (2004) 'Deflation and Monetary Policy in a Historical Perspective: Remembering the Past or Being Condemned to Repeat It?' NBER Working Paper No. 10833.

Bordo, M. D. and F. E. Kydland (1995) 'The Gold Standard as a Rule: An Essay in Exploration,' *Explorations in Economic History*, 32: 423–64.

Bordo, M. D. and H. Rockoff (1996) 'The Gold Standard as a Good Housekeeping Seal of Approval,' *Journal of Economic History*, 56: 389–428.

Cabarello, R. J. and M. L. Hammour (2000) 'Creative Destruction and Development: Institutions, Crises, and Restructuring,' NBER Working Paper Series 7849.

Cassel, G. (1924) 'The Restoration of the Gold Standard,' *Economica*, 9: 171–85.

Cho, Y. (2001) *Showa Kyoko* (*The Showa Depression*), Tokyo: Iwanami Shoten (originally published in 1973, revised in 1994; in Japanese).

DeLong, J. B. (1990) '"Liquidation Cycles": Old Fashioned Real Business Cycle Theory and the Great Depression,' NBER Working Paper Series 3546.

Dixit, A. K. (1996) *The Making of Economic Policy: A Transaction-Cost Politics Perspective*, Cambridge, Mass.: MIT Press.

Eichengreen, B. (1992) *Golden Fetters: The Gold Standard and the Great Depression, 1919–1939*, New York: Oxford University Press.

Faini, R. and G. Toniolo (1992) 'Reconsidering Japanese Deflation during the 1920s,' *Explorations in Economic History*, 29: 121–43.

Fisher, I. (1928) *The Money Illusion*, New York: Aldelphi Company.

Fukai, E. (1938) *Kin Honni Sei ridatsu go no Tsuka Seisaku* (*Currency Policy after Leaving the Gold Standard*), Tokyo: Chikura Shobo (in Japanese).

Fukai, E. (1941) *Kaiko 70 Nenn* (*Seventy Years in Retrospect*), Tokyo: Iwanami Shoten (in Japanese).

Fukuda, T. (1930) *Kosei Keizai Kennkyu* (*Studies on Welfare Economics*), Tokyo: Toko Syoin (in Japanese).

Gao, B. (1997) *Economic Ideology and Japanese Industrial Policy: Developmentalism from 1931 to 1965*, Cambridge: Cambridge University Press.

Gregory, T. E. (1925) *The Return to Gold*, London: E. Benn Limited.

Hamada, K. and A. Noguchi (2005) 'The Role of Preconceived Ideas in Macroeconomic Policy: Japan's Experiences in the Two Deflationary Periods,' *International Economics and Economic Policy*, 2: 101–26.

Hashimoto, J. (1989) 'Kyodai Sangyo no Bokko (The Rise of Large Scale Industries),' in T. Nakamura and K. Odaka (eds.) *Nihon Keizai Shi* (*Japanese Economic History*), vol. 6, Tokyo: Iwanami Shoten, Chapter 2 (in Japanese).

Hawtrey, R. G. (1922) 'The Genoa Resolutions on Currency,' *Economic Journal*, 32: 290–304.

Hawtrey, R. G. (1931) *Trade Depression and the Way Out*, London: Longmans, Green and Co.

Hijikata, S. (1929) *Kin Kaikin* (*Lifting the Embargo on the Gold Exports*), Tokyo: Nihon Hyoron Sya (in Japanese).

Ide, E. (2001) 'Shinkihakko no Nichiginhikiukehakko Seido wo Meguru Nihon Ginko-Ohkurasho no Seisakushiso (Policy Ideas of the BOJ and the MOF on the BOJ Purchase of Newly Issued Bonds),' *Kinyu Kenkyu* (Monetary Studies Bank of Japan), 20: 171–202 (in Japanese).

Inoue, J. (1930) *Sekai Fukeiki to Waga Kokumin no Kakugo* (*The World Depression and the Resolution of Our Nation*), Tokyo: Keizai Chishiki Sya (in Japanese).

Inoue, T. and K. Yagi (1998) 'Two Inquirers on the Divide: Tokuzo Fukuda and Hajime Kawakami,' in S. Sugihara and T. Tanaka (eds.) *Economic Thought and Modernization in Japan*, Cheltenham: Edward Elgar, Chapter 4.

Ishibashi, T. (1970–2) *Ishibashi Tanzan Zenshu* (*The Works of Tanzan Ishibashi*), Tokyo: Toyo Keizai Shimpo Sha, 15 vols (in Japanese).

James, H. (1986) *The German Slump: Politics and Economics, 1924–1936*, Oxford: Clarendon Press.

James, H. (2001) *The End of Globalization: Lessons from the Great Depression*, Cambridge: Harvard University Press.

Johnson, C. (1982) *MITI and the Japanese Miracle: The Growth of Industrial Policy, 1925–1975*, Stanford: Stanford University Press.

Kanamori, T. (1999) *Oboegaki Kin Yusyutsu Kaikinn Ronso Shi* (*Notes on the History of the Controversy over the Lifting of the Embargo on the Gold Exports*), privately circulated (in Japanese).

Keynes, J. M. (1930) *A Treatise on Money: The Pure Theory of Money*, London: Macmillan.

Keynes, J. M. (1971) *The Collected Writings of John Maynard Keynes*, vol. 4, London: Macmillan (originally published in 1923).

Laidler, D. (1991) *The Golden Age of the Quantity Theory*, New York: P. Allan.

Laidler, D. (1999) *Fabricating the Keynesian Revolution: Studies of the Inter-War Literature on Money, the Cycle, and Unemployment*, Cambridge: Cambridge University Press.

Laidler, D. (2001) 'The Role of the History of Economic Thought in Modern Macroeconomics,' Mimeo.

Matsuura, M. (2002) *Zaikai no Seiji Keizai Shi* (*The Political Influence of the Business Elites' Network in Modern Japan*), Tokyo: University of Tokyo Press (in Japanese).

Miwa, R. (2003) *Senkan Ki Nihon no Keizai Seisakusi-teki Kenkyu* (*Japanese Economic Policy in the Inter-War Period*), Tokyo: University of Tokyo Press (in Japanese).

Moggridge, D. E. (1972) *British Monetary Policy 1924–31: The Norman Conquest of $4.86*, Cambridge: Cambridge University Press.

Mouré, K. (2002) *The Gold Standard Illusion: France, the Bank of France, and the International Gold Standard, 1914–1939*, Oxford: Oxford University Press.

Nakamura, T. (1989) 'Keiki Hendo to Keizai Seisaku (Business Cycles and Economic Policy),' in T. Nakamura and K. Odaka (eds.) *Nihon Keizai Shi* (*Japanese Economic History*), vol. 6, Tokyo: Iwanami Shoten, Chapter 6 (in Japanese).

Nakamura, T. (1994) *Showa Kyoko to Keizai Seisaku* (*The Showa Crisis and Economic Policy*), Tokyo: Kodansha (in Japanese; originally published in 1967).

Nakamura, T. (1997) 'Depression, Recovery, and War,' in Kozo Yamamura (ed.) *The Economic Emergence of Modern Japan*, Cambridge: Cambridge University Press, Chapter 3.

Nakamura, T. and K. Odaka (1989) 'Gaisetsu 1914–37 nenn (General Overview 1914–37),' in T. Nakamura and K. Odaka (eds.), *Nihon Keizai Shi* (*Japanese Economic History*), vol. 6, Tokyo: Iwanami Shoten, Chapter 1 (in Japanese).

Nihon Ginko Chosa-kyoku (Bureau of Research, the Bank of Japan) (1968) *Nihon Kinyushi Showa hen* (*Documents of Monetary and Financial History of Japan, Showa Era*), vols. 20–3, Tokyo: Bank of Japan (in Japanese).

Nolte, S. H. (1987), *Liberalism in Modern Japan: Ishibashi Tanzan and His Teachers, 1905–1960*, Berkeley, Calif.: University of California Press.

Ogura, Seitaro (ed.) (1955) *Toyo Keizai Shimpo Gennron Rokujyu-nen (Sixty Years of Journalism by Toyo Keizai Shimpo Sha)*, Tokyo: Toyo Keizai Shimpo Sha (in Japanese).

Okada, Y., A. Seiji and I. Kikuo (2002) 'Dai Kyoko to Showa Kyoko ni miru Regime Tenkan to Gendai Nihon no Kinyu Seisaku (Regime Change in the Great Depression and the Showa Crisis and Its Implications for Current Monetary Policy of Japan),' in Y. Harada and K. Iwata (eds.) *Defure Fukyo no Jissyo Kenkyu (Empirical Studies on Deflationary Recessions)*, Tokyo: Toyo Keizai Shimpo Sha, Chapter 8 (in Japanese).

Patrick, H. T. (1971) 'The Economic Muddle of the 1920s,' in J. W. Morley (ed.) *The Dilemmas of Growth in Prewar Japan*, Princeton, NJ: Princeton University Press, pp. 211–66.

Pollard, S. (ed.) (1970) *The Gold Standard and Employment Policies between the Wars*, London: Methuen & Co.

Romer, C. and D. Romer (2002) 'The Evolution of Economic Understanding and Postwar Stabilization Policy,' NBER Working Paper Series 9274.

Schlitz, M. (2011) 'Money on the Road to Empire: Japan's Adoption of Gold Monometallism, 1873–97,' *Economic History Review*, 65, 3. http://onlinelibrary.wiley.com/doi/10.1111/j.1468-0289.2011.00619.x/pdf.

Smethurst, R. J. (2007) *From Foot Soldier to Finance Minister: Takahashi Korekiyo, Japan's Keynes*, Cambridge, Mass.: Harvard University Asia Center.

Sussman, N. and Y. Yafeh (2000) 'Institutions, Reforms, and Country Risk: Lessons from Japanese Government Debt in the Meiji Period,' *Journal of Economic History*, 60: 442–67.

Takahashi, K. (Kamekichi Takahashi) (1930a) *Kinyusyutsu Sai Kinshi Ron (Reembargo of the Gold Exports)*, Tokyo: Senshin Sha (in Japanese).

Takahashi, K. (Kamekichi Takahashi) (1930b) *Kabushiki Kaisha Bokoku Ron (Corporations are Ruining our Country)*, Tokyo: Banrikaku Shobo (in Japanese).

Takahashi, K. (Kamekichi Takahashi) (1931) *Keiki ha Do naru (What is Happening to the Recession?)*, Tokyo: Chikura Shobo (in Japanese).

Takahashi, K. (Kamekichi Takahashi) (1954–5) *Taisho Showa Zaikai Hendo Shi (History of Economic Changes during the Taisho and Showa Era)*, Tokyo: Toyo Keizai Shimpo Sha (in Japanese).

Takahashi, K. (Korekiyo Takahashi) (1936) *Takashi Korekiyo Keizairon (Korekiyo Takahashi on the Economy)*, Tokyo: Chikura Shobo (in Japanese).

Takenaka, H. (2002) *Senzen Nihon ni Okeru Minsyuka Tojyo Taisei no Zasetsu (The Breakdown of Developing Democracy in Pre-war Japan)*, Tokyo: Bokutaku sha (in Japanese).

Temin, P. (1989) *Lessons from the Great Depression*, Cambridge, Mass.: MIT Press.

Teranishi, J. (1989) 'Fukinko Seicho to Kinyu (Unbalanced Growth and Finance),' in T. Nakamura and K. Odaka (eds.) *Nihon Keizai Shi (Japanese Economic History)*, vol. 6, Tokyo: Iwanami Shoten, Chapter 4 (in Japanese).

Tokyo Shoko Kaigi Sho (Tokyo Chamber of Commerce) (1927) *Kin Yusyutsu Kaikin Mondai ni kann suru Sanko Siryo (Supplementary Document concerning the Lifting of the Embargo on Gold Exports)*, privately circulated (in Japanese).

Wakatabe, M. (2005) 'Was the Great Depression the Watershed of Macroeconomics?: The Impact of the Great Depression on Economic Thought Reconsidered,' Paper presented at the History of Macroeconomics Conference, Leuvan-la-Neuve, Belgium, January 2005.

White, L. H. (2008) 'Did Hayek and Robbins Deepen the Great Depression?' *Journal of Money, Credit and Banking*, 40: 751–68.

Yamamoto, T. (1981) *Kindai Nihon no Sinbun Dokusya So* (*Who Read Newspapers in Modern Japan?*), Tokyo: Hosei University Press.

Yamazaki, Y. (1929a) *Kin Yusyutsu Kaikin Mondai* (*Problem of the Lifting the Embargo on the Gold Exports*), Tokyo: Ritsumeikan University Press (in Japanese).

Yamazaki, Y. (1929b) *Kokumin Keizai no Tatenaoshi ka Hakai ka* (*Construction or Destruction of our Economy*), Tokyo: Shubun Kaku (in Japanese).

Young, L. (1998) *Japan's Total Empire: Manchuria and the Culture of Wartime Imperialism*, Berkeley: University of California Press.

2 Prof. Aoyama's study on Robertson and Keynes in interwar Japan in comparison with my interpretation

"With or without" Dynamic General Equilibrium Theory (DGET)

Toshiaki Hirai

1 Introduction

The present chapter has two objectives. One is to examine the study of Robertson and Keynes conducted by Prof. Hideo Aoyama (1910–1992)—one of the leading theoretical economists—concentrating on his activities in the interwar period, and the other is to present my own study in the same sphere for the sake of comparison.

This might seem a slightly odd approach given the time span of over 60 years. At first I had planned to focus on Aoyama's study alone. As my research proceeded, however, I came to notice the need to clarify my own understanding in the area concerned in order to fulfill the initial purpose, for my approach and understanding are rather different from his. That is why I chose to juxtapose them, adding my assessment of his study from my own stance.

The chapter runs as follows. First, the economics situation in interwar Japan is briefly sketched out (section 2). Then the following themes are discussed in various ways, juxtaposing Aoyama's interpretation together with my interpretation: Robertson's trade cycle theory (section 3); Walrasian general equilibrium theory and the Wicksell Connection (section 4); and Keynes's theory, including the *Treatise* (1930) and the *General Theory* (1936).

2 Economics in interwar Japan: an outline

Few, if any, economists would fail to mention as the greatest economists who contributed to and influenced the development of economics in interwar Japan the following three—Tokuzo Fukuda (1874–1930), Yasuma Takata (1883–1972) and Hajime Kawakami (1879–1946). The latter is a Marxian economist; the former two are relevant to the present paper.

Fukuda started his academic career as the leader of the Young Historical School in Japan, after studying economics under Lujo Brentano in Germany. He was very eager to study economics widely, with the aspiration of improving the "welfare" of Japanese society. While he was Professor of the Tokyo High School of Commerce (now Hitotsubashi University) and Keio University, he contributed to the development of economics through his academic and educational activities. Fukuda is also well known as a leader of the "Taisho Democracy" movement after World War I.

It should be noted here, among other things, that he continued to show interest in the Cambridge School. He used Marshall's *Principles* as a textbook at Keio University, eventually bringing out a volume published as Fukuda (1907), in which Marshall's views are juxtaposed with his own views. He was a keen reader of Pigou and Hawtrey (as well as Hobson and Cannan). In "From Price Struggle to Welfare Struggle" in *Social Policy and the Class Struggle* (1922), Fukuda emphasized the Welfare Struggle for the improvement of the people's conditions, while criticizing the Price Struggle as price mechanism. It was from this stance that he praised Book 1, criticizing Books 5 and 6 in Marshall's *Principles*.

Fukuda, a very influential leader of public opinion, continued to show interest in what was happening in both the world scene and Japan. As for the former, he was wont to praise Keynes's analysis and proposals put forward in *The Economic Consequences of the Peace* (1919).

Fukuda trained many leading economists. Above all, Ichiro Nakayama's accomplishment (1898–1980) was remarkable. Nakayama, after graduating from the Tokyo High School of Commerce, studied economics under Schumpeter at Bonn University (1927–1929), who introduced him to Walrasian general equilibrium theory and his own dynamic theory. He then tried to integrate the two by introducing an idea of "equilibrium in the development process",[1] which is greatly influenced by Keynes's "under-employment equilibrium" in the *General Theory*, the result of which was *Equilibrium Analysis of Development Process* (1939). Through these activities, Nakayama became a great pioneer in these fields.[2]

Yasuma Takata was another pioneering economist (as well as sociologist) at Kyoto University, eager to study Walrasian general equilibrium theory and Keynes's economics. He also trained many leading economists, including Hideo Aoyama, whose accomplishment was remarkable. Aoyama, Professor at Kyoto University, has some claim to a creditable place in the history of economic thought as a Japanese scholar who studied not only Walrasian General Equilibrium (WGE) theory and Dynamic General Equilibrium Theory (DGET), but also the Cambridge School and the Stockholm School at the highest level in the interwar period.[3]

Negishi referred to Takata, Aoyama and Kei Shibata (1902–1986) as the "Trio of the Kyoto School". Shibata—a disciple of Hajime Kawakami—became internationally famous for his paper integrating Marxian economics with Walrasian general equilibrium theory.

All in all, Nakayama, Aoyama and Takuma Yasui (1909–1995), whom we need to add here—a maverick at Tokyo University famous for his pioneering stability analysis of Walrasian general equilibrium—were the leading economists of the then so-called "Pure Economics" in interwar Japan.

Turning to the economic policy scene, Keynes was, again, very influential, as can be seen in the Kinkaikin (Lifting of Gold Embargo) Controversy over how the Japanese monetary system should be rectified—one of the two biggest economic controversies in the 1920s in Japan.

Kamekichi Takahashi and Tanzan Ishibashi—both excellent economic journalists—were advocates of the return to the gold standard at a new parity with public spending policy based on Keynes's stance. They were supported by Korekiyo Takahashi—a banker and politician, who is also particularly famous for his Keynesian-type policy in the 1930s and is dubbed the "Keynes of Japan". They were critical of Jyunnosuke Inoue—the Minister of Finance who advocated a return to the gold standard at the prewar parity as soon as possible with austerity measures.

Turning back to academic activities in Japan, Keynes's *Treatise* and *General Theory* came under intensive study by the economists of "Pure Economics", as emerges from the above account. In the 1940s, the Pacific War period, their interest came to shift toward Hicks' *Value and Capital* (1939) and monetary theory of trade cycle as represented by the Stockholm School, although the center of attention was the so-called "Political Economy School", which came under the political influence of Japanese militarism.

3 Robertson's trade cycle theory

The Cambridge School, which had initially inherited Marshall's credit cycle theory, took a different line with the new theoretical developments introduced by *Banking Policy and the Price Level* (Robertson, 1926; hereafter *BP*). Although he was influenced not so much by Wicksell[4] as by Aftalion and Cassel, his theory incorporated the same ideas as Wicksell's. Let us recall that Robertson's theory was highly rated by the Wicksell Connection on the grounds that it analyzes a similar problem by means of a similar method.

Greatly influenced by Robertson, Keynes was spurred on to evolve from the *Tract* (1923) to the *Treatise* (1930).

In this section we aim to show how Robertson actually developed his trade cycle theory—theory of "lacking", and then examine how Aoyama evaluated Robertson's theory and, at the same time, criticized it.

3.1 Trade cycle theory

Unlike the monetary theories found in Hawtrey (1923) and Keynes (1923), and the psychological theories in Pigou (1920), Robertson's trade cycle theory interweaves the real factors with the monetary factors in terms of the relations between saving, credit-creation and capital growth.

With regard to the real factors, Robertson classifies the output fluctuations in terms of "appropriate" and "inappropriate". Entrepreneurs often alter the volume of output based on reasonable considerations. The appropriate volume of output follows a rhythmical pattern of justifiable increases and decreases, being in accord with the technical and legal structure of the modern economy. Inappropriate fluctuations, as excess of actual fluctuations in the volume of output over "appropriate" fluctuations, occur in relation to the use of large and expensive durable means of production.

Robertson (1949, p. 39) then goes on to observe that the objective of monetary theory should "be ... to permit ... appropriate alterations in output and to repress [inappropriate alterations]".

Monetary factors are related to the activities of the banking system. In order to increase the volume of output, real circulating capital is required in advance. In order to purchase it, short lacking is required. If firms do not possess the whole amount of the short "lacking", the banking system provides the balance. Thus the banking system assists the productive activities by enabling consumption goods to go to the firms as circulating capital. When the firms' demand for circulating capital is strong, the public is deprived of consumption goods. It is by dint of an increase in the prices of consumption goods due to the use of credit that the banking system induces "forced saving".[5]

Robertson adopts a variant of the quantity theory of money (QT)[6] to the effect that the price level of consumption goods depends on the quantity of money channeled toward consumption. If the real balance of the quantity of money possessed by the public increases (decreases), they try to increase (decrease) their expenditure in order to restore consumption to the desirable level.

"Lacking" is defined thus: a man is lacking if during a given period he consumes less than the value of his current economic output (Robertson, 1949, 41).

The "lacking" is given by the portion of products not consumed. As this portion is purchased by firms with money, "lacking" might be thought of as money to purchase it (we would omit an explanation of his complicated lacking taxonomy here).

Robertson develops his trade cycle theory in the case of short lacking, and in the case of short and long lacking. Let us focus here on the former case.

Here a notion of the "demand and supply of short lacking" plays a central role. According to the trade cycle phase, the demand does not change in the same way as the supply in short lacking. How the economy deals with this difference depends on the behavior of the banking system. Here let us examine the upward phase.

In order to increase the volume of output, circulating capital is required. For this, short lacking is indispensable. If it cannot be procured as would be hoped, no planned increase in production can be implemented. The supply of short lacking is made by (Abortive) Lacking, which occurs when the income from sales of current output is saved with no resort to the creation of capital. Supply of it does not increase quickly enough to cope with a large and discontinuous increase in the demand for it.

The large excess demand for short lacking is met only by the provision of credit by the banking system. The consequence is (Imposed) Lacking.

When short lacking is met, the required circulating capital is procured, so that the volume of production increases. The amount of money in the economy increases, and the price level consequently rises.

Thus increase in the volume of production is in trade-off with stability in the price level.

Let us suppose that the banking system supplies the required money: the excess demand for short lacking is thus met, but the price level rises. Once this occurs, excess demand for short lacking persists for several reasons.[7]

If the banking system goes on supplying money to cope with the excess demand, the price level goes on rising cumulatively.

3.2 Aoyama's two-track evaluation

What interested Aoyama most was, then, a new theory, a "dynamic general equilibrium theory" (DGET), to be explained below—a dynamic version of Walrasian general equilibrium theory as initiated by Volpe, Frisch and Hicks.

Aoyama argues that Robertson (1926) pioneered a business cycle theory based on DGET,[8] for Robertson's model, he states, possesses a feature to the effect that the variables, determined at each point of time in a simultaneous equations system incorporating "period analysis" (together with a distinction between "ex-ante" and "ex-post" concepts), move on over time. This led him to show a keen interest in Robertson's theory.[9]

Robertson developed his theory by dynamizing the Cambridge-type quantity theory, applying "period analysis". Aoyama elegantly clarified the functioning of Robertson's model as analyzing, by means of four co-efficiencies, how the price level goes up and down according to whether the period of money circulation is longer or shorter than the average production period. Aoyama goes on to remark that, seeing that price fluctuations can be explained with an investment and saving analysis, Robertson might as well have done so.

Marshall did not conceive the idea of using his quantity theory ($m = kpy$) to account for economic fluctuations. Rather, he developed another theory for them, focusing on credit instability. Pigou (1917) and Keynes (1923) explained economic fluctuations based on a variant of Marshall's quantity theory, allowing for variations in parameters. Aoyama, for his part, arguably states that only Robertson eventually succeeded in dynamizing Marshall's quantity theory.

That is the positive evaluation. At the same time, however, Aoyama sees some difficulty or limitation in Robertson's theory. He argues that Robertson's theory as a dynamic extension of the quantity theory cannot deal with the monetary aspect of the actual economy. The difficulty derives from the quantity theory per se, which states that prices can be determined by expenditure on consumption over output. Especially when alternative forms of holding wealth is allowed for, it will meet the difficulty of treating them.[10]

In this respect, Aoyama claims that Keynes's bearishness function theory (in the *Treatise*) and liquidity preference theory (in the *General Theory*) are major contributions[11] to economic theory, for they are, in essence, anti-quantity theories of money which illustrate how the price level is determined by incorporating assets other than cash balances.

Aoyama argues that Robertson's attempt to extend his period analysis in such a way, incorporating savings account (as is seen in the *Treatise*, in which it is inextricably linked to the stock market), is fundamentally flawed. He even goes so far as to claim that period analysis cannot deal with the problem of the rate of interest.[12]

Aoyama, moreover, criticizes Robertson's theory in that it assumes a social economy in which entrepreneurs are inseparable from laborers, ergo neglecting saving from entrepreneurs' profits.

Thus Aoyama's evaluation of Robertson's theory should be actually seen as two-track.

Aoyama seems to overact to Robertson's theory. First, it is doubtful if Robertson's theory of trade cycle can be, in essence, characterized as dynamizing the quantity theory. Second, Robertson himself neither refers to nor shows any interest in Walrasian general equilibrium theory. I observe this from the history of economics point of view.

4 General equilibrium theory and the Wicksell Connection: with or without DGET

How should we think of the relationship between general equilibrium theory (GET) and the Wicksell Connection? This is very important in understanding the features of economic doctrines developed in the interwar period. When it comes to Aoyama's papers, however, we find his understanding rather different from ours. The main reason is that he tries to grasp the whole picture exclusively from a DGET point of view as the dynamic version of GET, while we do so in terms of GET vs. the Wicksell Connection without considering DGET. "With or without DGET", therefore, could be a crucial diverging point.

Therefore, we will first present our version, and then critically examine Aoyama's. It should be noted that the difference between the two, notwithstanding the fact that our interpretation derives, in essence, from the same literature as considered by Aoyama, which means that we form different pictures from the same literature, could lead to differences in evaluation of Robertson's and Keynes's theories.

4.1 Our interpretation

Wicksell (1898[1936]) put forward the so-called theory of cumulative process (hereafter TCP), which was to have great influence over the monetary economics of the economists in the 1920s and 1930s through critical interpretations (now called the "Wicksell Connection") such as Hayek (the Austrian School), Myrdal (the Stockholm School) and Keynes (as the author of the *Treatise*) (the Cambridge School). Although Wicksell endorsed WGE (except for the capital theory), Myrdal and Hayek put forward their own monetary economics, explicitly criticizing WGE, while Keynes developed his own, including criticism of the quantity theory but making no reference to WGE. The theoretical models put forward by Wicksell and the Wicksell Connection are not dealt with here.[13]

We see the Wicksell Connection as bringing together those economists who, reacting against neoclassical economics, developed monetary economics. The Connection is also indispensable for an understanding of the evolution of Keynes's ideas in the 1920s, which culminated in the *Treatise* (1930; hereafter *TM*).

Classifying economic theories between real and monetary economics[14] has the great, if rough, merit of identifying a fundamental distinction between economic theories: while real economics regards the market economy as stable and converging toward full employment, monetary economics regards it as inherently unstable and incessantly fluctuating. The difference derives from a difference in opinion as to the role of money and credit.

Real economics regards money as having neutral effect on the real economy, while monetary economics sees it as having a certain effect. That is, real economics accepts the classical dichotomy, the quantity theory of money and Say's Law, whereas monetary economics rejects them, focusing attention on transitional periods.

Real economics, embraced by the classical economists as well as the neoclassical economists, represents mainstream economics. It should be noted that WGE is real economics. Monetary economics came to the fore with Wicksell (1898[1936]), a century after Thornton (1802),[15] followed by the "Wicksell Connection", which can be further classified between two types:

i The hard-core version: Monetary economists who endeavor to construct their own theories of economic fluctuations in terms of the divergence either between the natural rate and the money rate of interest or between investment and saving, based on immanent criticism of Wicksell's theory: Myrdal, Lindahl, Mises, Hayek and Keynes (1930).[16] They consciously criticize neoclassical orthodoxy.

ii The peripheral version: Monetary economists who unwittingly do the same thing as the hard-core version. To that degree they are less critical of neoclassical orthodoxy: Robertson (1926) and Hawtrey (1913).

Picking out Wicksell, Myrdal, Hayek and Keynes, let us examine the similarities and differences.

1 Hayek takes the most extreme position in the sense that only he develops an argument to the effect that the way money is injected into the economy never fails to influence the relation between the price levels of consumption goods and many producers' goods, bringing about a prolongation (or shortening) of the production structure. In addition, Hayek alone regards the case of voluntary saving as an ideal state of affairs, and thinks the case of forced saving to be an awkward state of affairs disturbed by the quantity of money.

2 Myrdal falls into a position second farthest from Wicksell, for he is farther from Wicksell than Keynes is, as he approves only the second of Wicksell's monetary equilibrium conditions and denies the first and third ones, while Keynes approves all of them. Moreover, Myrdal has doubts about the bank

rate operations performed by the banking system, while Keynes stresses their importance, following Wicksell.

3   Myrdal and Keynes adopt a common position as far as the determination of the price level of consumption goods is concerned. They also develop similar arguments concerning the value of capital, and both attribute investment and saving to a central role in analysis.

The difference lies, first, in how investment should be dealt with. Second, concerning a theory of production, Myrdal adopts a theory of roundabout production, while Keynes adopts the TM supply function (to be explained later). Third, Myrdal consistently adopts an investment and saving analysis, while Keynes's analysis is rather ambiguous. Finally, the definitions of income and profit differ in that Myrdal takes them as ex-ante concepts.

4.2 Aoyama's interpretation examined

As already stated, in the 1940s "Pure Economics" turned its attention to Hicks' *Value and Capital* (1939) and the Stockholm School. Aoyama, who also studied WGE as well as the Wicksell Connection under the supervision of Takata, was a leading young economist in this period.

Aoyama started his studies with Hayek's *Monetary Theory and the Trade Cycle* (1933) and *Prices and Production* (1931), which led him to go on studying the Tugan-Baranovsky School, which endorsed Say's Law. Then he came to have doubts about the school and embraced Aftalion–Robertson's analysis, which criticized Say's Law. He was also strongly attracted by the then latest theory—DGET as represented by Volpe and Hicks. He eventually hit upon the idea that the separate development of WGE and theories of economic fluctuations could be overcome by means of DGET. He understood Aftalion–Robertson's analysis as showing DGET in terms of period analysis. He even insisted that only DGET can effectively refute Say's Law while Keynes's *General Theory* cannot, in spite of Keynes's claim that his theory of effective demand did away with the Law.

We now need a rough outline of DGET[17]—what Aoyama (1942) presented as Volpe's model. DGET is a dynamic version of WGE which is static, while retaining the main elements as far as possible—i.e., utility maximization by households; profit maximization by firms; contemporary interdependent relation between agents; Walras's Law; numéraire and so on. The main difference between the two lies in whether inter-temporal relation and expected prices are included or not.

First, a household behaves in such a way as to maximize its utility defined as a function of demand for goods over the period from the present to the year of its (expected) death. From this, an individual demand function is obtained as a function of the time series of the prices of numerous goods.

Second, a firm is assumed to produce goods in such a way as to maximize profit by means of goods obtained at the period ω earlier than the present period. From this an individual supply function is obtained as a function of the time series of the prices of numerous goods.

Third, general equilibrium in the market is formulated. There at each time all the prices are determined, which means that over the entire period the time series of prices and quantities of numerous goods are determined.

This is a basic idea of DGET.

Aoyama's understanding of WGE and the Wicksell Connection is different from ours as shown in section 4.1. The main difference lies in the interpretation of what Wicksell and the Wicksell Connection were aiming at.

It was, above all, DGET that attracted Aoyama's keenest interest, so he then set out to interpret theoretical economics from the DGET point of view. Because DGET is a dynamic version of WGE, WGE itself also occupied a central place in his studies. It was from this stance that he viewed Wicksell and the Wicksell Connection. That is, while in our interpretation DGET has no place in understanding Wicksell and the Wicksell Connection, in Aoyama's interpretation it has a central place.

In consequence Aoyama was not concerned with the critical stance the Wicksell Connection took on WGE, the quantity theory of money and the classical dichotomy. It was, therefore, hardly surprising that when he examined Wicksell's theory, he focused on the natural rate of interest within the framework of WGE rather than on TCP, and saw Myrdal as a theorist of general equilibrium cum ex-ante concept rather than a harsh critic of WGE.[18]

In our understanding, moreover, it is impossible for us to take the Wicksell Connection within the framework of DGET, for they were critical of GET per se, although their models were, in essence, dynamic—DGET might be one form of dynamics, but dynamics could have other forms.

Turning to the Cambridge School, there was not even one of them who studied WGE seriously. Keynes, Pigou, Robertson, Hawtrey and so forth did not publish a book or article examining or studying WGE. Moreover, they did not incorporate DGET into their economic theories. That is to say, Cambridge economists in the interwar period never referred to Walras, or WGE, and still less to DGET.

Schumpeter is famous for his two separate theories: GET as statics and *The Theory of Economic Development* (1934) as dynamics (it was Nakayama who tried to incorporate the two). Schumpeter praised Robertson (1926) very highly because it aimed at analyzing economy from the same point of view as Schumpeter's dynamic theory did. This praise is different from Aoyama's, although both rank Robertson (1926) very highly.

Turning to the Stockholm School, the scholars belonging to it studied WGE in earnest, influenced by Wicksell and Cassell. Because of this, Myrdal, for example, set out to put forward a new dynamic theory, criticizing WGE, the Quantity Theory and Say's Law.

As Aoyama saw it, WGE and theory of economic fluctuations evolved separately. The path toward integration of the two, however, was finally opened by DGET as typified by Robertson (1926).

We might sum up ours as a history of economic theory approach, while Aoyama's as a theoretical economics approach.

5 Keynes's *Treatise* and *General Theory*

In this section, I propose my interpretation of the theoretical framework of the *Treatise* and the *General Theory*, and then examine Aoyama's evaluation of Keynes's theories. I eventually decided that I might as well present my interpretation, having formed it on the perusal of these books, rather than set out other scholars' divergent interpretations.

5.1 The Treatise[19]

The most significant feature of the *Treatise* theory seems to be the coexistence of a Wicksellian-type theory and "Keynes's own theory".

The *Treatise* belongs to the Wicksellian strand of thought. The principal grounds on which Keynes regards his theory as belonging to the Wicksellian stream lie in his adoption of the idea that the bank rate influences investment and saving. In the *Treatise* this idea is used to present a mechanism in which economic stability (stability of the price level and the volume of output) can be attained by means of a bank rate policy.

At the same time, Keynes develops "Keynes's own theory", which we will explain below.

5.1.1 The basic assumptions

Let us begin with the production of goods. Goods are classified in two groups: consumption goods and investment goods. The output of each good is determined at the beginning of the current period based on the amount of profit in the previous period.[20] Units of quantities of goods are defined in such a way that each unit has the same cost of production. This means that the average cost of each good is constant and the output of each group thus measured does not change during the current period.

The production cost of each group of goods defined as the unit cost multiplied by the volume of output is determined at the beginning of the current period. It is paid as the earnings of the factors of production at the beginning of the current period. Part of the earnings is spent on consumption goods while the rest is saved.[21]

We turn next to the price level of investment goods. This is determined in the capital stock market, for the output of investment goods is small as compared with capital stock as accumulated over a long period. Keynes then discusses the price level of investment goods in two ways. One is related to the stock market. Investment goods are additions to capital stock. Capital stock is in a one-to-one relation to securities. Therefore the price level of investment goods is determined on the stock market. In order to understand it, we need to examine the financial structure. Money is defined as including not only state money and bank money, but also short-term and long-term bonds. Each bears its own rate of interest. Against "money" stand equities.[22]

In the *Treatise*, money, which includes bonds and yields interest, is compared with equities, which are in a one-to-one relation to capital goods. The public make a portfolio selection between them.

(Assumption 1) The rate of interest is a policy variable. The money supply changes as the rate of interest changes.[23]

The other formulation concerning the determination of the price level of investment goods is as follows:

(Assumption 2) The demand price of capital goods (and therefore that of investment goods) can be obtained by discounting the prospective yields by the rate of interest. It is realized as the market price of capital stock (and therefore that of investment goods). If the rate of interest rises, then the demand price of capital stock goes down and investment expenditure decreases.

5.1.2 The market mechanism

The market mechanism in the *Treatise* is composed of two parts. One has to do with the determination of variables in "each period". The other concerns the determination between one period and the next.

Let us first explain the former. In the case of the consumption goods sector, the determination in each period is constructed as follows:

(Mechanism 1) The determination of the consumption goods sector in each period.

The production cost and the volume of supply are determined at the beginning of the current period. Once the expenditure on consumption goods is determined mechanically on the basis of the earnings, it is automatically realized as the sale of consumption goods proceeds, and both the price level and the profit are simultaneously determined.

This mechanism is simple but somewhat unclear. It is simple for the following reasons:

i   The output is supposed to be realized according to the entrepreneurs' plan, and the sale proceeds are supposed to be realized at the consumers' will;
ii As a result, profit is ascertained and entrepreneurs are supposed to determine the output in the next period.

It is somewhat unclear because it is not explained how the expenditure on consumption goods (the sale proceeds) is determined.

In the case of the investment goods sector, the determination of variables in each period is constructed as follows:

(Mechanism 2) The determination of the investment goods sector in each period.

The production cost and the volume of supply is determined at the beginning of the current period. The price level of investment goods is determined in the capital stock market. As a result of the above, profit is ascertained.

Let us turn to the determination between one period and the next. This is shown as follows:

(Mechanism 3) The behavior of the entrepreneurs (the "TM supply function"). Entrepreneurs behave in such a way that they expand output in the next period, according as they make a profit in the current period. Conversely they behave in such a way that they contract output in the next period, according as they make a loss in the current period.[24]

This mechanism suggests that Keynes deals with the relation between profit and output in terms of a one-period time-lag. We will refer to the supply function, which is expressed as the function of profit, as the "TM supply function". It is peculiar to the *Treatise* and can be formulated as follows;

$$\Delta R = f_1 (Q_1 <t>)$$

$$\Delta C = f_2 (Q_2 <t>)$$

(where R stands for the output of consumption goods, C the output of investment goods, Δ an increment, Q_1 the profit of consumption goods, Q_2 the profit of investment goods, $<t>$ time t).

The TM supply function occupies an important place in Keynes's theoretical development from the *Treatise* to the *General Theory*.[25]

From the above argument, the theoretical structure of *A Treatise on Money* can be expressed as the dynamic process of Mechanisms 1 and 2 through the TM supply function. In the consumption goods sector, "each period" is determined by Mechanism 1, while in the investment goods sector "each period" is determined by Mechanism 2. The profits thus ascertained determine the output in the next period through the TM supply function.

After that, the economy returns to both Mechanism 1 and Mechanism 2, and then moves forward through the two TM supply functions. This is the dynamic mechanism which is developed in the *Treatise*.

5.2 The whole picture

Now that I have outlined my interpretation of the theoretical structure of the *Treatise* and the Wicksell Connection (at section 4.1), it is time to view the whole picture (Figure 2.1) of my understanding of the relation between the *Treatise*, the Wicksell Connection and the *General Theory*, although we will be looking into the *General Theory* a little later (at section 5.3).

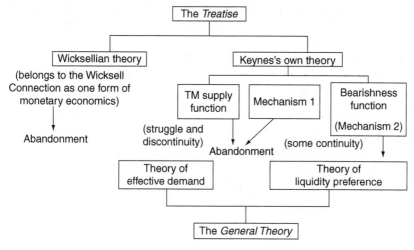

Figure 2.1 Relation between the *Treatise*, the Wicksell Connection and the *General Theory*.

We regarded the *Treatise* as propounding monetary economics critical of neo-classical orthodoxy. How, then, did Keynes develop his theory after the *Treatise* to arrive at the *General Theory*? This theme was, in fact, developed in great detail in Hirai (2008, Chs. 6–12), and is outlined as follows.

After the *Treatise*, Keynes went on applying "Keynes's own theory", disregarding a Wicksellian theory. In the *Treatise*, the importance of the relation between profits and the volume of output (the "TM supply function") is stressed as expressing the dynamic mechanism. Keynes adhered to this function after the *Treatise*. Toward the end of 1932, however, he eventually abandoned it, and put forward a new formula of a system of commodity markets—a turning point on the way to the *General Theory*. The revolutionary feature of the *General Theory* lies in showing, through presentation of a clear-cut model, that the market economy, if left to itself, falls into an underemployment equilibrium. It was not until 1933, however, that Keynes came to put forward a model of how the volume of employment is determined. Thereafter he took pains to elaborate his model. At the same time, we argue that the *General Theory* sees the market economy as fraught with instability, uncertainty and complexity.

5.3 The theoretical model of the General Theory: an interpretation[26]

Keynes states that only two fundamental units of quantity—quantities of money-value and those of employment (adopting the wage-unit as a unit of employment)—should be used in a theory of employment, arguing that the concepts of national dividend, the stock of real capital and the general price-level lack precision. As to prices, he uses only the price of an individual commodity, and prices occur as endogenous variables. More importantly, Keynes takes for granted the existence of many kinds of goods and capital assets[27] and expectations, including long-term and short-term expectations.[28]

The main problem is to see how his model was to be constructed, once all these factors were taken into account. Our answer is that Keynes aimed at building a theory of underemployment equilibrium, assuming the existence of various kinds of goods and expectations, in terms of the two fundamental units only. In carrying out this task we need to consider the relation between the micro- and macro-structures in his theory.

Our conclusions are summarized in Figure 2.2, which offers a bird's-eye view of the structure of the *General Theory*.

Let us go through the main conclusions, dividing them into four areas.

<u>The First Area</u> concerns the principal corrections and clarifications that need to be introduced, namely:

1   using the first postulate of classical economics only to describe the behavior of an individual firm in the multiple-goods economy;

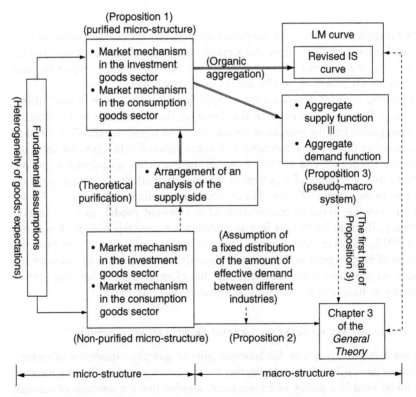

Figure 2.2 Structure of demonstration.

2   taking the concept of the "marginal efficiency of capital"[29] only as express-
     ing the demand for investment goods;
3   explicitly showing the supply side in the consumption goods sector.

The Second Area is a matter of our cleaned-up version of the commodity market
mechanism. Let us refer to the micro-structure of the *General Theory* with the
above-described ambiguities removed as the "purified micro-structure".

> (Proposition 1) The commodity market mechanism of the *General Theory*
> can be expressed in terms of the purified micro-structure and the macro-
> structure expressed as the "revised IS curve". The purified micro-structure is
> composed of the market mechanisms in the investment and consumption
> goods sectors while the revised IS curve is derived from the purified micro-
> structure.

The Third Area comprises our understanding of the commodity market mechanism as it stands in the *General Theory*.

> (Proposition 2) The mechanism of the commodity market actually described
> in the *General Theory* can be expressed in terms of the "non-purified micro-
> structure" and the macro-structure as described in Chapter 3. The latter is
> derived from the non-purified micro-structure, given the distribution of the
> existing amount of effective demand among different industries is fixed.

The Fourth Area relates to certain propositions which differ from other interpretations of the *General Theory*.

> (Proposition 3) The aggregate supply and the aggregate demand functions
> describe one and the same purified micro-structure from different angles, so
> that both are equilibrium concepts. Chapter 3 provides not so much a sup-
> ply–demand equilibrium analysis as a "pseudo-macro system".

> (Proposition 4) There are two, mutually incompatible, consumption theo-
> ries: the theory based on the heterogeneity-expectations approach and the
> "consumption function" theory. What is required in the theoretical structure
> of the *General Theory* should be the former.

The consumption theory based on the heterogeneity-expectations approach is
as follows: the market price, the volume of production and the volume of
employment in an individual consumption good industry are determined in
such a way that the effective demand for the consumption good, generated
through the multiplier process with the income in the investment goods sector
as the prime mover, intersects a "sales proceeds function" for that industry,
which describes the relationship between the volume of employment and the
sales proceeds.

(Proposition 5) Determination of the equilibrium values. The national income and the rate of interest are determined where the "revised IS curve" intersects the LM curve (to be explained below).

In our view, the aggregate supply and the aggregate demand functions should be replaced by the "revised IS curve", which expresses the whole real economy in terms of a functional relationship between the rate of interest and the national income. In order for the system to be determinate, we need another equation, which is the LM curve, showing the state of equilibrium in the money market.

The *General Theory* is a form of monetary economics. Keynes assumes the exogeneity of money supply, and argues that money's "own-rate of interest" falls most slowly because of the highest liquidity-premium.

Keynes develops the theory of liquidity preference.[30] The rate of interest is treated as a purely monetary and psychological phenomenon.

$$M = L_1(Y) + L_2(r)$$

where M is the total amount of money; L_1 the liquidity preference function due to the transactions and precautionary motives; L_2 the liquidity preference function due to the speculative motive; Y income; and r interest.

The essence of his theory of money rests with $L_2(r)$. The rate of interest is determined between the monetary authority and the public in the debts market. Keynes stresses that the degree of success of any monetary policy depends on psychological and conventional phenomena. Monetary policy should not be changed drastically,[31] for this would imply the risk of increasing the volatility of the economic system through the collapse of public confidence.

(Proposition 6) A dual (or two tier) adjustment mechanism. The rate of interest plays an essential role in adjusting the whole system, while individual prices in the investment goods sector and the "multiplier process" in the consumption goods sector play subsidiary roles.

The rate of interest plays a primary role in the adjustment of the whole system, for it alone can adjust any discrepancy between the level of national income determined through the mechanism of the commodity markets and the level of national income that would bring about equilibrium in the money market. Individual prices play a role in bringing about equilibrium in the investment goods markets, in which, given the rate of interest, is ascertained a demand curve which meets a supply curve. The multiplier process, through which purchases of consumption goods occur one after another until they converge at a certain point, plays a role in the adjustment of the consumption goods markets.

Finally, one point is worth emphasizing. The *General Theory* theoretical model cannot be confined within a mathematical framework, for Keynes presents a clear-cut theoretical model, but at the same time his theory is constructed on rather subtle and complex realities.

5.4 Aoyama's evaluation of Keynes's theory[32]

Aoyama's evaluation of Keynes's theory might be seen as reflecting his assessment of Robertson's theory.

On the one hand, Aoyama did not regard the *General Theory* as revolutionary. He argued that, although Keynes criticized Say's Law from his theory of effective demand, the *General Theory* is, in fact, not a theory of underemployment equilibrium.[33] He maintained that DGET can effectively be applied to criticize Say's Law, and that this stance was, rather, to be discerned in Robertson's analysis.

> To sum up, the criticism of Say's Law by Aftalion and Robertson was the most penetrating in theories of economic fluctuations. We insist, moreover, that by using DGET as the recent product in theories of economic fluctuations we could assure Aftalion-Robertson's stance definitely.
>
> (Aoyama, 1942, p. 245)

On the other hand, Aoyama evaluated Keynes's theory of money—the bearishness function theory (in the *Treatise*), and the liquidity preference theory (in the *General Theory*). He argued that Keynes's two theories of money are, by their very nature, against the quantity theory, and stressed the importance of Keynes's approach, which takes account of the influence of portfolio selection on the price level of goods.

More interestingly, he sees some difficulty and limitation in Robertson's period analysis, arguing that Robertson's analysis is a dynamic extension of the quantity theory and can deal with neither the bearishness function nor the theory of liquidity preference. Here we see, again, Aoyama's two-track evaluation of Robertson's theory as well as Keynes's theory.

6 Conclusion: a brief outline of post World War II[34]

After World War II, economics, like everything else, was imported from the US and came to dominate Japan, which meant that the development of economics in the interwar period made through influences from Europe came to a halt.

In the field of macroeconomics, the Keynesian revolution which occurred in the shape of IS-LM cum 45 degree line arrived. This was a different interpretation from the one that had evolved in interwar Japan, which took Keynes's theory mainly as monetary economics. A dynamic version of Keynesian macroeconomics (trade cycle theory put forward by Samuelson, Hicks and others) as well as econometrics followed suit.

In the field of microeconomics, WGE arrived with more mathematical elaboration as represented by the proof of the existence of, and the stability conditions for, an equilibrium point. As can be surmised from the above description of the development of "pure theory" in interwar Japan, this field showed no gaps and stood at the same level as the US counterpart, as attested by the achievements of, to mention but a few, Morishima (a disciple of Takata and Aoyama), Uzawa and Negishi.

The combination of Keynesian macroeconomics with WGE was called the "Neoclassical Synthesis" and ruled the roost in the field of economics up until the 1970s.

Subsequently, over the last three decades, anti-Keynesian schools such as Monetarism and New Classical School have become increasingly predominant.

Even on the Keynesian side, there emerged schools critical of Keynesian macroeconomics as one pillar of the Neoclassical Synthesis (the Income–Expenditure approach), as represented by the Disequilibrium Keynesians (Leijonhufvud, Negishi and so forth), Post Keynesians and New Keynesians. Thanks to Leijonhufvud (who coined the term), the Wicksell Connection drew the spotlight once again.

WGE, another pillar of the Neoclassical Synthesis, also came under attack both from within and from outside.

In the 1970s, the Arrow-Debreu model was proved neither to retain equilibrium nor to guarantee global stability—the Sonnenshine–Mantel–Debreu theory. Efforts then went into modeling WGE under disequilibrium—the Neo-Walrasian model.[35]

With regard to the criticism of WGE from outside, it was objected that the axiomatic methodology adopted in it does not explain actual economic phenomena and, what is more, economics was moving in the wrong direction due to Debreu's elaboration of WGE. Israel (2007) insists that the "genuine" game theory based on cooperative games which von Neumann and Morgenstern originally aimed at establishing should be pursued. This type of criticism could be one reason why Market Design Mechanism theory came to flourish recently.

What about DGET? One can say that this line became predominant neither in Japan nor in the world in general. Although at present we have the "New Neo-Classical Synthesis" as represented by Woodford, which has a name similar to DGET (i.e., DSGE), it emerged from an intellectual background different to that of DGET.

Notes

1 This idea was severely criticized by Nisaburo Kitoh, a leading Keynesian and a Professor of the Tokyo High School of Commerce.
2 Eiichi Sugimoto (1901–1952), who was also a disciple of Fukuda, rated Marshall's contribution highly because of its dynamic nature, while criticizing Walras. See Sugimoto (1950[1981]).
3 For the academic circumstances surrounding his studies in Japan at the time, see Ikeo (1994, 2006). For Aoyama as an economist, see Negishi and Ikeo (1999).
4 He tried to examine the industrial fluctuations in terms of a natural and a market rate of interest only in Robertson (1934).
5 Forced saving was already in Robertson (1922, pp. 90–93), although the term "lacking" was not. See Presley (1979, pp. 10–104) and Bridel (1987, pp. 85–88).
6 See *BP*, pp. 59–62.
7 See *BP*, pp. 72–76. For the same argument, see Robertson (1922, pp. 157–158).
8 See Aoyama (1944, pp. 7–8).
9 He also regards Lindahl (1939) as elaborating on Robertson's theory. See Aoyama (1940, p. 304).

10 See Aoyama (1939a, pp. 213–214).

11 See Aoyama (1939b, Ch.7).

12 See Aoyama (1941, pp. 236–237).

13 For them, see Hirai (2008, pp. 17–30).

14 On which, see Hicks (1976).

15 Wicksell (1898, 1936[the original in 1906]) does not refer to Thornton. The similarity was pointed out in 1916 by Davidson to Wicksell. See Laidler (1991, p. 150).

16 Marco Fanno put forward his own theory of business fluctuations as early as 1912, succeeding Wicksell's theory critically. See Spiller and Pomini (2007).

17 For details, see Aoyama (1942, pp. 192–217).

18 See Aoyama (1944, pp. 14–15).

19 For more details, see Hirai (2008, pp. 56–70).

20 The "constancy of output" needs to be understood in a dynamic context, as it is here. In "A Note on the *Treatise*" (in Hicks, 1967), this is "stage one", at which the price levels of investment and consumption goods change, while the volume of output and the level of employment remain constant. See also the fourth lecture in Kahn (1984).

21 Cf. *TM*.1, p. 122. Hicks (1967, p. 196) explains this by introducing the propensity to save explicitly.

22 Cf. *TM*.1, p. 127 and pp. 179–180.

23 Cf. *TM*.1, p. 194.

24 Cf. *TM*.1, pp. 141, 179–180. Myrdal (1939) interprets Wicksell's investment theory in a similar way, and refers to a formula now known as Tobin's "q theory". Cf. Myrdal (1939, pp. 76–78 and p. 65).

25 The term "TM supply function" is apposite for the following reasons. "TM" simply refers to the *Treatise* (the only book in which Keynes uses this function). "Supply function" is appropriate given that Keynes himself referred to the mechanism as the "supply curve". In Asano (1985 [6], pp. 37–40), the role of the TM supply function is similarly stressed. In Yoshikawa (1984, p. 129), it is interpreted in connection with Tobin's "q theory". On the other hand, in the version of Keynes's development from the *Treatise* to the *General Theory* in Klein (1947), the TM supply function makes no appearance at all (cf. pp. 189–192). This is also true of Chapter 7 of Harrod (1969). This is the case, notwithstanding that all stress the importance of the *Treatise*.

26 The detailed analysis is developed in Hirai (1981). The above text owes to its abstract version seen in Hirai (2008), pp. 184–191 except for Figure 2.2.

27 See Hirai (1981, p. 225), which shows how the heterogeneity of goods runs through the *General Theory*.

28 See Hirai (1981, pp. 180–183), which shows how expectations run through the *General Theory*.

29 Minsky maintains that Keynes failed to construct an appropriate investment theory because he put too much emphasis on the marginal efficiency of capital. An appropriate investment theory, argues Minsky, should aim to determine the demand price of investment goods by capitalizing the prospective yields of capital. Keynes thought the two approaches identical, and emphasized the former approach. See Minsky (1975, Ch.5). Joan Robinson upholds Minsky's argument. See Eatwell and Milgate (eds.) (1983, p. 71).

30 Harrod (1936) seems to accept Keynes's claim that there exists no established theory of the rate of interest, but takes a rather neutral position, stating that the theory of liquidity preference is neither in conflict with nor necessary to what he has to argue. See p. 135. Harrod (1948), however, supports the theory of liquidity preference on the grounds that it is much more realistic than either of the loanable fund theories or the theory which attributes far too much foresight to the market, and defends it against several criticisms, claiming that it should be properly regarded as an attempt to fill a void. See pp. 63–72.

31 With regard to monetary policy, Keynes points out the following: (i) in reality the monetary authority cannot perform the ideal operations; (ii) there could be some contingencies in which the monetary authority would fail to attain a certain rate of interest.

32 Takahashi (1936), probably the only book of its time that examined the *Treatise* in detail from a critical, but not ideological, point of view, attributes the vital defect of the fundamental equations to the fact that Keynes takes equality between the earnings and the cost of production for granted and neglects the cost of capital depreciation. See Takahashi (1936, Chs. 4 and 5). Kitoh (1942), the most sophisticated book dealing with both the *Treatise* and the *General Theory* published in Japan before World War II, considers that the most essence in the two books lies in the instability of the monetary economy. He criticizes the fundamental equations on the grounds that Keynes neglects the fluctuations of goods in stock as well as the cost of capital depreciation. See Kitoh (1942, pp. 124–139). However, Kitoh rates the fundamental equations highly for connecting the price level with the distinction between the act of saving and the act of investing. See Kitoh (1942, pp. 73–80). Kitoh translated the *Treatise* in five volumes over the period 1932–1934.

33 See Aoyama (1942, p. 274).

34 For details, see Hirai (2008).

35 See, e.g., Cartelier (2007).

References

Aoyama, H. (1939a) "Robertson no bukka hendou riron" (Robertson's theory of price fluctuations), *Keizai Ronsou* (*The Economic Review*), 49–1: 153–169 (Kyoto University; in Japanese; reprinted as Chapter VI of Aoyama, 1999).

Aoyama, H. (1939b) "Kahei-suuryousetu no dougakuka to siteno kikan—bunseki" (Period analysis of a quantity theory of money as a dynamic version), *Keizai Ronsou* (*The Economic Review*), 49–2: 343–361 (Kyoto University; in Japanese; reprinted as Chapter VII of Aoyama, 1999).

Aoyama, H. (1940) "Kikan bunseki to kinkou gainen" (Period analysis and equilibrium analysis), *Keizai Ronsou* (*The Economic Review*), 50–4: 474–488 (Kyoto University; in Japanese; reprinted as Chapter IX of Aoyama, 1999).

Aoyama, H. (1941) "Robertson no kakaku suijun hendou riron to sono hihan" (Robertson's theory of price fluctuations critically examined) (in Japanese; reprinted as Chapter VIII of Aoyama, 1999; this is a paper which put together and arranged the four papers contributed to *Keizai Ronsou*).

Aoyama, H. (1942) "Gendai keiki riron ni okeru hanro housoku no mondai" (The problem of Say's Law in the modern theory of trade cycle), *Nihon Keizai Gakkai Nenpou* (*Annual of the Japanese Economic Association*), No. 2 (in Japanese; reprinted as Chapter IV of Aoyama, 1999).

Aoyama, H. (1944) "Kinkou riron no dougakuteki hatten" (A dynamic development of equilibrium theory), in The Newspaper Section of Kobe University of Commerce (ed.) *Keizai oyobi keizaigaku no saishuppatu* (*Economy and Economics Restarted*), Tokyo: Nihon Hyoron-sha (in Japanese; reprinted as Chapter I of Aoyama, 1999).

Aoyama, H. (1999) *Keizai hendou riron no kenkyu* (*A Study on the Theory of Economic Fluctuations*), Vol. 3, Tokyo: Sobunsha (in Japanese).

Asano, E. (1979–1985) "Ippan Riron Seiritushiron" (How did the *General Theory* come into being? (1)–(6)), *Shogaku Ronsou* (*Bulletin of Commerce*), Chuo University (in Japanese).

Bridel, P. (1987) *Cambridge Monetary Thought—The Development of Saving-Investment Analysis from Marshall to Keynes*, London: Macmillan.

Cartelier, J. (2007) "Money and markets as twin concepts?", in Giacomin, A. and Marcuzzo, M. C. (eds.) *Money and Markets*, London and New York: Routledge, Chapter 6.

Eatwell, J. and Milgate, M. eds. (1983) *Keynes's Economics and the Theory of Value and Distribution*, Oxford: Duckworth.

Fukuda, T. (1907) *Keizaigaku Kougi* (*Lecture on Economics*), Tokyo: Ookura Shoten (in Japanese).

Fukuda, T. (1922) *Shakai Seisaku to Kaikyu Tousou (Social Policy and the Class Struggle)*, Tokyo: Ookura Shoten (in Japanese).

Harrod, R. (1936) *The Trade Cycle*, Oxford: Clarendon Press.

Harrod, R. (1948) *Towards a Dynamic Economics*, London: Macmillan.

Harrod, R. (1969) *Money*, London: Macmillan.

Hawtrey, R. (1913) *Good and Bad Trade—An inquiry into the causes of trade fluctuations*, London: Constable & Company.

Hawtrey, R. (1923) *Monetary Reconstruction*, London: Longmans, Green and Co.

Hayek, F. (1931) *Prices and Production*, London: Routledge & Kegan Paul.

Hayek, F. (1933) *Monetary Theory and the Trade Cycle*, London: Routledge & Kegan Paul (translated from the German by Kaldor, N. and Croome, H. M.).

Hicks, J. R. (1939) *Value and Capital*, Oxford: Clarendon Press.

Hicks, J. R. (1967) *Critical Essays in Monetary Theory*, Oxford: Clarendon Press.

Hicks, J. R. (1976) "'Revolutions' in Economics", in Latsis, S. (ed.) *Method and Appraisal in Economics*, Cambridge: Cambridge University Press, Chapter 8.

Hirai, T. (1981) *Keynes Ippan Riron no Saikouchiku* (*A Reconstruction of Keynes's General Theory*), Tokyo: Hakuto Shobo (in Japanese).

Hirai, T. (2008) *Keynes's Theoretical Development: From the Tract to the General Theory*, London and New York: Routledge.

Ikeo, A. (1994) "When economics harmonized mathematics in Japan: A history of stability analysis", *European Journal of the History of Economic Thought*, 1–3: 577–599.

Ikeo, A. (2006) *Nihon no Keizaigaku—20 Seiki ni okeru Kokusaika no Rekishi (Economics in Japan—The Internationalization of Economics in the Twentieth Century)*, Nagoya: Nagoya University Press (in Japanese).

Israel, G. (2007) "Does game theory offer 'new' mathematical images of economic reality?", in Giacomin, A. and Marcuzzo, M. C. (eds.) *Money and Markets*, London and New York: Routledge, Chapter 4.

Kahn, R. (1984) *The Making of Keynes' General Theory*, Cambridge: Cambridge University Press.

Keynes, J. M. (1919) *The Economic Consequences of the Peace*, London: Macmillan.

Keynes, J. M. (1923) *A Tract on Monetary Reform*, London: Macmillan.

Keynes, J. M. (1930) *A Treatise on Money I, II*, London: Macmillan.

Keynes, J. M. (1936) *The General Theory of Employment, Interest and Money*, London: Macmillan.

Kitoh, N. (1942) *Kahei to Rishi no Doutai* (*Dynamics of Money and Interest*), Tokyo: Iwanami (in Japanese).

Klein, L. (1947) *The Keynesian Revolution*, London: Macmillan.

Laidler, D. (1991) *The Golden Age of the Quantity Theory*, Princeton: Princeton University Press.

Lindahl, E. (1939) *Studies in the Theory of Money and Capital*, London: George Allen and Unwin.

Marshall, A. (1920) *Principles of Economics*, eighth edition. London: Macmillan.

Minsky, H. (1975) *John Maynard Keynes*, New York: Columbia University Press.

Myrdal, G. (1939) *Monetary Equilibrium*, Glasgow: W. Hodge.

Nakayama, I. (1939) *Hatten Katei no Kinkou Bunseki* (*Equilibrium Analysis of Developmental Process*), Tokyo: Iwanami (in Japanese).

Negishi, T. and Ikeo, A. (1999) "Aoyama Hideo Kyouju to Keizaigaku" (Prof. Hideo Aoyama and Economics), in Aoyama Hideo Chosakushu Kankoukai ed., *Aoyama Hideo Sensei no Gakumon to Kyoiku* (*Prof. Aoyama's Learning and Education*, Tokyo: Sobunsha (in Japanese).

Pigou, A. (1917) "The value of money", *Quarterly Journal of Economics*, 32: 38–65.

Pigou, A. (1920) *The Economics of Welfare*, London: Macmillan.

Presley, J. (1979) *Robertsonian Economics: An Examination of the Work of Sir D.H. Robertson on Industrial Fluctuation*, London: Macmillan.

Robertson, D. (1922) *Money*, London: Nisbet & Co.

Robertson, D. (1926; 2nd ed. 1949) *Banking Policy and the Price Level—An Essay in the Theory of the Trade Cycle*, London: Staples Press Limited.

Robertson, D. (1934) "Industrial fluctuation and the natural rate of interest", *Economic Journal*, 44: 650–656.

Schumpeter, J. (1934) *The Theory of Economic Development*, Oxford: Oxford University Press (translated from the German, 1911, by Opie, R.).

Spiller, C. and Pomini, M. (2007) "Profit rate, money and economic dynamics in Fanno's thought", in Giacomin, A. and Marcuzzo, M. C. (eds.) *Money and Markets*, London and New York: Routledge, Chapter 14.

Sugimoto, E. (1981) *Kindai Keizaigaku no Kaimei* (*Elucidation of Modern Economics*) (1)(2), Tokyo: Iwanami (1st ed. in 1950) (in Japanese).

Takahashi, M. (1936) *Kaheiron no Kenkyu* (*A Study of the Treatise*), Tokyo: Nankosha (in Japanese).

Thornton, H. (1802) *An Inquiry into the Nature and Effects of the Paper Credit of Great Britain* (Hayek, F. ed.), London: George Allen & Unwin, 1939.

Wicksell, K. (1936) *Interest and Prices* (translated from the German, 1898, by Kahn, R.), London: Macmillan.

Yoshikawa, H. (1984) *Makuro Keizaigaku Kenkyu* (*Study on Macroeconomics*), Tokyo: University of Tokyo Press (in Japanese).

3 Japanese contributions to dynamic economic theories from the 1940s to the 1970s

A historical survey

Toichiro Asada

1 Introduction

Although this chapter is mainly concerned with the international contributions by Japanese theoretical economists in the post-World War II period (after 1945), in this section, we shall briefly refer to some important contributions before 1945. Until the end of World War II, Japan was a pure importer of economic theory and had nothing to export except only a few exceptional contributions.[1] Kei Shibata and Masazo Sono are two such exceptional Japanese scholars who were able to add something new to modern economic theory of that period.

Shibata was a very creative theoretical economist at Kyoto University. He studied mathematical Walrasian/Casselian general equilibrium theory as well as Marxian economic theory. In 1930, he found that Cassel's (1918) system of equations of general economic equilibrium may not have a meaningful solution because there is the possibility that a subsystem becomes over-determinate. Unfortunately, his paper (Shibata 1930) was written in Japanese, so that his contribution remained unknown amongst western economists. But his assertion was in fact the same as that of von Stackelberg (1933), which appeared three years *after* the publication of Shibata (1930).[2] Shibata (1933), which was written in English, tried to formulate Marx's scheme of reproduction by means of a simplified two sector Walrasian general equilibrium system of equations, and this paper was referred to by Oscar Lange (1935). He also published a critical review of Keynes' General Theory (Keynes 1936) in English only a year after the publication of Keynes' book (cf. Shibata 1937). Masazo Sono was a mathematician rather than economist, but his mathematical analysis of the 'separable goods' problem, which was done during World War II, is an important contribution to consumer theory (cf. Sono 1943).[3] The contributions by such economists as Shibata and Sono were the pioneering works which foreshowed the striking international contributions by several Japanese theoretical economists after World War II, especially in the period between the 1940s and the 1970s.

In the following sections, we shall consider international contributions by Japanese economists to the development of economic theory after World War II, especially focusing on the development of dynamic economic theories from the

1940s to the 1970s. We take up the theoretical contributions by Takuma Yasui, Michio Morishima, Hirofumi Uzawa, Takashi Negishi, Nobuo Okishio and Hukukane Nikaido.[4]

2 Takuma Yasui as a pioneer of dynamic analysis of economic stability and nonlinear analysis of business cycles

Takuma Yasui, who was a Professor of Economics at Tohoku University, Osaka University and other universities in Japan, is considered to be the father of mathematical economics in Japan. He began to study Walrasian general equilibrium theory during World War II. But he was frustrated because he could not find the correct *method* to deal with the dynamic analysis of Walras' *tâtonnement* (trial and error) process of price adjustment. Soon after World War II, he found the correct method in the mathematical theory of differential and difference equations. He published in Japanese a series of papers that dealt with the mathematical conditions for the dynamic stability (cf. Yasui 1948a, 1948b, 1950). Yasui (1948b) described the Routh-Hurwitz conditions for the local stability of an n-dimensional system of differential equations[5] and provided their economic applications to Walrasian/Hicksian general equilibrium system and Keynesian system. Yasui (1948b) also clearly described the Cohn-Schur conditions for the local stability of an n-dimensional system of difference equations without economic application.[6] In the postscript to his collected papers (Yasui 1971), he noted that these papers were written *before* he read Samuelson's famous book *Foundations of Economic Analysis* (Samuelson 1947), and Cohn-Schur conditions are not referred to by Samuelson (1947), although the Routh-Hurwitz conditions are contained in Samuelson (1947). In Yasui (1950), he referred to Liapunov's theorem on the global stability of a system of differential equations, due to Liapunov (Liapounoff 1907).[7] At that time, this theorem was not well known even among western mathematical economists. This means that Yasui is one of the first economists to realize the analytical power of Liapunov's theorem for economic analysis, as Weintraub (1987, 1991) correctly pointed out. Although Yasui (1950) did not provide economic application of this theorem, later this theorem was effectively used by Arrow and Hurwicz (1958) and Arrow, Block and Hurwicz (1959) to prove the global stability of Walrasian competitive equilibrium under the assumption of gross substitutability.

Another important contribution of Yasui to dynamic economic theory is a reformulation of Kaldor's (1940) business cycle theory by means of nonlinear differential equation. Kaldor (1940) presented an ingenious graphical presentation of his business cycle theory by means of an S-shaped nonlinear investment function (cf. Figure 3.1). In Figure 3.1, Y is real national income, the line ff represents the saving function $S = S(Y)$ and the S-shaped curves φ_{ei} ($i = 1, 2, 3, \ldots$) represent the investment function $I = I(Y, K)$, where the real investment I is supposed to be an S-shaped increasing function of real national income Y and decreasing function of real capital stock K. Kaldor (1940) assumes that the speed of the quantity adjustment in the goods market is very high, while the real capital

stock moves slowly. In Figure 3.1, the downward (upward) shift of the investment function is caused by an increase (decrease) of K, and the endogenous business cycle along the closed curve in Figure 3.1 occurs in his model.

Yasui (1953) reformulated Kaldor's (1940) theory by means of the following
system of dynamic equations omitting the asymmetry between the movement of
income and that of capital stock:

$$i = f(y) - \mu k \quad (f'(y) > 0, \mu > 0), \tag{1}$$

$$\varepsilon \dot{y} = i - sy \quad (\varepsilon > 0, 0 < s < 1), \tag{2}$$

$$\dot{k} = i - \delta k \quad (0 < \delta < 1), \tag{3}$$

$$y = Y - Y_0, i = I - I_0, k = K - K_0, \tag{4}$$

where Y=real national income, I=real investment demand, K=real capital stock.
The values Y_0, I_0, and K_0 are equilibrium values of these variables. The parameters μ, ε, s and δ are the sensitivity of investment with respect to the changes of
the capital stock, the reciprocal of the speed of the quantity adjustment in the
goods market, the average propensity to save and the rate of capital depreciation
respectively. Eq. (1) is the Kaldorian investment function where $f(y)$ is S-shaped,
Eq. (2) is the disequilibrium adjustment equation in the goods market and finally
Eq. (3) is the capital accumulation equation.

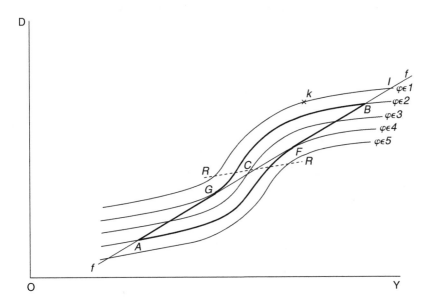

Figure 3.1 Kaldor's business cycle model (source: Kaldor 1960, p. 189).

Yasui (1953) derived the following single nonlinear second-order differential equation from the above system of equations:

$$\varepsilon\ddot{y} + [\varepsilon(\mu + \delta) + s - f'(y)]\dot{y} + s(\mu + \delta)y - \delta f(y) = 0 \tag{5}$$

Under some additional assumptions, he showed that this equation is mathematically equivalent to the following type of the generalized van der Pole equation (or Liénard equation) with $zF(z) > 0$ for $|z| > 0$.

$$\ddot{z} + F(z)\dot{z} + G(z) = 0 \tag{6}$$

Yasui (1953) noted that this type of equation had already been treated by Goodwin (1951) and that it produces the dynamic behavior of cyclical fluctuations by means of limit cycles, as represented by Figure 3.2 under some additional assumptions.[8]

It is worth noting that Kaldor himself referred to Yasui's (1953) paper in the preface of his collected papers (Kaldor 1960). Kaldor wrote as follows.

> The paper on 'A Model of the Trade Cycle', written shortly before the war, put forward a new idea—that the postulate of non-linear investment and/or savings functions produces a 'limit cycle' which is neither damped, nor anti-damped, and which does not presuppose for its operation that the various parameters assume values which fall within narrow range, as was the case with the earlier models of Frisch, Tinbergen or Kalecki. This idea attracted relatively little attention until some ten years later when Goodwin and Hicks published, quite independently, models of the trade cycle based on non-linear investment

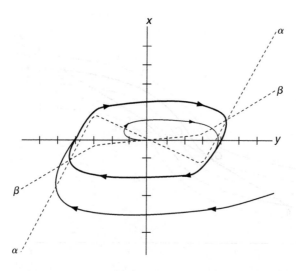

Figure 3.2 Yasui's graphical representation (source: Yasui 1971, p. 236).

functions and Yasui showed that the model could be translated into mathematical terms with the aid of van der Pol's theory of relaxation oscillations.

(Kaldor 1960, p. 9)[9]

Incidentally, Yasui's (1953) model as well as Kaldor's (1940) original model produces the cycles around the constant equilibrium values of income and capital. In other words, these models cannot produce cyclical growth (cycles around the growth trend). Yasui (1954) tried to reformulate such a Kaldorian model to produce cyclical growth. We shall interpret Yasui's (1954) model after we interpret Morishima's (1955) model of cyclical growth, because both models are closely related to each other.

3 Michio Morishima as a pioneer of nonlinear analysis of business cycles and cyclical growth

Michio Morishima was a distinguished Japanese mathematical economist, although he was a Professor of the London School of Economics from 1970 to 1988. He entered Kyoto University (Kyoto Imperial University at that time) in 1942 as a student, and studied Hicks' *Value and Capital* (Hicks 1939) under the guidance of his teacher Hideo Aoyama. After World War II, he taught economic theory at Kyoto University, Osaka University, the University of Essex, the London School of Economics and the University of Siena in Italy. In the 1950s and the 1960s, he was a colleague of Takuma Yasui at Osaka University. In 1964, he became the first Japanese economist to undertake the role of the President of the Econometric Society. At that time, he was 41 years old.[10] Since the 1950s, he published numerous quite original and creative papers and books on dynamic economic theory both in English and in Japanese (cf. Morishima 1950, 1953, 1955, 1958, 1964, 1969, 1996). In particular, he studied nonlinear macrodynamic models of economic fluctuations and multisectoral dynamic models of economic growth à la von Neumann. He also studied mathematical approaches to Marxian, Ricardian and Walrasian economic theories (cf. Morishima and Seton 1957; Morishima and Catephores 1978; Morishima 1973, 1977, 1989).[11]

In this section, we take up Morishima's contribution to nonlinear business cycle theories in the 1950s, which are closely related to Yasui's works, which we considered in the previous section. First, we shall take up the model of Morishima (1953, 1958), which was called the 'Ichimura-Morishima model' by Velupillai (2008).[12]

Morishima's (1953, 1958) model consists of the following system of equations (cf. Velupillai 2008).

$$C_t = \alpha Y_{t-\tau} + \beta(t), 0 < \alpha < 1 \tag{7}$$

$$I_t = v(Q_t + L_t - K_t), v > 0 \tag{8}$$

$$\dot{Q}_t = \phi(\dot{Y}_t), \phi' > 0 \tag{9}$$

$$Y_t = C_t + I_t + l(t), l(t) = \dot{L}_t \tag{10}$$

where Y=national income, C=consumption expenditure, I=induced investment expenditure, Q=desired capital stock, L=capital stock required for innovational investment, K=actual capital stock, and $l(t)$=autonomous or innovational investment expenditure. The subscript denotes time period.

Eq. (7) is the consumption function with an expenditure time lag. Eq. (8) together with Eq. (9) constitute the investment function of the nonlinear accelerator type. Eq. (10) is the equilibrium condition of the goods market.

The above system is a nonlinear system of mixed difference and differential equations. But, by expanding Eq. (7) in a Taylor series and neglecting the terms of higher order than the first, Morishima approximates Eq. (7) by the following equation.[13]

$$C_t = \alpha Y_t - \varepsilon \dot{Y}_t + \beta(t), \varepsilon = \alpha \tau > 0 \tag{11}$$

Furthermore, he adopted the simplifying assumption that $\beta(t)$ and $l(t)$ are constant. Then, he derived the following single nonlinear second order differential equation from the system of equations (8)–(11).

$$\varepsilon \theta \ddot{y} + [\varepsilon + (1-\alpha)\theta - \phi(\dot{y})/\dot{y}]\dot{y} + (1-\alpha)y = 0; \theta = 1/v, y = Y - Y^* \tag{12}$$

where Y^* is the equilibrium value of Y.[14] As Morishima (1958) noted, this is a Rayleigh type nonlinear differential equation rather than the Liénard equation. He proved the existence of a limit cycle in this model under some restrictive assumptions. As Velupillai (2008) pointed out, however, it is worth noting that it is possible to prove the existence of a limit cycle in Morishima's (1953, 1958) model as well as Yasui's (1953) model under less restrictive assumptions than that they imposed by applying the Hopf-bifurcation theorem.[15]

If it is assumed that the autonomous expenditures $\beta(t)$ and $l(t)$ are increasing functions of time, the equilibrium level of national income itself becomes an increasing function of time. In this case, the system of equations (8)–(11) can produce cyclical growth around a moving equilibrium. Morishima (1955, chap. 4) applied the same idea to Kaldor's (1940) model of business cycle. He wrote as follows.

> Basic consumption increases as the population and the standard of living increase, while the population increases as time passes, and the standard of living also tends to increase as time passes, so that we can suppose that basic consumption increases as time passes. Therefore, $b(t)$ becomes an increasing function of t where $b(t)$ is the basic consumption at the time period t.
>
> (Morishima 1955, p. 102; original text is in Japanese)

Then, Morishima (1955) presented Figure 3.3, which describes the process of cyclical growth in the Kaldorian setting. In this figure, the increase of basic consumption induces the rightward shift of the saving function S_i^*, so that cyclical growth along the trajectory *abcde*... is brought out.

Yasui (1954) provided a more complex version of the Kaldorian cyclical growth, which is represented by Figure 3.4. It must be noted that Yasui's (1954) model is an adaptation of Morishima's (1955) model and not the other way round, although Yasui's paper was published a year before the publication of Morishima's book. In fact, Yasui (1954) referred to Morishima's forthcoming book at that time. In Morishima's (1955) model, it is simply assumed that the saving function continues to shift rightward because of the increase in autonomous consumption expenditure, while Yasui (1954) adopted the more sophisticated 'ratchet effect' approach of Duesenberry (1949), which means that the consumption does not return to the previous low level even if the national income decreases because of the inertia effect of consumers having become accustomed to high consumption levels. Another difference between these two models is that in Yasui's (1954) model the cyclical growth can persist forever because the trajectory moves continually toward the north-east direction, while in Morishima's (1955) model the process of the cyclical growth must stop eventually because the trajectory moves toward the south-east direction.

4 Hirofumi Uzawa's investment function and Tobin's q theory

Hirofumi Uzawa is one of the most distinguished Japanese mathematical economists, together with Michio Morishima and Hukukane Nikaido. He studied mathematics at the University of Tokyo, and moved to Stanford University to

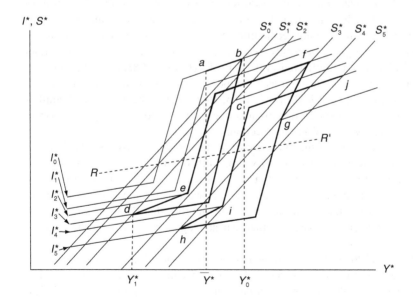

Figure 3.3 Morishima's model of cyclical growth (source: Morishima 1955, p. 106).

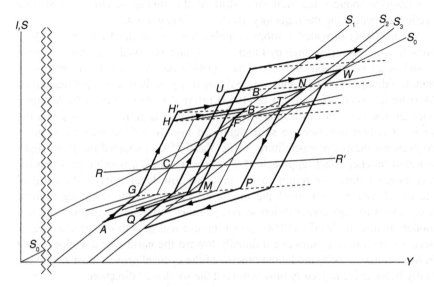

Figure 3.4 Yasui's model of cyclical growth (source: Yasui 1971, p. 255).

complete joint research on mathematical programming with Kenneth Arrow and Leonid Hurwicz in 1956. The output of this joint research was published in Arrow, Hurwicz and Uzawa (1958). He became a Professor of Economics at the University of Chicago in 1964. At that time, he was 36 years old. In 1969, he went back to Japan and became a Professor of Economics at the University of Tokyo. In 1977, he was elected as the President of the Econometric Society. After retiring from teaching economics at the University of Tokyo, he taught economics at Niigata University and Chuo University. Most of his important theoretical works are collected in three books (Uzawa 1988a, 1988b, 1990). In the 1960s, he published a series of important papers on neoclassical growth theory (Uzawa 1961a, 1961b, 1963, 1965, 1969) and Walrasian general equilibrium theory (Uzawa 1962). In particular, we shall refer to three important papers (Uzawa 1962, 1965, 1969) in this section.

It is well known that the existence of Walrasian competitive equilibrium can be proved by means of Brouwer's fixed point theorem.[16] This means that Brouwer's fixed point theorem implies Walras's existence theorem. On the other hand, Uzawa (1962) proved that the existence of Walrasian competitive equilibrium implies Brouwer's fixed point theorem. This implies that Brouwer's fixed point theorem and Walras's existence theorem are logically equivalent. This is the famous theorem of Uzawa.

In Uzawa (1961a), he studied the mathematical condition for 'neutral' technical progress. In this paper, however, the rate of technical progress was treated as an exogenous variable. On the other hand, in Uzawa (1965), the rate of technical progress becomes an endogenous variable which depends on the amount of the investment on human capital (education of the workers). In this sense, Uzawa (1965) is a pioneering work which became a predecessor of the so-called 'endogenous growth theory' by Lucas (1988), Romer (1990), etc., which flourished in the 1980s and the 1990s. In fact, Lucas (1988) quoted Uzawa (1965) as the direct source of his idea.[17]

The above works of Uzawa to which we referred are very famous among economic theorists. Now we shall take up the relatively less known contribution of Uzawa—that is, Uzawa (1969). In this paper, he presents a dynamic optimization model of a Keynesian type investment function by adopting the hypothesis of increasing adjustment cost of investment.[18] This contribution is quite important because later Yoshikawa (1980) and Hayashi (1982), both of whom were Uzawa's students at the University of Tokyo, showed that Uzawa's (1969) investment function provides a microeconomic foundation of Tobin's q theory, due to Tobin (1969, 1980). In fact, they proved that Uzawa's (1969) investment theory implies Tobin's q theory.

Uzawa (1969) formulated the following typical firm's dynamic optimization problem of investment:

$$\text{Maximize} \int_0^\infty \{r - \varphi(g(t))\} p_K K(t) e^{-\rho t} dt \tag{13}$$

$$\text{subject to } \dot{K}(t) = g(t)K(t), \, K(0) = K_0 = \text{constant.} \tag{14}$$

where K=real capital stock, g=rate of investment (rate of capital accumulation), r=rate of profit, p_K=price of the capital goods, ρ=rate of discount and t denotes the time period. It is assumed that r, p_K, and ρ are positive parameters. The function $\varphi(g)$ is the adjustment cost function of investment with the following properties:[19]

$$\varphi(0) = 0, \, \varphi'(g) > 0, \, \varphi''(g) > 0, \, \varphi'(0) = 1 \tag{15}$$

The control variable is the rate of investment (g).

Uzawa (1969) derived the following optimal solution to this problem:[20]

For all $t \geq 0$, keep $g(t)$ constant at the level g^* such that

$$\frac{r - \varphi(g^*)}{\rho - g^*} = \varphi'(g^*). \tag{16}$$

Uzawa (1969) illustrated this solution by using a graph, such as Figure 3.5, from which it follows that

$$g^* = g^*(r, \rho); \quad \partial g^* / \partial r > 0, \, \partial g^* / \partial \rho < 0, \tag{17}$$

which is nothing but Uzawa's (1969) investment function.

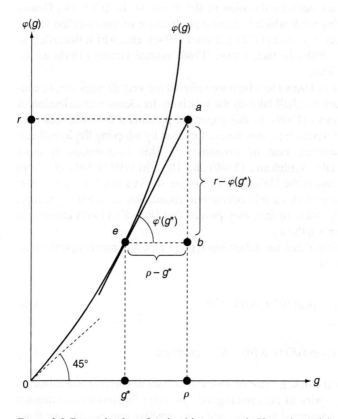

Figure 3.5 Determination of optimal investment in Uzawa's model.

Incidentally, Yoshikawa (1980) showed that this investment function is equivalent to Tobin's q theory. We can summarize his argument as follows. Suppose that $g(t) = g^* < \rho$ for all $t \geq 0$. In this case, the market value of the firm becomes

$$V(t) = \int_t^\infty \{r - \varphi(g^*)\} p_K K(s) e^{-\rho(s-t)} ds$$

$$= \int_t^\infty \{r - \varphi(g^*)\} p_K K(t) e^{-(\rho-g^*)(s-t)} ds = \frac{r - \varphi(g^*)}{\rho - g^*} p_K K(t). \qquad (18)$$

Therefore, Tobin's q, which is defined as the ratio of the market value of the firm to the value of the real capital stock, becomes

$$q = \frac{V(t)}{p_K K(t)} = \frac{r - \varphi(g^*)}{\rho - g^*}. \qquad (19)$$

From equations (16) and (19), we have

$$q = \varphi'(g^*). \tag{20}$$

Solving this equation with respect to g^*, we obtain the following famous 'q investment function':

$$g^* = f(q); \quad f'(q) > 0, \, f(1) = 0 \tag{21}$$

This demonstrates that Uzawa's (1969) approach can serve as a microeconomic foundation of Tobin's q theory.

5 Takashi Negishi as a pioneer of dynamic stability analysis of the Walrasian competitive equilibrium

Takashi Negishi, who became a Professor of Economics at the University of Tokyo after studying economics at the same university, published a series of pioneering mathematical papers on general equilibrium theory in the 1950s and the 1960s (cf. Negishi 1958, 1960, 1961, 1962). In the 1970s, he utilized the method of general equilibrium analysis to investigate the microeconomic foundations of Keynesian Macroeconomics (cf. Negishi 1979). In the 1980s, he shifted his attention to the study of the history of economic theory (cf. Negishi 1989). After retiring from teaching economics at the University of Tokyo, he taught economics at Aoyama Gakuin University. He became the President of the Econometric Society in 1993. In this section, we shall focus on Negishi's remarkable contributions to the dynamic stability analysis of the Walrasian competitive equilibrium in the 1950s and the 1960s.

Walras' tâtonnement process is the price adjustment process in which the prices of the goods with positive (negative) excess demand increase (decrease). But there is no *a priori* reason to guarantee that this process is dynamically stable unless we impose some restrictions on the properties of the excess demand functions. Hicks (1939) proposed a set of particular mathematical 'stability conditions', but Samuelson (1944) pointed out that Hicks' stability conditions are not identical to the 'true' Routh-Hurwitz conditions for local stability of a system of differential equations. Metzler (1945) found that Hicks' stability conditions become identical to the 'true' local stability conditions if it is assumed that all goods are 'gross substitutes'.[21]

In 1958, remarkable progress was made on the related research areas by two papers which were published in *Econometrica*, that is, Hahn (1958) and Negishi (1958). They arrived at the same conclusion independently of each other. Namely, the 'true' local stability conditions are satisfied automatically in the system with 'gross substitutes'. Next, we shall summarize Negishi's (1958) approach. He effectively used the Perron–Frobenius theorem concerning the indecomposable nonnegative matrices to prove the local stability of the Walrasian price adjustment in a system with gross substitutes.[22]

Negishi (1958) considers the following Walrasian price adjustment process by means of a system of differential equations.

$$\dot{p}_j = E_j(p_1, p_2, \cdots, p_{m-1}, p_m), \; j = 1, 2, \cdots, m-1, \tag{22}$$

$$p_m = 1, \tag{23}$$

$$\sum_{j=1}^{m} p_j E_j(p_1, p_2, \cdots, p_{m-1}, p_m) = 0, \tag{24}$$

where p_j is the price of good j, and E_j is the excess demand (the difference between demand and supply) of good j. It is assumed that the excess demand function is differentiable and the following conditions for gross substitutability are satisfied:

$$\frac{\partial E_j}{\partial p_j} < 0, \; \frac{\partial E_j}{\partial p_k} > 0 \text{ if } j \ne k \; (j, k = 1, 2, \cdots, m-1, m). \tag{25}$$

Eq. (23) means that the m'th good is selected as the numéraire and its price is always fixed at the level 1. In addition, it is assumed that there exists the unique strictly positive equilibrium price vector $\bar{p} = [\bar{p}_1, \bar{p}_2, \ldots, \bar{p}_{m-1}]'$ which satisfies[23]

$$E_j(\bar{p}) = 0 \text{ for all } j \in \{1, 2, \ldots, m-1, m\} \tag{26}$$

Eq. (24) is the so called 'Walras law', which means that the total excess demand is always zero even in a disequilibrium situation.[24]

Expanding the right-hand side of Eq. (22) in a Taylor series at the equilibrium point and neglecting the terms of higher order than the first, Negishi (1958) derived the following linear system of differential equations:

$$\dot{p}_j = \sum_{k=1}^{m-1} \frac{\partial E_j(\bar{p})}{\partial p_k}(p_k - \bar{p}_k), \; j = 1, 2, \ldots, m-1. \tag{27}$$

By using matrix notation, we can rewrite this system as follows:

$$\dot{p} = A(p - \bar{p}), \tag{28}$$

$$p = [p_1, p_2, \cdots, p_{m-1}]', \tag{29}$$

$$A = \begin{bmatrix} a_{11} & a_{12} & \cdots & a_{1m-1} \\ a_{21} & a_{22} & \cdots & a_{2m-1} \\ \vdots & \vdots & \ddots & \vdots \\ a_{m-11} & a_{m-12} & \cdots & a_{m-1m-1} \end{bmatrix}, \tag{30}$$

$$a_{jk} = \frac{\partial E_j(\bar{p})}{\partial p_k} \quad (j,k = 1,2,\ldots,m-1). \tag{31}$$

The characteristic equation of this linear system of differential equation becomes

$$\Delta(\lambda) = |\lambda I - A| = 0. \tag{32}$$

It is well known that the equilibrium point of the original (nonlinear) dynamical system (22) is locally stable if all the roots of Eq. (32) have negative real parts. As Yasui (1948b) pointed out, such a stability condition is equivalent to the quite complicated Routh–Hurwitz conditions. The direct application of the Routh–Hurwitz conditions to such a high-dimensional system is, however, highly impractical. Negishi (1958) solved the problem ingeniously by applying the Perron–Frobenis theorem for indecomposable nonnegative matrices rather than the Routh–Hurwitz theorem to this system of equations. In his derivation, the Walras law (Eq. 24) as well as the gross substitutability postulate (inequalities 25) plays the crucial role.

By differentiating Eq. (24) with respect to p_k, he obtains the following expression:

$$\sum_{j=1}^{m} p_j \frac{\partial E_j(p)}{\partial p_k} + E_k(p) = 0 \quad (k = 1,2,\cdots,m-1). \tag{33}$$

At the equilibrium point $E_k(\bar{p})=0$ is satisfied, so that he obtains

$$-\sum_{j=1}^{m-1} \bar{p}_j \frac{\partial E_j(\bar{p})}{\partial p_k} = \frac{\partial E_m(\bar{p})}{\partial p_k} \quad (k = 1,2,\cdots,m-1), \tag{34}$$

or in matrix notation,

$$-xA = z, \tag{35}$$

$$x = \bar{p}' = [\bar{p}_1, \bar{p}_2, \cdots, \bar{p}_{m-1}] > 0, \tag{36}$$

$$z = \left[\frac{\partial E_m(\bar{p})}{\partial p_1}, \frac{\partial E_m(\bar{p})}{\partial p_2}, \cdots, \frac{\partial E_m(\bar{p})}{\partial p_{m-1}} \right] > 0. \tag{37}$$

Since all of the non-diagonal elements of the matrix A are positive, he is able to define the following positive matrix M by selecting the sufficiently large positive scalar t:

$$M = tI + A > 0. \tag{38}$$

Substituting this equation into Eq. (35), he obtains the equation

$$x[tI - M] = z, M > 0, x > 0, z > 0, t > 0. \tag{39}$$

Now, let us consider the characteristic equation

$$\Delta(\rho) = |\rho I - M| = 0. \tag{40}$$

Since the positive matrix M is a special case of an indecomposable nonnegative matrix, we can use the following results of the Perron-Frobenius theorem concerning indecomposable nonnegative matrices.[25]

The characteristic root of Eq. (40) which has the largest absolute value (ρ_M), which is called the 'Frobenius root', is a positive real root.

Suppose that the positive vectors x, z, and positive real number t satisfy the relationship (39). Then, we have the inequality $t > \rho_M$.

Therefore, we have the following inequality for any characteristic root ρ of Eq. (40):

$$t > \rho_M \geq |\rho|. \tag{41}$$

It follows from equations (32) and (38) that $\rho = \lambda + t$, so that inequality (41) implies that

$$t > |\lambda + t| \geq \text{Re}(\lambda + t) = (\text{Re}\,\lambda) + t \tag{42}$$

where Reχ means the real part of the complex number χ.[26] Inequality (42) implies that we have Re$\lambda < 0$ for any characteristic root λ of Eq.(32). This completes Negishi's (1958) proof of local stability of the equilibrium point of the Walrasian dynamic adjustment process with gross substitutes (22)–(24).

Arrow and Hurwicz (1958) proved the *global* rather than local stability of the competitive equilibrium under the Walrasian adjustment process with gross substitutability in a paper which was also published in *Econometrica* in 1958 by using Liapunov's theorem, so that it seems that the proofs of *local* stability of the same system by Hahn (1958) and Negishi (1958) immediately became obsolete in 1958.[27] Nevertheless, Negishi's (1958) proof has its own value as an example of the ingenious application of the Perron-Frobenius theorem concerning the indecomposable nonnegative matrices to economic analysis in a research area other than Leontief-type input–output analysis. A few years later, Negishi published an exhaustive survey article on the stability of the Walrasian competitive equilibrium, including the evaluations of the contributions by himself, Hahn, Arrow and Hurwicz and others, and his survey article (Negishi 1962) had much influence on researchers working on the related topics (cf. Weintraub 1991, chap. 7).

Incidentally, in the disequilibrium situation in the Walrasian tâtonnement process, transactions are not allowed. On the other hand, in the so-called non-tâtonnement process the transactions are allowed, even in the disequilibrium situation. Hahn and Negishi (1962) proved the dynamic stability of equilibrium in such a non-tâtonnement process.

6 Nobuo Okishio on the mathematical formulation of Harrodian instability

Nobuo Okishio, who was a Professor of Economic Theory at Kobe University, was a world-famous pioneer of mathematical Marxian economics. The mathematical study of the classical and Marxian economic systems was begun in the early period of the twentieth century by a few economists such as Dmitriev and Bortkiewicz (cf. Dmitriev 1904 [1974] for the Ricardian system and Bortkiewicz 1907 [1949] for the Marxian system). But, up to the 1950s, there was very little progress in this research area. In 1960, Sraffa published a small but important book on the mathematical study of the Ricardian system (Sraffa 1960) and the revival of the mathematical study of classical economics began. But, in the 1950s, Okishio had already begun to study the Marxian theory of value and price by using the mathematical theory on nonnegative matrices which had become well known among economists through the study of the Leontief-type input–output system. Earlier mathematical works by Okishio on Marxian value and price theory were published in Japanese (cf. Okishio 1957, 1965), but his works which include the essence of his analytical results were published in English later (cf. Okishio 1963 and Okishio 1993). In fact, Morishima's work on mathematical Marxian economics—for example, Morishima (1973)—owes a great debt to Okishio's work and not the other way round.

Another notable contribution by Okishio is the mathematical formulation of the Harrodian instability principle in the models of economic growth and economic fluctuations (cf. Okishio 1964, 1976, 1977). Okishio reconsidered Harrod's (1948) dynamic theory of economic growth from a Marxian point of view. He thought that Harrod's idea on the instability of the capital accumulation process could be utilized to construct a mathematical Marxian theory of the reproduction process of the capitalist economy. Next, we shall reproduce the simplest version of Okishio's analysis of Harrodian instability by means of the difference equation which is contained in Okishio (1964).

Okishio (1964) summarizes the steady-growth solution of the so-called 'Harrod-Domar model' as follows:

$$sY=I, \tag{43}$$

$$Y=\sigma K, \tag{44}$$

$$I=\Delta K, \tag{45}$$

where Y=real national income, I=real investment expenditure, K=real capital stock, s= average propensity to save $(0<s<1)$ and σ=output–capital ratio (average productivity of capital) in the case of the full utilization of capital stock>0. It is assumed that s and σ are constant parameters.

The system of equations (43)–(45) can determine the movement of the three endogenous variables Y, I and K. In fact, Okishio obtains the following solution of the growth rates of these variables from the above system of equations:

$$s\sigma = \frac{\Delta K}{K} = \frac{\Delta I}{I} = \frac{\Delta Y}{Y}. \tag{46}$$

This equation determines the equilibrium growth rates of capital, investment and income at the steady state with full capacity utilization. Okishio (1964) correctly pointed out, however, that there is no investment function in this model, and he wrote as follows:

> Though this model determines the value of new investment I, this value is the required value of new investment to guarantee the steady growth and is not the actual value which capitalists invest. Therefore it remains as a problem whether the actual growth path converges to the steady growth.
> (Okishio 1993, p. 191)

He pointed out that in actual situations, there is no guarantee that the full utilization of the capital stock is realized and the degree of capital utilization must become an endogenous variable. Therefore, according to Okishio (1964), the actual growth process must be reformulated as follows:[28]

$$sY_t = I_t, \tag{47}$$

$$Y_t = \delta_t \sigma K_t, \tag{48}$$

$$I_t = \Delta K_t, \tag{49}$$

where δ is the degree of the utilization of the capital stock. This is a system of three equations with four endogenous variables (Y, I, K, δ). Okishio (1964) pointed out that one more equation is required to close the system and the missing additional equation is nothing but the firms' investment function. He proposed to close this system by adding the following type of investment function:

$$\frac{I_{t+1}}{K_{t+1}} = \frac{I_t}{K_t} + F(\delta_t), \quad F(1) = 0, \quad F' > 0. \tag{50}$$

This equation means that the entrepreneurs determine their investment expenditures according to the degree of capital utilization. In fact, it is possible to interpret this type of investment function as a mathematical formalization of Harrod's (1948) idea.[29]

From equations (47) and (48), Okishio (1964) obtains the expression

$$s\sigma\delta_t = \frac{I_t}{K_t}.$$
(51)

Substituting this equation into Eq. (50), he derived the following difference equation for the single endogenous variable δ:

$$\delta_{t+1} = \delta_t + \frac{1}{s\sigma}F(\delta_t)$$
(52)

Differentiating this equation with respect to δ_t, he derived the inequality

$$\frac{d\delta_{t+1}}{d\delta_t} = 1 + \frac{1}{s\sigma}F'(\delta_t) > 1.$$
(53)

This inequality means that the equilibrium point of this system which satisfies $\delta = 1$ is dynamically unstable. Okishio (1964) illustrated this instability proposition by using a graph such as Figure 3.6.

One of the causes of instability in this model is the dual nature of investment. In other words, an increase in investment means an increase of effective demand as well as an increase in the productive capacity. The increase (decrease) of the rate of capacity utilization of capital stock which is caused by the increase

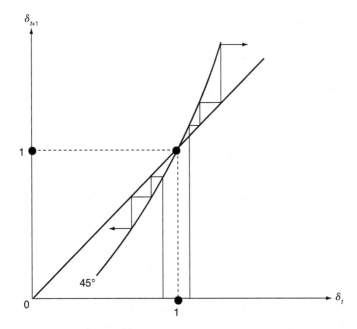

Figure 3.6 Harrodian instability in Okishio's model.

(decrease) of the effective demand induces the increase (decrease) of investment expenditure, which causes further increase (further decrease) of the rate of capacity utilization through further increase (further decrease) of the effective demand. This is the destabilizing positive feedback mechanism in the model. Another cause of instability is the postulated myopic bounded-rational investment behavior of the entrepreneurs, which exclusively depends on the current rate of capacity utilization of the capital stock. This process of the 'cumulative disequilibrium' will continue until the floor and the ceiling which are created by financial, labor or other markets prevent the investment expenditure from the upward or downward infinite divergence. Okishio (1976) developed his theory of the business cycle by introducing such ceilings and floors into the model, which somewhat resembles Hicks' (1950) theory of the business cycle.

7 Hukukane Nikaido on Harrodian instability and the irrelevance of smooth factor substitution

Hukukane Nikaido, who was a Professor of Mathematical Economics at Osaka University, Hitotsubashi University and other universities in Japan, is one of the most brilliant Japanese mathematical economists. After studying mathematics at the University of Tokyo, he began to write a series of brilliant papers on mathematical economics in the 1950s. His earlier important contribution is Nikaido (1956), which provided a rigorous but elegant proof of the existence of the Walrasian competitive equilibrium by means of Kakutani's fixed point theorem quite independently of the papers by McKenzie (1954), Arrow and Debreu (1954) and Gale (1955).[30] He also wrote a joint paper with Uzawa on the stability of the competitive equilibrium (Nikaido and Uzawa 1960) and a joint paper with Gale on sufficient conditions for the uniqueness of the equilibrium solution (Gale and Nikaido 1965). He also succeeded in presenting a complete mathematically rigorous characterization of Radner's (1961) turnpike theorem (cf. Nikaido 1964). Nikaido (1968) is the exhaustive advanced textbook of mathematical economics, in which his original contributions up to this period are contained.

After the 1970s, he shifted his attention from the mathematical study of the Walrasian/neoclassical microeconomic theories to the mathematical study of the imperfect competition and Keynesian/Harrodian/Marxian macrodynamic theories (cf. Nikaido 1975a, 1975b, 1979, 1980, 1983). In the introduction to his collected papers on economic dynamics, which was published in 1996, he wrote as follows:

> These early results[31] dealt with statics and dynamics within the Hicksian week of a generic Walrasian Arrow–Debreu economy, one that is solely composed of production, exchange and consumption but devoid of capital formation, credit, and money. In my view, such models describe ideal resource allocation in an institutional framework of complete private ownership, rather than the working of the market economy in the real world. They are best thought of as normative, rather than positive, construction.
>
> (Nikaido 1996, p. xiii)

The principal view, which drives me most, is that the working of the real world capitalist economy can better be elucidated along the lines suggested by Keynes (1936) in his criticism of the Classical school rather than along the lines currently pursued by the rational expectations and new Classicals as descendants of the old Classicals. It is especially his grand vision that the economy is unstable and can be ill-behaved that seems most important (Nikaido 1996, p. xiv).

In this section, we consider Nikaido (1975b), which proved that the assumption of smooth factor substitution is not sufficient to deny the Harrodian instability principle contrary to a common belief among economists.[32] Nikaido (1975b) formulates the following system of equations:

$$\dot{L}/L = n, \tag{54}$$

$$y = \min[I/s, F(K,L)], \tag{55}$$

$$\dot{K} = sy, \tag{56}$$

$$I/s = \theta F(K,L) = F(\theta K, \theta L), \tag{57}$$

$$\frac{d}{dt}(I/K) = \varphi(\theta - 1), \ \varphi(0) = 0, \ \varphi' > 0, \tag{58}$$

where L=labor supply, n=growth rate of labor supply >0, y=real national income, I=real investment demand, K=real capital stock, s=average propensity to save $(0<s<1)$, θ=a measure of the degree of capital shortage, and $F(K, L)$ is a neoclassical linear homogeneous production function with smooth factor substitution. It is assumed that n and s are constant parameters.

Eq. (54) states that the labor supply grows at the constant rate. According to Eq. (55), the real national income (y) is determined by the 'short side' between the Keynesian effective demand (I/s) and the potential full employment level ($F(K, L)$). Eq. (56) implies that capital accumulation is determined by the rule

$$\dot{K} = \begin{cases} sF(K,L) & \text{if} \quad I/s > F(K,L), \\ I & \text{if} \quad I/s \le F(K,L). \end{cases} \tag{59}$$

Eq. (57) defines the measure of the degree of the capital shortage (θ). The inequality $\theta > 1$ means capital shortage, while $\theta < 1$ means excess capacity of capital. Eq. (58) is a Harrod-type investment function, which implies that the entrepreneurs accelerate (decelerate) investment in the case of capital shortage (excess capacity of capital). The dynamic system of five equations (54)–(58) determines the movement of the five endogenous variables (L, y, K, θ, I).

Nikaido (1975b) proved that the rate of investment (I/K) continues to decrease indefinitely if the following set of inequalities is satisfied at the initial period (period 0):

$$I(0)/s < F(K(0), L(0)), \tag{60}$$

$$\dot{K}(0)/K(0) \le \dot{L}(0)/L(0) = n. \tag{61}$$

His reasoning is as follows. Since Eq. (57) implies that

$$I/s - F(K, L) = (\theta - 1)F(K, L), \tag{62}$$

we have $\theta < 1$ at the initial period if the inequality (60) is satisfied. In this case, we have $\dfrac{d}{dt}(I/K) < 0$ at $t=0$. This result guarantees that there exists the time period $\tau > 0$ such that there holds the set of inequalities

$$I(t)/s < F(K(t), L(t)), \quad \dot{K}(t)/K(t) < n \tag{63}$$

for all $t \in (0, \tau)$, which also implies that we have $\dfrac{d}{dt}(I/K) < 0$ for all $t \in (0, \tau)$. On the other hand, we have the expression

$$\frac{d}{dt}\left[\frac{I}{sK} - \frac{F(K,L)}{K}\right] = \frac{1}{s}\frac{d}{dt}\left(\frac{I}{K}\right) - \left(\frac{L}{K}\right)\left(n - \frac{\dot{K}}{K}\right)\frac{\partial}{\partial(L/K)}F(1, L/K). \tag{64}$$

It follows from the inequalities (63) and Eq. (64) that

$$\frac{d}{dt}\left[\frac{I}{sK} - \frac{F(K,L)}{K}\right] < 0 \tag{65}$$

for all $t \in (0, \tau)$. This inequality means that we can extend the time period τ which satisfies a set of inequalities (63) for all $t \in (0, \tau)$ indefinitely. Therefore, the rate of investment I/K continues to decrease indefinitely if a set of initial conditions (60) and (61) is satisfied. This completes Nikaido's (1975b) proof of Harrodian instability in a system with smooth factor substitution. This is the rationale of Nikaido's following assertion.

The stability of the Solovian neoclassical growth equilibrium heavily relies upon its particular investment habits of capitalists in which investment automatically equals savings, rather than factor substitution.[33] On the other hand, one of the most crucial points in Harrod's analysis is that the investment behaviors of capitalists are primarily responsible for the growth equilibrium balanced on the knife-edge. Thus instability is likely to occur even under flexible smooth factor substitution, depending on the investment habit (Nikaido 1996, p. 159).

8 Theoretical contributions of other Japanese economists from the 1950s to the 1980s

In this final section, we shall refer to some other important theoretical contributions of Japanese economists from the 1950s to the 1980s.

Kenjiro Ara, who was a Professor of Economics at Hitotsubashi University, was the first Japanese economist to publish a paper in the *Economic Journal* (cf. Ara 1958). Ara (1958) is one of the earliest papers on the neoclassical aggregative theory of economic growth which was formulated independent of Solow (1956) and Swan (1956). Ara (1959), which was published in *Econometrica*, is a theoretical contribution to the aggregation problem of the Leontief-type multisectoral input–output system, which is somewhat related to the paper by Morishima and Seton (1957). He also provided a pioneering analysis of the two sector model of unbalanced growth, although it was written in Japanese (cf. Ara 1969, Appendix 1).

Kenichi Inada and Yoichi Shinkai, both of whom were Professors of Economics at Osaka University, also contributed to the theory of economic growth in the 1960s (cf. Inada 1964, 1966; Shinkai 1960). In particular, the name of Inada is well known because of the so called 'Inada conditions' concerning the shape of the neoclassical production function.[34]

Although the theme of this chapter is the Japanese contribution to dynamic economic theory from the 1940s to the 1970s, we shall refer to an important contribution by a Japanese economist in the 1980s. Koichi Hamada, who was Professor of Economics at the University of Tokyo and Yale University, made a pioneering contribution to the dynamic as well as static game theoretical approach to the international monetary economics (cf. Hamada 1985, 1996).

In this chapter, we have concentrated on some of the notable contributions of Japanese economists to dynamic economic theories from the 1940s to the 1970s. Although the contributions which were taken up in this chapter are by no means exhaustive, it is unquestionable that all of them are important contributions to economic theory.

Acknowledgment

This chapter is the revised version of the paper that was written in December 2009 while the author was staying at the School of Finance and Economics, University of Technology Sydney (UTS) as a Visiting Professor under the 'Chuo University Leave Program for Special Research Project'. Thanks are due to Professor Carl Chiarella of UTS, who kindly checked and corrected the expressions in English. The author is also grateful to Professor Harutaka Takahashi of Meiji Gakuin University in Tokyo, who kindly provided the evidence that shows the importance of McKenzie's relatively less known contribution to the general equilibrium theory and Ara's contribution to the two sector model of unbalanced growth. Needless to say, however, only the author is responsible for possible remaining errors. This research was financially supported by the Japan Society for the Promotion of Science (Grant-in Aid for Scientific Research (C) 25380238) and Chuo University, Grant for Special Research.

Notes

1 The newest imported economics in this period in Japan was Marxian economics, but the Japanese government oppressed it because the government considered it politically dangerous, and the Japanese mainstream economics in this period was quite domestic, nationalistic, and illogical economics written in Japanese, which had no international influence.

2 Zeuthen (1933) presented the correct way to solve this problem by means of inequalities rather than equations, and Wald (1936) managed to solve the problem mathematically. See also Yasui, Kumagai and Fukuoka (1977) for related topics.

3 The goods X and Y are said to be separable from the good Z if the marginal rate of substitution between X and Y is independent of the quantity of Z (cf. Ikeo 2006, p. 99; according to Ikeo 2006, this is the definition by Takuma Yasui.) Sono's paper in Japanese (1943) was later translated into English (Sono 1961).

4 Other important economists who are not taken up in this chapter are Ichiro Nakayama (study of Walrasian general equilibrium theory and Schumpeter's economics), Eiichi Sugimoto (synthesis of Marshallian and Marxian economics) and Hideo Aoyama (study of the theory of imperfect competition and the sociological study of Max Weber) because most of their contributions were written in Japanese and it seems that they had little international impact. As for the expositions of their contributions, see Ikeo (1999) and Ikeo (ed.) (2006). Another influential economist who is not taken up in this chapter is Shigeto Tsuru, a Marxian-oriented 'institutional' economist who is internationally well known (cf. Tsuru 1993).

5 Let us consider the following n-th order polynomial characteristic equation,

$$\lambda^n + a_1\lambda^{n-1} + a_2\lambda^{n-2} + \cdots + a_{n-1}\lambda + a_n = 0.$$

The Routh–Hurwitz conditions mean that all of the roots of this characteristic equation have negative real parts *if and only if* the following set of inequalities is satisfied (the following expressions are the same as those adopted by Yasui 1948b):

$$a_1 > 0, \begin{vmatrix} a_1 & a_3 \\ 1 & a_2 \end{vmatrix} > 0, \begin{vmatrix} a_1 & a_3 & a_5 \\ 1 & a_2 & a_4 \\ 0 & a_1 & a_3 \end{vmatrix} > 0, \begin{vmatrix} a_1 & a_3 & a_5 & a_7 \\ 1 & a_2 & a_4 & a_6 \\ 0 & a_1 & a_3 & a_5 \\ 0 & 1 & a_2 & a_4 \end{vmatrix} > 0, \ldots$$

6 The Cohn–Schur conditions mean that all the roots of the characteristic equation

$$\lambda^n + a_1\lambda^{n-1} + a_2\lambda^{n-2} + \cdots + a_{n-1}\lambda + a_n = 0$$

have absolute values which are less than 1 *if and only if* the following set of inequalities is satisfied (again the following expressions are the same as those by Yasui 1948b):

$$\begin{vmatrix} 1 & a_n \\ a_n & 1 \end{vmatrix} > 0, \begin{vmatrix} 1 & a_1 & a_n & 0 \\ 0 & 1 & a_{n-1} & a_n \\ a_n & a_{n-1} & 1 & 0 \\ 0 & a_n & a_1 & 1 \end{vmatrix} > 0, \begin{vmatrix} 1 & a_1 & a_2 & a_n & 0 & 0 \\ 0 & 1 & a_1 & a_{n-1} & a_n & 0 \\ 0 & 0 & 1 & a_{n-2} & a_{n-1} & a_n \\ a_n & a_{n-1} & a_{n-2} & 1 & 0 & 0 \\ 0 & a_n & a_{n-1} & a_1 & 1 & 0 \\ 0 & 0 & a_n & a_2 & a_1 & 1 \end{vmatrix} > 0, \ldots$$

7 We can summarize a version of Liapunov's theorem as follows.

Let $\dot{x}=f(x)$, $x=[x_1, x_2,\ldots, x_n]\in R^n$ be an n-dimensional system of differential equations that have the unique equilibrium point $x^*=[x_1{}^*, x_2{}^*,\ldots, x_n{}^*]$ such that $f(x^*)=0$. Suppose that there exists a scalar function $V=V(x-x^*)$ with continuous first derivatives and with the following properties (1)–(5):

1 $V\geq 0$,
2 $V=0$ if and only if $x_i-x_i{}^*=0$ for all $i\in \{1, 2,\ldots, n\}$,
3 $V\rightarrow +\infty$ as $\|x-x^*\|\rightarrow +\infty$,

4 $\dot{V} = \displaystyle\sum_{i=1}^{n}\frac{\partial V}{\partial(x_i - x_i{}^*)}\dot{x}_i \leq 0,$

5 $\dot{V} = 0$ if and only if $x_i-x_i{}^*=0$ for all $i\in \{1, 2,\ldots, n\}$.

Then, the equilibrium point x^* of the above system is globally asymptotically stable.

The above function $V=V(x-x^*)$ is called a 'Liapunov function'. By the way, this version of Liapunov's theorem is not quoted from Yasui (1950) but it is quoted from Gandolfo (2009, p. 404). In the postscript to Yasui (1971), he confessed that he found Liapunov's paper in French, which was published in 1907, in the library of Tohoku University and he struggled with this huge paper of 260 pages in order to write Yasui (1950).

8 In Figure 3.2, we have $x = \dot{y}$.

9 In the footnotes to this sentence, Kaldor referred to Yasui (1953) and Morishima (1958), as well as Hicks (1950) and Goodwin (1951). Although he did not refer to the paper by Kalecki in the footnotes, apparently he discussed Kalecki (1935) in the text which we quoted.

10 The second and the third Japanese economists to become President of the Econometric Society were Hirofumi Uzawa and Takashi Negishi.

11 With respect to the mathematical study of Marxian economics, it seems that Morishima was much influenced by another creative Japanese economist, Nobuo Okishio, who is the true pioneer of mathematical Marxian economics.

12 This name stems from the fact that Shinichi Ichimura, who was a colleague of Morishima at Osaka University, published a paper with a similar idea (cf. Ichimura 1955).

13 This procedure was also adopted by Goodwin (1951). Needless to say, it can be rationalized only when the time lag τ is sufficiently small.

14 In this expression, we omit the subscript which describes time period for notational simplicity.

15 See Gandolfo (2009, p. 481) for the exposition of the Hopf-bifurcation theorem.

16 See Nikaido (1968) for an exposition of Brouwer's fixed point theorem.

17 Two other important predecessors of endogenous growth theory which entails endogenous technical progress are Kaldor (1957) and Arrow (1962).

18 Uzawa's (1969) approach is called the 'adjustment cost approach' and is in the same sprit as similar approaches by Lucas (1967) and Treadway (1969).

19 These mean that the marginal adjustment cost as well as the total adjustment cost of investment increases as the rate of investment increases. Uzawa (1969) called this effect the 'Penrose effect' after Penrose (1959).

20 We can solve this problem by means of Pontryagin's maximum principle as follows (cf. Gandolfo 2009, chap. 27 for Pontryagin's maximum principle). First, we define the current value Hamiltonian as

$$H(t) = \{r - \varphi(g(t))\}p_K K(t) + \mu(t)g(t)K(t),$$

where $\mu(t)$ is the co-state variable. Then, the set of necessary conditions for the optimal solution can be written as

$$\dot{K}(t) = \partial H(t)/\partial \mu(t). \qquad\qquad \dot{\mu}(t) = \rho\mu(t) - \partial H(t)/\partial K(t).$$

Select $g(t)$ which maximizes $H(t)$ for all $t \geq 0$.

$$\lim_{t\to\infty} \mu(t)e^{-\rho t} = 0.$$

Solving this system of equations, we have the result which is described in the text.

21 The good i is said to be a gross substitute for the good j if the excess demand of the good i (E_i) is an *increasing* function of the price of the good j (p_j).

22 See also Negishi (1965) for a restatement of the result of his analysis.

23 In this expression, the dash is the notation of transposition of the vector. In other words, we define the price vector p as a column vector.

24 Usually this equality is derived from the budget constraints of the economic agents (cf. Negishi 1965).

25 See Nikaido (1968, chap. 2) for an exposition of the Perron-Frobenius theorem.

26 Note that the absolute value of a complex number is not smaller than the value of its real part.

27 See also Arrow *et al.* (1959).

28 The subscript t denotes the time period in this formulation.

29 It follows from Eq. (48) that $C_t \equiv K_t / Y_t = 1/(\delta_t \sigma)$, $C^* \equiv (K_t / Y_t)|_{\delta=1} = 1/\sigma$, where C_t is the 'actual' capital–output ratio and C^* is the 'required' capital–output ratio. Therefore, we can rewrite Eq. (50) as

$$\frac{I_{t+1}}{K_{t+1}} = \frac{I_t}{K_t} + H(C_t), \quad H(C^*) = 0, \quad H' < 0.$$

This means that entrepreneurs accelerate (decelerate) investment expenditures in case of the shortage (surplus) of the capital stock, which is nothing but the investment attitude of the entrepreneurs which Harrod (1948) postulated in his verbal explanation of the model.

30 McKenzie's (1954) paper is relatively less known compared with Arrow and Debreu's (1954) paper, but it does not mean that McKenzie's contribution is less important. In fact, McKenzie's contribution was published in *Econometrica* before Arrow and Debreu's contribution was published in the same journal. See Weintraub (2011) for the detailed exposition.

31 'These early results' mean the analytical results which Nikaido derived in his early works.

32 Nikaido (1980) is the more complicated sequel to Nikaido (1975b).

33 Needless to say, the word 'Solovian' that was used by Nikaido stems from Solow's (1956) famous paper that formulated a prototype of the neoclassical growth model. See also Swan (1956) as an example of similar formulation.

34 The neoclassical production function is formulated as $y=f(k)$, $f'(k)>0$, $f''(k)<0$, where $y=Y/L$ is the output–labor ratio (average labor productivity) and $k=K/L$ is the capital–labor ratio (capital intensity). The 'Inada conditions' are the additional conditions such that $\lim_{k\to 0} f'(k) = +\infty$ and $\lim_{k\to +\infty} f'(k) = 0$. For example, the Cobb Douglas production function $y=Ak^\alpha$, $A>0$, $0<\alpha<1$ satisfies all of these conditions.

References

Ara, K. (1958) 'Capital theory and economic growth', *Economic Journal* 118: 511–527.

Ara, K. (1959) 'The aggregation problem in input-output analysis', *Econometrica* 27: 257–262.

Ara, K. (1969) *Keizai Seichou Ron (Theory of Economic Growth)*, Tokyo: Iwanami Shoten (in Japanese).

Arrow, K. J. (1962) 'The economic implications of learning by doing', *Review of Economic Studies* 29: 155–173.

Arrow, K. J. and G. Debreu (1954) 'Existence of an equilibrium for a competitive economy', *Econometrica* 22: 265–290.

Arrow, K. J. and L. Hurwicz, (1958) 'On the stability of the competitive equilibrium', *Econometrica* 26: 522–552.

Arrow, K. J., H. D. Block and L. Hurwicz, (1959) 'On the stability of the competitive equilibrium II', *Econometrica* 27: 88–109.

Arrow, K. J., L. Hurwicz and H. Uzawa (1958) *Studies in Linear and Nonlinear Programming*, Stanford: Stanford University Press.

Bortkiewicz, L. V. (1949) 'On the correction of Marx's fundamental theoretical construction in third volume of Capital', in P. M. Sweezy (ed.) *Karl Marx and the Close of His System*, New York: Kelly (original German version 1907).

Cassel, G. (1918) *Theoretische Sozialökonomie*, Leipzig: C. F. Winter.

Dmitriev, V. K. (1974) *Economic Essays on Value, Competition and Utility*, D. M. Nuti (ed.), Cambridge: Cambridge University Press (original Russian version 1904).

Duesenberry, J. S. (1949) *Income, Saving and the Theory of Consumer Behavior*, Cambridge, Massachusetts: Harvard University Press.

Gale, D. (1955) 'The law of supply and demand', *Mathematica Scandinavia* 3: 155–169.

Gale, D. and H. Nikaido (1965) 'The Jacobian matrix and global univalence of mappings', *Mathematischen Annalen* 159: 81–93.

Gandolfo, G. (2009) *Economic Dynamics (Fourth Edition)*. Berlin: Springer.

Goodwin, R. (1951) 'The nonlinear accelerator and the persistence of business cycles', *Econometrica* 19: 1–17.

Hahn, F. H. (1958) 'Gross substitutes and the dynamic stability of general equilibrium', *Econometrica* 26: 169–170.

Hahn, F. H. and T. Negishi (1962) 'A theorem on non-tatonnement stability', *Econometrica* 30: 463–469.

Hamada, K. (1985) *The Political Economy of International Monetary Interdependence*, Cambridge, Massachusetts: MIT Press.

Hamada, K. (1996) *Strategic Approaches to the International Economy: Selected Essays of Koichi Hamada*, Cheltenham, UK, Edward Elgar.

Harrod, R. F. (1948) *Towards a Dynamic Economics*, London: Macmillan.

Hayashi, H. (1982) 'Tobin's marginal q and average q: A neoclassical interpretation', *Econometrica* 50: 213–224.

Hicks, J. R. (1939) *Value and Capital*, Oxford: Clarendon Press.

Hicks, J. R. (1950) *A Contribution to the Theory of the Trade Cycle*, Oxford: Clarendon Press.

Ichimura, S. (1955) 'Toward a general nonlinear macrodynamic theory of economic fluctuations', in K. K. Kurihara (ed.) *Post-Keynesian Economics*, London: George Allen & Unwin.

Ikeo, A. (ed.) (1999) *Nihon no Keizaigaku to Keizai Gakusha (Economics and Economists in Japan)*, Tokyo: Nihon Keizai Hyoron-sha (in Japanese).

Ikeo, A. (2006) *Nihon no Keizaigaku (Economics in Japan)*, Tokyo: Nihon Keizai Hyoron-sha (in Japanese).

Inada, K. (1964) 'On the stability of growth equilibria in two-sector models', *Review of Economic Studies* 31: 127–142.

Inada, K. (1966) 'Investment in fixed capital and the stability of growth equilibrium', *Review of Economic Studies* 33: 19–30.

Kaldor, N. (1940) 'A model of the trade cycle', *Economic Journal* 50: 78–92 (reprinted in Kaldor 1960).

Kaldor, N. (1957) 'A model of economic growth', *Economic Journal* 67: 591–624 (reprinted in Kaldor 1960).

Kaldor, N. (1960) *Essays on Economic Stability and Growth*, London: Duckworth.

Kalecki, M. (1935) 'A macrodynamic theory of business cycles', *Econometrica* 3: 327–344.

Keynes, J. M. (1936) *The General Theory of Employment, Interest and Money*. London: Macmillan.

Lange, O. (1935) 'Marxian economics and modern economic theory', *Review of Economic Studies* 2: 189–201.

Liapounoff, A. M. (1907) 'Problème général de la stabilité du movement', *Annales de la Faculte des Sciences de Toulouse* 9. (English version: A. M. Liapunov (1966) *Stability of Motion*, translated by F. Abramovici and M. Shimshoni, New York: Academic Press.)

Lucas, R. E. (1967) 'Adjustment cost and the theory of supply', *Journal of Political Economy* 75: 321–334.

Lucas, R. E. (1988) 'On the mechanics of economic development', *Journal of Monetary Economics* 22: 1–42.

McKenzie, L. W. (1954) 'On equilibrium in Graham's model of world trade and other competitive systems', *Econometrica* 22: 147–161.

Metzler, L. (1945) 'Stability of multiple market: The Hicksian condition', *Econometrica* 13: 277–292.

Morishima, M. (1950) *Dougakuteki Keizai Riron (Dynamic Economic Theory)*, Tokyo: Kobundo (in Japanese).

Morishima, M. (1953) 'Mittsu no hisenkei moderu (Three nonlinear models)', *Kikan Riron Keizaigaku (Economic Studies Quarterly)* 4: 213–219 (in Japanese).

Morishima, M. (1955) *Shihonshugi Keizai no Hendo Riron (Theory of Fluctuations in a Capitalist Economy)*, Tokyo: Sobunsha (in Japanese).

Morishima, M. (1958) 'A contribution to the nonlinear theory of the trade cycle', *Zeitschrift für Nationalökonomie* 18: 165–173 (reprinted in Morishima 1996 as an addendum).

Morishima, M. (1964) *Equilibrium, Stability and Growth*, Oxford: Clarendon Press.

Morishima, M. (1969) *Theory of Economic Growth*, Oxford: Clarendon Press.

Morishima, M. (1973) *Marx's Economics*, Cambridge: Cambridge University Press.

Morishima, M. (1977) *Walras' Economics*, Cambridge: Cambridge University Press.

Morishima, M. (1989) *Ricardo's Economics*, Cambridge: Cambridge University Press.

Morishima, M. (1996) *Dynamic Economic Theory*, Cambridge: Cambridge University Press (extended version of Morishima 1950 in English).

Morishima, M. and G. Catephores (1978) *Value, Exploitation and Growth*, London: McGraw Hill.

Morishima, M. and F. Seton (1957) 'Aggregation in Leontief matrices and the labour theory of value', *Econometrica* 29: 203–220.

Negishi, T. (1958) 'A note on the stability of an economy where all goods are gross substitutes', *Econometrica* 26: 445–447.

Negishi, T. (1960) 'Welfare economics and existence of an equilibrium for a competitive economy', *Metroeconomica* 12: 92–97.

Negishi, T. (1961) 'Monopolistic competition and general equilibrium', *Review of Economic Studies* 28: 196–201.

Negishi, T. (1962) 'The stability of a competitive economy: A survey article', *Econometrica* 30: 635–669.

Negishi, T. (1965) *Kakaku to Haibun no Riron (Theory of Prices and Allocation)*, Tokyo: Toyo Keizai Shinpo-sha (in Japanese).

Negishi, T. (1979) *Microeconomic Foundations of Keynesian Macroeconomics*, Amsterdam: North-Holland.

Negishi, T. (1989) *History of Economic Theory*, Amsterdam: North-Holland.

Nikaido, H. (1956) 'On the classical multilateral exchange problem', *Metroeconomica* 8: 135–145.

Nikaido, H. (1964) 'Persistence of continual growth near the von Neumann ray: A strong version of the Radner turnpike theorem', *Econometrica* 32: 151–162 (reprinted in Nikaido 1996).

Nikaido, H. (1968) *Convex Structures and Economic Theory*, New York: Academic Press.

Nikaido, H. (1975a) *Monopolistic Competition and Effective Demand*, Princeton: Princeton University Press.

Nikaido, H. (1975b) 'Factor substitution and Harrod's knife-edge', *Zeitschrift für Nationalökonomie* 35: 149–154 (reprinted in Nikaido 1996).

Nikaido, H. (1979) 'Wage-price spirals under monopoly: 'What is an objective demand function?' Set in motion', *Zeitschrift für Nationalökonomie* 39: 299–313 (reprinted in Nikaido 1996).

Nikaido, H. (1980) 'Harrodian pathology of neoclassical growth: The irrelevance of smooth factor substitution', *Zeitschrift für Nationalökonomie* 40: 111–134 (reprinted in Nikaido 1996).

Nikaido, H. (1983) 'Marx on competition', *Zeitschrift für Nationalökonomie* 43: 337–362 (reprinted in Nikaido 1996).

Nikaido, H. (1996) *Prices, Cycles, and Growth*, Cambridge, Massachusetts: MIT Press.

Nikaido, H. and H. Uzawa (1960) 'Stability and non-negativity in a Walrasian tâtonnement process', *International Economic Review* 1: 50–59 (reprinted in Nikaido 1996).

Okishio, N. (1957) *Saiseisan no Riron (Theory of Reproduction)*, Tokyo: Sobunsha (in Japanese).

Okishio, N. (1963) 'A mathematical note on Marxian theorems', *Weltwirtschaftliches Archiv* 91: 287–299 (reprinted in Okishio 1993).

Okishio, N. (1964) 'Instability of Harrod-Domar's steady growth', *Kobe University Economic Review* (reprinted in Okishio 1977, 1993).

Okishio, N. (1965) *Shihonsei Keizai no Kiso Riron (Basic Theory of the Capitalist Economy)*, Tokyo: Sobunsha (in Japanese; second edition, 1978).

Okishio, N. (1976) *Chikuseki Ron (Theory of Accumulation)* (second edition), Tokyo: Chikuma Shobo (in Japanese).

Okishio, N. (1977) *Gendai Keizaigaku (Modern Economics)*, Tokyo: Chikuma Shobo (in Japanese).

Okishio, N. (1993) *Essays on Political Economy*, M. Krüger and P. Flaschel (eds.), Frankfurt am Main: Peter Lang.

Penrose, E. T. (1959) *The Theory of the Growth of the Firm*, Oxford: Basil Blackwell & Mott.

Radner, R. (1961) 'Paths of economic growth that are optimal with regard only to final states: A Turnpike Theorem', *Review of Economic Studies* 28: 98–104.

Romer, P. (1990) 'Endogenous technological change', *Journal of Political Economy* 94: S71–S102.

Samuelson, P. (1944) 'The relation between Hicksian stability and true dynamic stability', *Econometrica* 10: 1–25.

Samuelson, P. A. (1947) *Foundations of Economic Analysis*, Cambridge, Massachusetts: Harvard University Press.

Shibata, K. (1930) 'Cassel shi no "Kakaku keisei no kikou" no ginmi (An examination of Mr. Cassel's "Mechanism of price formation")', *Keizai Ronsou (Economic Review)* 30: 916–936 (Kyoto University; in Japanese).

Shibata, K. (1933) 'Marx's analysis of capitalism and the general equilibrium theory of the Lausanne School', *Kyoto University Economic Review* 8: 107–136.

Shibata, K. (1937) 'Some questions on Mr. Keynes' General Theory of Employment, Interest and Money', *Kyoto University Economic Review* 12: 83–96.

Shinkai, Y. (1960) 'On the equilibrium growth of capital and labor', *International Economic Review* 1: 107–111.

Solow, R. M. (1956) 'A contribution to the theory of economic growth', *Quarterly Journal of Economics* 70: 65–94.

Sono, M. (1943) 'Kakaku hendo ni tomonau bunri kanou zai no jukyu hendou (Changes of demand and supply of separable goods due to price changes)', *Kokumin Keizai Zasshi (Journal of National Economy)* 74: 1–51 (Kobe University; in Japanese)

Sono, M. (1961) 'The effect of price changes in the demand and supply of separable goods', *International Economic Review* 2: 239–271 (English version of Sono 1943, translated by K. Sato).

Sraffa, P. (1960) *Production of Commodities by Means of Commodities: Prelude to a Critique of Economic Theory*, Cambridge: Cambridge University Press.

Stackelberg, H. von (1933) 'Zwei kritische Bemerkungen zur Preistheorie Gustav Cassels', *Zeithshrift für Nationalökonomie* 4.

Swan, T. W. (1956) 'Economic growth and capital accumulation', *Economic Record* 32: 334–361.

Tobin, J. (1969) 'A general equilibrium approach to monetary theory', *Journal of Money, Credit and Banking* 1: 15–29.

Tobin, J. (1980) *Asset Accumulation and Economic Activity*, Oxford: Basil Blackwell & Mott.

Treadway, A. B. (1969) 'On rational entrepreneurial behavior and the demand for investment', *Review of Economic Studies* 36: 227–239.

Tsuru, S. (1993) *Institutional Economics Revisited*, Cambridge: Cambridge University Press.

Uzawa, H. (1961a) 'Neutral inventions and the stability of growth equilibrium', *Review of Economic Studies* 28: 448–468.

Uzawa, H. (1961b) 'On a two-sector model of economic growth', *Review of Economic Studies* 29: 40–47.

Uzawa, H. (1962) 'Walras's existence theorem and Brouwer's fixed point theorem', *Economic Studies Quarterly* 13: 59–62 (reprinted in Uzawa 1988a).

Uzawa, H. (1963) 'On a two-sector model of economic growth II', *Review of Economic Studies* 30: 105–118.

Uzawa, H. (1965) 'Optimal technical change in an aggregative model of economic growth', *International Economic Review* 6: 1–24.

Uzawa, H. (1969) 'Time preference and the Penrose effect in a two-class model of economic growth', *Journal of Political Economy* 77: 628–652.

Uzawa, H. (1988a) *Preference, Production, and Capital: Selected Papers of Hirofumi Uzawa*, Cambridge: Cambridge University Press.

Uzawa, H. (1988b) *Optimality, Equilibrium, and Growth: Selected Papers of Hirifumi Uzawa*, Tokyo: University of Tokyo Press.

Uzawa, H. (1990) *Keizai Kaiseki: Kisohen (Economic Analysis: Foundations)*, Tokyo: Iwanami Shoten (in Japanese).

Velupillai, K. V. (2008) 'Japanese contributions to nonlinear cycle theory in the 1950s', *The Japanese Economic Review* 59: 54–74.

Wald, A. (1936) 'Über einige Gleichungssysteme der mathematischen Ökonomie', *Zeitschrift für Nationalökonomie* 7: 637–670. (English version: 'On some system of equations of mathematical economics', *Econometrica* 14: 368–403.)

Weintraub, E. R. (1987) 'Stability theory via Liapunov's method: A note on the contribution of Takuma Yasui', *History of Political Economy* 19: 615–620.

Weintraub, E. R. (1991) *Stabilizing Dynamics: Constructing Economic Knowledge*, Cambridge: Cambridge University Press.

Weintraub, E. R. (2011) 'Lionel W. McKenzie and the proof of the existence of a competitive equilibrium', *Journal of Economic Perspectives* 25: 199–215.

Yasui, T. (1948a) 'Shurensei no koujun to dougakuteki antei jouken (Postulate of convergence and conditions of dynamic stability)', *Shakai Kagaku Hyoron (Review of Social Sciences)* 1/2 (in Japanese; reprinted in Yasui 1971).

Yasui, T. (1948b) 'Keizaiteki kinkou no dougakuteki antei jouken (Conditions for dynamic stability of economic equilibrium)', *Keizai Shichou (Trend of Economic Thought)* 9 (in Japanese; reprinted in Yasui 1971).

Yasui, T. (1950) 'Antei no ippan riron (General theory of stability)', *Kikan Riron Keizaigaku (Economic Studies Quarterly)* 1: 13–32 (in Japanese; reprinted in Yasui 1971).

Yasui, T. (1953) 'Self-excited oscillations and the business cycle', *Cowles Commission Discussion Paper: Economics* No. 2065 (reprinted in Yasui 1971).

Yasui, T. (1954) 'Junkanteki seichou ni kansuru ichishiron (An essay on cyclical growth)', *Keizai Kenkyu (Economic Review)* 5 (Hitotsubashi University; in Japanese; reprinted in Yasui 1971).

Yasui, T. (1971) *Yasui Takuma Chosakushu Dai 3 Kan: Keizai Dougaku no Shomondai (Collected Papers of Takuma Yasui Vol. 3: Problems of Economic Dynamics)*, Tokyo: Sobunsha. (Ten papers in Japanese and five papers in English are contained.)

Yasui, T., H. Kumagai and M. Fukuoka (1977) *Kindai Keizaigaku no Riron Kouzou (Structure of Modern Economic Theory)*, Tokyo: Chikuma Shobo (in Japanese).

Yoshikawa, H. (1980) 'On the "q" theory of investment', *American Economic Review* 70: 739–743.

Zeuthen, F. (1933) 'Das prizip der knappheit, technische kombination und ökonomische qualität', *Zeitschrift für Nationalökonomie* 4: 1–24.

Part II

Economics of the lost twenty years in Japan from the 1990s to the 2000s

4 Controversies regarding monetary policy and deflation in Japan from the 1990s to the early 2000s

Asahi Noguchi

1 Introduction

The global economic crisis initiated by the burst of the US subprime bubble and the subsequent bankruptcy of Lehman Brothers Holdings Inc. in September 2008, the "Lehman Shock," drastically changed the way that governments and central banks throughout the world conducted macroeconomic policies. The crisis restored the concept of Keynesian fiscal policy and the use of fiscal measures of governmental spending and taxation to stabilize output and employment in an economy by expanding or contracting its aggregate spending. Since John Maynard Keynes (1883–1946) manifested this concept in *The General Theory* (1936), it occupied the way politicians and policy officials thought about macroeconomic policies, at least until the 1960s (Keynes, 1978). However, subsequent criticism by certain leading economists of Keynesian macroeconomics crucially undermined the notion. It gradually decayed thereafter and was supposed to be literally useless precisely until the crisis began. The gravity of the crisis eventually forced many governments to resort to the Keynesian fiscal policy that was ignored for a long time, although stubborn opposition to the policy was rampant.

The change was no less drastic for monetary policy. Until the crisis, few countries experienced reaching the lower bound of interest rates. In *The General Theory* (1936), Keynes referred to a situation in which injections of money into an economy by a central bank could no longer lower interest rates, later called a "liquidity trap." Although the concept of a liquidity trap subsequently became prevalent in Keynesian literature, the actual case cited as its historical example was usually confined to that of the US in the 1930s when the short-term interest rate as measured by three-month Treasuries was lowered to 0.05 percent during the Great Depression. However, as the latest global crisis proceeded, most of the major developed countries, including the US, the UK, Japan, and the countries in the euro region, consequently had to encounter a situation in which the short-term interest rate was lowered to its minimal level. Therefore, the central banks could no longer use the conventional way of lowering policy interest rates to stimulate investment and consumption of private corporations and households. This situation compelled the central banks to initiate various measures of unconventional monetary policies, or monetary policies other than manipulating the policy interest rate.[1]

This article examines the controversies surrounding monetary policy and deflation in Japan from the 1990s to the early 2000s. The purpose is to obtain insights and lessons on how novel and unconventional economic policies are accommodated and implemented during economic crises. Although many countries confronted the annoying situation of a lower bound on interest rates after the Lehman Shock for the first time since World War II, the case was not new for Japan. Japan already experienced the same situation before the most recent global economic crisis. In February 1999, the Bank of Japan (BOJ) first introduced a zero interest rate policy (ZIRP) in the face of an economic downturn triggered by the successive bankruptcies of several major financial institutions from the end of 1997 to the middle of 1998. This first attempt of the policy was temporary because the BOJ suspended the ZIRP in August 2000 and rejected various oppositions to its suspension. Unfortunately for the BOJ, just after this suspension, the worldwide economic boom motivated by the development of information technology (IT) that swelled around the end of the 1990s collapsed. This situation forced the BOJ to return to the ZIRP and to establish an unconventional monetary policy called quantitative easing (QE). Consequently, this quantitative monetary easing policy executed by the BOJ from March 2001 to March 2006 paved the way for the unconventional monetary policies that the central banks around the world adopted after the Lehman Shock.

Many similarities existed between Japan's case and the cases after the Lehman Shock regarding the process of implementing an unconventional monetary policy and its general background. The latest global economic crisis was primarily initiated by the bursting of the US subprime bubble. Similarly, Japan's economy experienced an unprecedented expansion of the bubble, in particular a cumulative increase in land prices and stock prices around the end of the 1980s, and then its burst at the beginning of the 1990s. The burst of the US subprime bubble and the subsequent decline in asset prices drastically worsened the financial positions of banking institutions. Similarly, the burst of Japan's bubble resulted in many formerly outstanding financial institutions facing difficulty. In both cases, the bankruptcy of some leading financial institutions eventually triggered the systematic crisis of the entire financial market, although realization of the financial panic in Japan was postponed until the end of 1997 by various measures invented both publicly and privately. In any event, both financial panics eventually caused a severe downturn in the economy as a whole.

As the global economic crisis after the Lehman Shock led many central banks to the lower bound of policy interest rates and forced them to set out unconventional monetary policies, the BOJ was also enforced to adopt ZIRP at the end of the 1990s and QE at the beginning of the 2000s. However, the process of adopting them was far from peaceful. These policies were introduced only after many twists and turns. Heated controversies in both journalism and academia ensued over whether or not unconventional monetary policies should be implemented. The BOJ itself was always rather reluctant to embark on any unpracticed policy measure. The BOJ adopted ZIRP and QE not so much in a keen manner as in a willy-nilly fashion. Therefore, that the BOJ initiated unconventional monetary policies ahead of the other central banks was very ironic because it was forced to do so for at least two reasons. One reason was the external and internal criticism of the BOJ's conservative policy stance. The other reason was the aggravation of deflation in Japan, particularly since the economic downturn of 1997–1998.

However, this latter reason was not as definite, at least in the beginning. When symptoms of deflation became conspicuous in the Japanese economy, specifically after 1997, deflation was not necessarily recognized as a bad thing. Rather, whether deflation should be accepted or contained was a main focus of the controversy at this stage. Apparently, the BOJ sympathized with the "good deflation" theory that was in fashion within journalistic circles until the beginning of the 2000s. Only after the harmful effects of deflation became sufficiently apparent and, thus, the call for measures against deflation became stronger did the BOJ take a reluctant step.

This process of implementing unconventional monetary policy in Japan clearly exemplifies the crucial role that the related arguments and controversies within journalism and academism might play on how unpracticed economic policies are accommodated during times of economic crisis. If not for the criticism toward the BOJ in these controversies, unconventional monetary policy in Japan would have been retarded at best or aborted at worst. Moreover, if unconventional monetary policy had not been implemented in Japan before the Lehman Shock, unconventional monetary policies in other countries after the shock would have been less definite. These conjectures highlight the importance of obtaining insights and lessons into economic policy making by focusing on how the controversies surrounding monetary policy and deflation in Japan developed during this critical period, which is presented in this article.

With respect to the controversies related to monetary policy, at least two major upsurges within the period occurred. First, the "money supply controversy" that occurred in the first half of the 1990s between economists who were critical of the BOJ's monetary policy around the burst of the bubble and those who attempted to defend it. This controversy marks, so to speak, the pre-history of a more extensive controversy on unconventional monetary policies under deflation that continued from the end of the 1990s to the early 2000s. Moreover, the latter controversy could be divided into two distinct but interrelated controversies; the first was on the goodness or badness of deflation and the other was on the validity or invalidity of unconventional monetary policies against deflation. Before arguing about these three controversies, the next section presents a general picture of Japan's economy during the period often called "Japan's lost decade." The following three sections successively examine the money supply controversy, the deflation controversy, and the controversy regarding unconventional monetary policies. The last section presents insights from these topics.

2 A concise picture of Japan's lost decade

Japan's economy went through an unprecedented long period of stagnation from the 1990s to the early 2000s. In the 1970s and the 1980s, Japan's real growth rates were constantly higher and its unemployment rates were constantly lower than those of most other developed countries. Until that time, the Japanese economy was regarded as the most vivid of all developed countries' economies. Naturally, the Japanese economy was hailed as the model to follow for developing countries that aspired to economic success. However, a sudden expansion of the bubble economy at the end of the 1980s and its burst at the beginning of the 1990s completely changed the picture. After these events, Japan turned into one of the most stagnating economies of all developed countries. This stagnation was most plainly expressed by lower GDP growth and increasing unemployment rates. From 1992 to 1994, Japan's GDP consistently grew at slower than 1 percent and eventually dropped to a negative range around 1998. In 1990, when Japan's economy was at the peak of its unusual boom, the country's unemployment rate was only 2.1 percent. Unemployment gradually increased and reached 4.7 percent in 1999 and 5.4 percent in 2002 (Table 4.1). In due course, the period came to be called "Japan's lost decade."

The burst of the bubble was most noticeable through the drastic fall in asset prices, particularly that of stock prices and land prices. The Nikkei Stock Average, the most widely quoted stock index of Japanese equities, grew at an unusual rate in the latter half of the 1980s, had hit its all-time high in December 1989, collapsed at this point, declined sharply over the next two years, and has drifted in a declining pattern since then (Figure 4.1). This feature is analogous to that of land prices, although the collapse of land prices occurred at the end of 1991, about two years later than the collapse of stock prices (Figure 4.2).

This drastic decline in asset prices crucially eroded the equity position of financial institutions, threatened their feasibility, and finally, led to an overall crisis in the entire financial system that was the most disastrous in postwar Japan. This period saw the non-performing loan (NPL) problem as continuously clouding Japan's economy and remained the situation until the mid-2000s. Although

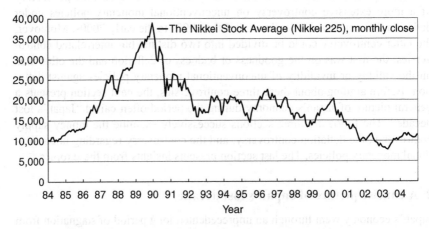

Figure 4.1 Nikkei Stock Average: 1984–2004 (source: Yahoo! Finance).

Table 4.1 Real GDP growth rate and unemployment rate in Japan: 1982–2008

Years	'82	'83	'84	'85	'86	'87	'88	'89	'90	'91	'92	'93	'94	'95	'96	'97	'98	'99	'00	'01	'02	'03	'04	'05	'06	'07	'08
Real GDP growth rate (%)*	3.4	3.1	4.5	6.3	2.8	4.1	7.1	5.4	5.6	3.3	0.8	0.2	0.9	1.9	2.6	1.6	−2.0	−0.0	2.9	0.2	0.3	1.4	2.7	1.9	2.0	2.4	−1.0
Unemployment rate (%)	2.4	2.6	2.7	2.6	2.8	2.8	2.5	2.3	2.1	2.1	2.2	2.5	2.9	3.2	3.4	3.4	4.1	4.7	4.7	5.0	5.4	5.3	4.7	4.4	4.1	3.9	4.0

Source: Economic and Social Research Institute, Cabinet Office, Government of Japan, and Statistics Bureau of the Ministry of Internal Affairs and Communications.

Note

* Expenditure approach, chain-linked.

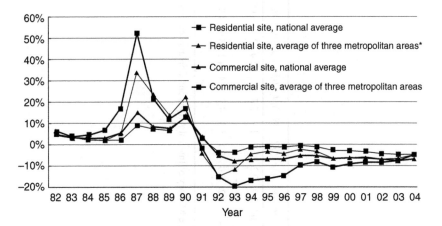

Figure 4.2 Change in land price in Japan: 1982–2004 (source: Land and Water Bureau, Ministry of Land, Infrastructure and Transport).

Note
* Three metropolitan areas include Tokyo, Osaka, and Nagoya.

Japan's NPL problem was in fact stubborn and serious, it did not appear this way in the beginning. During the heyday of Japan's bubble in the latter half of the 1980s, many Japanese banks, anticipating additional rising land prices, rushed into mortgage loans. Once the bubble burst, a large portion of these loans naturally turned into NPLs. However, the initial supposition was that financial institutions could easily tolerate the burden because they had already accumulated sufficient earnings during previous years of the bubble. Moreover, at the time, Japan's financial institutions were highly regulated by the Ministry of Finance (MOF) in the name of financial stability. This public protection system was called "the convoy banking system." Although some regional banks failed around the mid-1990s, they supposedly did not represent the general situation. During 1997, the problem finally turned into a panic. In April 1997, Japan's consumption tax increased from 3 to 5 percent as a way to improve the Japanese government's general financial condition, which had fallen into a deficit after the bubble burst. In July 1997, Thailand's system of pegging its national currency, the baht, to the US dollar collapsed because of a speculative attack on that currency. The same type of currency turmoil rapidly spread to other Asian countries and, finally, brought about a region-wide economic dispute called the Asian financial crisis. As a result of these downside pressures, Japan's economy began to slide into a recession in the autumn of 1997. On November 3, 1997, Sanyo Securities Company Limited failed, which triggered the overall collapse of the Japanese financial market. Until the end of 1998, many major financial institutions, including Hokkaido Takushoku Bank Limited, Yamaichi Securities Company Limited, Long-Term Credit Bank of Japan, and Nippon Credit Bank Limited, failed one after another. Precisely at this time, Japan's economy was involved in the most serious financial and economic crisis that had occurred since the Showa Crisis during the Great Depression of the 1930s.

The Japanese economy showed signs of recovery in 1999 as a result of the boldest Keynesian financial policy for stimulating economic recovery conducted by the then Obuchi Keizo government in the latter half of 1998 and the world-wide IT dot-com boom that occurred during the period. However, during the previous period of serious economic contraction, the Japanese economy was caught by chronic deflation, one of the most troublesome diseases destined to hinder the economy from sufficient recovery. During the 1980s, the rate of change in Japan's consumer price index (CPI) was kept relatively low, except during the initial years of the decade. A sudden rise in the yen exchange rate after the so-called Plaza Accord in 1985 lowered the CPI during the following few years. Moreover, the increase in the CPI was relatively small until the end of the decade despite this period coming precisely at the peak of the bubble. Only in the final phase of the bubble did general prices show an upward tendency. However, when the bubble burst and asset prices drastically declined during the first half of the 1990s, general prices also began to decline—not drastically but gradually. Eventually, CPI growth became negative in the mid-1990s, partially as a result of a sharp appreciation in the yen exchange rate (Figure 4.3). Although Japan's economy enjoyed a short period of recovery from 1996 to the beginning of 1997, the change in CPI turned positive with a slight margin. Then, the financial and economic crisis occurred in late 1997, which eventually placed Japan's economy in almost a continuous state of deflation (Figure 4.4).

The recovery of Japan's economy since 1999 as a result of the Obuchi government's stimulating policy and the worldwide dot-com boom was short-lived. The dot-com boom soon turned into another bubble. The NASDAQ collapsed from its historical peak in March 2000, which signaled the beginning of the worldwide recession. Once again, Japan's economy slid into a recession, this

Figure 4.3 The yen/US dollar exchange rate: 1982–2008 (source: The Bank of Japan).

Figure 4.4 Annual increase in Japan's consumer price index (CPI): 1982–2008 (source: Statistics Bureau of the Ministry of Internal Affairs and Communications).

Note

* Consumption tax hikes in April 1989 from 0 to 3 percent and in April 1997 from 3 to 5 percent were not adjusted.

time with worsening deflation. During the most stagnating years of 2001 and 2002, Japan's CPI declined to nearly −1 percent. Meanwhile, the unemployment rate continued to increase and temporarily reached 5.5 percent, the then highest rate for postwar Japan. The situation appeared almost like the "deflation spiral," meaning that the stagnation prompted deflation and, in turn, the deflation worsened the stagnation.

During the worst economic period of April 2001, the Junichiro Koizumi cabinet was installed. The Koizumi administration initially received enthusiastic support from Japanese voters by adopting the slogan "structural reform" to reflect its intent to revitalize the Japanese economy. Basically, the structural reform entailed the reorganization of public and private relationships in the economy. More specifically, deregulation, privatization, and rationalization of administrations were supposed to be typical realizations of structural reform. As these policies suggested, the structural reform was supply-side oriented and unrelated to macroeconomic problems such as deflation and unemployment. However, the worsening business and employment conditions at that time forced the Koizumi administration to shift its policy focus gradually from supply-side to demand-side. In October 2002, the government unveiled an economic package of "comprehensive policy measures against deflation." This name was misleading because the package was actually concerned with remedies for the NPL problem and did not contain macroeconomic policies to fight deflation. Nevertheless, this policy proclamation was significant in that the government formally designated deflation as a policy target to overcome. Monetary and currency policies were actually utilized to remedy the deflationary situation. In March 2003, the government appointed Toshihiko Fukui, former Deputy Governor of the BOJ, as the twenty-ninth Governor of the BOJ. Governor Fukui immediately activated a quantitative monetary easing policy that the former governor, Masaru

Hayami, introduced but left inactive. In January 2003, the MOF embarked on a continuous and large-scale intervention in the foreign exchange market to prevent the appreciation of the yen. Taylor (2006) called this massive intervention the Great Intervention, which lasted until March 2004 at an increasing pace and eventually amounted to the largest intervention in history.

After the cyclical bottom of 2002, Japan's economy went through a long, obscure period of economic recovery until the global economic crisis occurred in 2008. From 2003 to 2007, the GDP growth rate was kept at around 2 percent, a figure satisfactory at least compared with that of the previous decade. Meanwhile, the unemployment rate decreased gradually from approximately the middle of 5 percent to less than 4 percent. The CPI increased from approximately −1 percent to almost 0 in 2003, and remained at approximately 0 until the middle of 2007. This period of economic recovery eventually became the longest of all postwar economic booms. However, it was called "the unnoticeable recovery" because the common people in Japan could hardly sense that the economy was recovering—the recovery depended exclusively on overseas demand and not on domestic demand. This period was precisely when the US economy rapidly recovered from the burst of the dot-com bubble and enjoyed another boom induced by the expansion of the subprime mortgage market. In addition, during this period some of the emerging economies represented by the BRICs, namely Brazil, Russia, India, and China, attained remarkable economic growth. Together with a gradual depreciation in the yen exchange rate after the Great Intervention of 2003–2004, these external factors contributed significantly to Japan's net exports, which supported the period's economic recovery. It was thus inevitable that Japan's economy was exposed to the most serious downside pressure once the world economy contracted and the yen appreciated after the Lehman Shock in 2008.

3 Japan's monetary policy controversy after the bubble burst at the turn of the 1990s

3.1 General background on the controversy

A decade after the second half of the 1980s, Japan's economy experienced significant macroeconomic fluctuations. The circumstance was most plainly shown through monetary aggregates. Both the annual rate of increase in the money supply and that of the monetary base rose abnormally during the bubble period of the late 1980s (Figure 4.5). This monetary expansion was apparently a result of the BOJ's policy to maintain a low interest rate to prevent appreciation of the yen against the US dollar that could be triggered by the Plaza Accord of 1985. The Plaza Accord called for macroeconomic policy coordination primarily among the US, Japan, and West Germany, which initially intended to correct an overestimated dollar exchange rate that prevailed in the first half of the 1980s. The result was too drastic. The dollar/yen exchange rate promptly changed directions and continued to decline until 1988. This acute appreciation of the yen

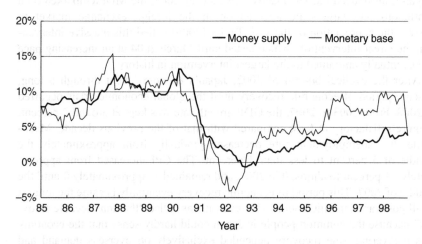

Figure 4.5 Annual rate of change in Japan's money supply and monetary base:
1985–1998 (source: The Bank of Japan).

exchange rate applied serious downside pressure on the Japanese economy,
which forced the BOJ to lower interest rates. In retrospect, this policy of keeping
interest rates very low continued for too long. Although the general business
condition did not appear so good, certain asset prices, particularly land prices
and stock prices, were diverging distinctly upward from the previous trend, at
least in 1987. This phenomenon was later noticed as the beginning of the bubble
economy.

Although the economy was apparently in a state of overheating, at least in
1988, the BOJ exited from the low interest rate policy of the post Plaza Accord
period only at the very end of the 1980s. In December 1989, Yasushi Mieno was
appointed as the twenty-sixth Governor of the BOJ and soon thereafter launched
an aggressive policy to increase the interest rate to halt the bubble. As a result,
the overnight call rate rose from 3 percent in 1989 to 8 percent in early 1991
(Figure 4.6). Along with this monetary tightening policy of the BOJ, Japan's
MOF introduced another regulatory policy to contain the bubble. On March 27,
1990, the MOF issued an official note to banks that directed them to restrain
from increasing loans to the real estate industry. This policy on mortgage loans
was intended to halt rising land prices, which was at the time the most common
topic of discomfort for the general population. These policies containing the
bubble were very effective and soon turned out to be too effective. At around the
end of 1991, land prices showed apparent signs of collapse and, consequently,
continued to decline during subsequent years until the middle of the 2000s. After
all, the BOJ's monetary tightening policy and the MOF's regulative policy on
mortgage loans perfectly completed their mission of bursting the bubble, with
the ironic effect of causing the economy to stagnate for the next two decades.[2]

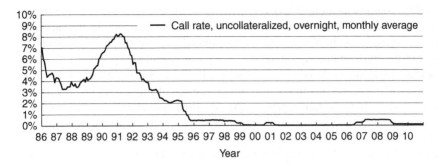

Figure 4.6 Short-term money market rate in Japan: 1986–2010 (source: The Bank of Japan).

The monetary expansion during the bubble period of the late 1980s was the result of the BOJ maintaining the low interest rate for too long. This apparent retardation of a policy response made the BOJ impatient to boldly and swiftly increase the interest rate around the turn of the 1990s, which caused the bubble to burst. This drastic shift in the BOJ's monetary stance to contain the bubble and its consequences were most conspicuously shown in the movement of monetary aggregates. The annual rate of change in the money supply and in the monetary base declined sharply in the middle of 1990, when the BOJ steadfastly increased the interest rate. These two aggregates continued to decline until around 1992. Faced with this situation, the BOJ decided to shift its policy stance once again from a tightening to an easing position in the spring of 1991. Since then, the BOJ gradually kept lowering its policy rate. Yet, in retrospect, the speed of easing money was far too slow to match the intensity of the negative monetary shocks, which took the form of a sudden decline in money supply and the monetary base. The CPI did not stop sliding downward, despite the lowered policy rate. Because of the diminishing inflation rate, the BOJ had to continue to lower the policy rate. By the end of 1995, the policy interest rate was lowered to an unparalleled 0.4 percent.

3.2 The money supply controversy and its alternative evaluations

The economist who first paid attention to this serious contraction in the money supply that broke out in the middle of 1990 and issued cautions about its consequences was Yuji Shimanaka, a representative monetarist in Japan. Shimanaka (1991) pointed out that the Japanese economy at the time, May 1991, was on the verge of "monetary depression." In the article, he referred to the "key propositions of monetarism" presented by Milton Friedman.[3] Using these propositions as guidance, Shimanaka (1991, pp. 32–33) cautioned that making little of the money supply index on prospecting business conditions was extremely dangerous if the increase in the money supply diverged at least "abnormally" either upward or downward from some stable range. Furthermore, Shimanaka emphasized the importance of appropriately controlling the money supply. In the beginning of 1992, when everyone noticed that the bubble had completely burst and the economy was shrinking, Shimanaka pointed out that the unusual continuation of the BOJ's monetary tightening policy was definitely a primal cause of the proceeding business downturn (Shimanaka, 1992, p. 48). He named the ongoing process of monetary contraction a "roller coaster of money supply," a phrase used frequently thereafter to refer to the situation. It gradually became apparent that Shimanaka had very precisely considered what was and would be occurring. However, his diagnosis was not necessarily regarded seriously, at least in the initial phase of the downturn, because the majority of the economists at that time viewed the situation as a mere correction of economic overheating.

In late 1992, a confrontation eventually broke out between the economists who were critical of the BOJ's way of conducting monetary policy and those who were in the BOJ. Kikuo Iwata represented the critics and Kunio Okina, then the BOJ economist, was the opposing figure in charge of refuting the criticism. Iwata (1992) triggered the controversy and strongly condemned the BOJ for fluctuating the money supply and the monetary base in a detrimental way, thus disturbing the economy itself. He ascribed this policy failure primarily to "the BOJ doctrine," a BOJ in-house policy principle. Okina (1992) immediately responded, retorting that the BOJ doctrine was not wrong. Thereafter, many economists entered the controversy, represented by Yutaka Harada (1992) and Yutaka Kosai (1992) on the critical side, Kagehide Kaku (1992) on the defending side, and Kazuo Ueda (1992) on the reconciling side. The entire argument was eventually called the money supply controversy. Iwata and Okina, the two prominent economists who confronted each other, subsequently summarized and reconstructed the issues related to the controversy from their own perspectives (Iwata 1993; Okina 1993b).

One of the most crucial points of the confrontation was "the BOJ doctrine." Ryutaro Komiya (1976) first used this phrase to denote the typical way of thinking about monetary policy in the BOJ during his time. In the article, Komiya criticized the BOJ's monetary policy in 1971 and 1972 for allowing a tremendous increase in the money supply, up to a 28 percent annual rate, thus causing the "skyrocketing inflation" that reached 25 percent of the annual rate of increase in 1974. In the same article, Komiya criticized the traditional BOJ thinking that it could not control the money supply and the monetary base because they were, in principle, determined passively by demand for money in the private sector. Komiya cynically named this line of thinking "the BOJ doctrine."

From a historical perspective, the BOJ doctrine is rightly called a descendant of the real bills doctrine. The primal tenet of the real bills doctrine is that issuing money accommodatingly to its demand based on real economic needs is not an inflationary action. The doctrine further implies that inflation is basically a matter of individual goods rather than money. For this reason, central banks historically employed the real bills doctrine as grounds for their claim that they were not responsible for inflation. The most typical example was found in the Bullionist Controversy of 1810 that was provoked between the Bank of England and few critical economists represented by Henry Thornton and David Ricardo. These economists, who attributed the inflation occurring in England during the Napoleonic War to the over-issuance of inconvertible paper money by the Bank of England, were later called the Bullionists. The controversy between Komiya and the BOJ in Japan in the middle of the 1970s has basically the same feature.

The most crucial failure of the real bills doctrine and the BOJ doctrine in the 1970s was in their contention that money supply and inflation were irrelevant for the discretion of a central bank. Apparently, this notion is incorrect because a central bank usually determines discretionally its policy interest rate even if it cannot directly control the money supply. Because the demand for money in the private sector is usually supposed to be negatively related to this policy interest rate, the discretion of a central bank is sure to influence the money supply and, thus, inflation.

When Okina (1992) responded to Iwata (1992) and retorted that the BOJ doctrine was not incorrect, he was not defending the doctrine, which was prevalent before the 1970s. Okina grasped Iwata's criticism of the BOJ as an argument that called for strict money supply targeting in line with monetarism. He compared it with interest-rate targeting that he assumed was the only feasible monetary framework for a central bank. In fact, the BOJ doctrine that Okina designated as such was not so much the one in the 1970s as it was the interest-rate targeting policy in which a central bank controls the policy interest rate instead of the money supply. In this renewed setting, Okina made his own argument that the BOJ doctrine is correct because the BOJ could control neither the money supply nor the monetary base once the policy interest rate was fixed.

Iwata (1993, chap. 6) named the theoretical position presented by Okina (1992) as "the sophisticated doctrine of the BOJ" and pointed out its defect. He argued that accepting interest rate targeting as a monetary policy framework does not necessarily mean accepting volatile movements in the money supply. To clarify the point, Iwata presented a monetary policy framework that he thought was the most proper. In this framework, three key policy variables must be distinguished: instrumental target, intermediate target, and policy goal (Iwata, 1993, chap. 7). The instrumental target is usually the policy interest rate. In Japan, the short-term money market rate, specifically the uncollateralized over-night call rate, has been used as the instrumental target. The policy goal is usually about the stability of certain crucial macroeconomic variables, especially the CPI increase rate and the unemployment rate. The intermediate target provides guidance that combines the instrumental target with the policy goal. Usually, the rate of increase in the money supply is supposed to be such an intermediate target.

In this framework, a central bank should manipulate the policy interest rate while monitoring the instrumental target, which is the rate of increase in the money supply that eventually influences the inflation rate and the unemployment rate. Therefore, that the rate of increase in the money supply diverges distinctively downward (upward) from a stable range more often than not means that a central bank should have lowered (raised) its policy interest rate more promptly. Thus, Iwata concluded that the BOJ's inability to control the money supply merely indicated its reluctance to preemptively manipulate the instrumental target. Actually, Iwata stated that an apparent tendency of the BOJ was to evaluate the stability of the policy interest rate, which was treated virtually as a policy goal rather than the instrumental target. Such adherence to the stability of a policy interest rate, which Iwata described as "accommodative monetary policy," would inevitably lead to an unstable economy (Iwata, 1993, chaps. 8–9). Thus, Iwata's understanding was that the "roller coaster of money supply" and the associated macroeconomic instability of the Japanese economy around the turn of the 1990s still resulted from the BOJ doctrine, although it might be more technically sophisticated.

These conflicts between both sides of the money supply controversy could never be resolved while it was in process. Even thereafter, the conflicts continued as to how both sides of these arguments should be evaluated. A typical evaluation in line with the BOJ's side is that the controversy consequently revealed the superiority of the interest-rate targeting framework to the money supply targeting framework. Ueda (1992), subtitled "reconciling the Iwata-Okina controversy," first presented the schema of "interest-rate targeting versus money supply targeting" to summarize the controversy and evaluate its arguments. This schematization might be reasonable, at least from Okina's side, because his arguments in the controversy were definitely confined to this setting. By mentioning the controversy, Okina (1993a) argued that the traditional monetarist thought emphasizing the crucial importance of stabilizing the increasing growth in the money supply was collapsing because a stable relationship between the money supply and the real economy became increasingly vague all over the world. Okina's point was probably correct because the monetary policy framework that gave a strategic role to the intermediate target of the rate of increase in the money supply prevalent in the 1980s among major central banks in developed countries was becoming obsolete and was virtually abandoned thereafter.[4] This perceptional change in policy practice that occurred around the time was rather fortunate for the BOJ, which wanted to be exempted from the responsibility of creating the "roller coaster of money supply" at the turn of the 1990s.

However, the evaluation is completely different if we grasp the true focus of the controversy, not as the choice of operational methodology on monetary policy but as the desirability of monetary policy actually conducted. When Iwata and the economists on his side criticized the manner in which the BOJ conducted monetary policy, they were also implying that the bank's monetary easing after the burst of the bubble was too late and too small, meaning that the BOJ should have lowered and should lower its policy rate more boldly. The movement in the money supply was sure to provide some precautionary information on that matter, regardless of whether or not it should be controlled.

Thereafter, the controversy shifted to its second stage and questioned directly the sufficiency of the BOJ's monetary easing in that particular phase. The answer to the question of which side was right is clear in every respect if we take a retro-spective look at what subsequently occurred in the Japanese economy. As the crit-ical economists cautioned, the BOJ's wait-and-see style of monetary easing turned out to be too timid to reverse the deflationary trend that was gradually fixating in the Japanese economy and that eventually urged it into persistent deflation.

3.3 The second stage of the controversy and an overall evaluation

The factors to which the critical economists paid special attention in the second stage were the negative balance sheet effects of asset deflation and the burden of the rising real interest rate attributable to ongoing disinflation. Takahiro Miyao first indicated how the burst of the bubble was depressing the economy. Miyao (1992) argued that declining stock prices and land prices worsened the balance sheet of financial institutions, private enterprises, and households that, in turn, generated downside pressure on the economy as a whole. Thus, Miyao charac-terized the incoming depression induced by the asset deflation as "the balance sheet depression" and called for decisive countermeasures for macroeconomic policies to cope with it. In addition, Miyao (1993) first reported the negative effects of deflation in that particular phase and argued that the Japanese economy at that time was shifting from a cycle of asset deflation to a novel stage of "genu-inely deflationary depression" accompanied by persistent deflation. Miyao pointed out that the existing interest rate that the BOJ described as "unprecedent-edly low" was not actually low because the real interest rate was possibly rising as a result of ongoing disinflation. Thus, Miyao called for a drastic reduction in the policy interest rate, desirably near to zero, to lower the real interest rate. Moreover, Iwata (1994) maintained that the monetary policy after the burst of the bubble was contractionary rather than expansionary in real terms despite the BOJ's lowering of the policy interest rate because the expected real interest rate was rising from the rapid disinflation developing at the same time. Seiji Shinpo (1994) similarly argued that the contraction of the money supply was caused by the BOJ's obsession with the nominal interest rate and its negligence of a rising real interest rate resulting from disinflation. He further criticized the failure of the BOJ, government, and majority of the economists to take into account the deflationary effect of asset deflation. Thus, Shinpo proposed the introduction of an ultra-low interest rate policy to lower the real interest rate to help restore the balance sheets in the private sector.

The BOJ's counterarguments to these criticisms were found in a speech given by Yasushi Mieno, the then BOJ governor, on November 10, 1993 (Mieno, 1995). In the speech, Mieno acknowledged that the Japanese economy was in a painful process of capital stock and balance sheet adjustment. However, contrary to the above critics, he perceived it as an unavoidable process of removing superfluous elements in an economy forged during the previous period of the bubble, and denied the efficacy of monetary policy in counteracting asset deflation. In contrast, he emphasized that the BOJ had already lowered its policy interest rate to a histori-cally low level, thus retorting to the criticism that the monetary easing was insufficient. Moreover, Mieno mentioned the criticism from the viewpoint of the real interest rate and denied the efficacy of this concept as a policy criterion, stating that the expected inflation rate was difficult to estimate.

Subsequent events decisively showed that the BOJ was wrong and the economists criticizing the BOJ were right. This evaluation might be confirmed most reliably by scholarly literature focused on the issue. The representative studies in the field, including Bernanke (2000), Jinushi, Kuroki, and Miyao (2000), and Ahearne *et al.* (2002), coincidentally stated that the BOJ's reluctance with monetary easing during the period after the burst of the bubble was the immediate cause of Japan's prolonged deflation. Bernanke (2000, pp. 150–151) argued that "the failure to ease policies adequately during the 1991–94 period, as asset prices, the banking system, and the economy declined precipitously" was one more important monetary policy mistake made by the BOJ. As a result of their ex-post evaluation of Japanese monetary policy using the Taylor rule, Jinushi *et al.* (2000, p. 122) reported that there was a delay in monetary easing from 1992 to early 1995 and concluded that "the BOJ should have continued to ease more." Ahearne *et al.* (2002) was the most precise in this respect.

> The 1993–94 period may have been particularly crucial for monetary policy, since that is the last time (with the exception of the short-lived response to the VAT hike in 1997) that inflation rates exceeded zero by a reasonable margin, so that a sufficiently large drop in the policy interest rate could have generated very low or negative short-term real interest rates. After the beginning of 1995, zero or negative inflation rates largely undermined the effectiveness of monetary policy by limiting the extent to which the real interest rate could be lowered.
>
> (Ahearne *et al.*, 2002, p. 13)

All of these studies decisively support the hypothesis that the delay in lowering the policy interest rate during the period after the burst of the bubble caused rapid disinflation and associated higher real interest rates, which eventually led to what Bernanke (2000) described as "self-induced paralysis."

A review of the money supply controversy and subsequent debates on monetary policy in the first half of the 1990s astonishingly shows that the economists who criticized the BOJ not only accurately grasped the vital elements of the particular situation but also proposed policy prescriptions that were actually workable. During the actual period when the situation changed from moment to moment, they pointed out the core elements of the problem that were later developed in Bernanke (2000) and Ahearne *et al.* (2002)—for example, the negative balance sheet effect from asset deflation and the suppressing effect of rising real interest rates from rapid disinflation. They further demanded an introduction of the near zero interest policy to overcome the problem. A few years later, although the BOJ actually adopted the ZIRP, it was too late. Until then, deflation had profoundly settled in the Japanese economy, which largely undermined the effectiveness of the policy.

4 Arguments on the goodness or badness of deflation

4.1 General background of the arguments related to deflation

As exposed in the previous section, the BOJ was indecisive in lowering the policy interest rate, particularly around 1993 and 1994. The BOJ even attempted to raise the rate in the second half of 1994. This symptom of the BOJ's reversal of its monetary stance was immediately transferred to the foreign exchange market, in which a gradual appreciation of the yen exchange rate had already begun at the turn of the 1990s. In the spring of 1995, an increase in the yen further accelerated, and the exchange rate eventually hit 79 yen per dollar in April 1995, a rate that remained the highest until 2011. This violent appreciation of the yen completely changed Japan's macro-economic circumstance and the BOJ was urged not only to abandon its reckless attempt to wishfully hike the policy interest rate but also to resume lowering it. In April 1995, the BOJ again set out a process of reducing the policy interest rate that settled at around 2.1 percent until then. Thereafter, the policy interest rate was successively and steadily lowered and eventually reached 0.4 percent in October 1995. This aggressive reduction in the policy interest rate was relatively exceptional because the BOJ completed its task and successfully helped reverse the direction of the movements in the yen exchange rate. A threat of the "strong-yen depression" ended. In 1996, the Japanese economy enjoyed a genuine recovery for the first time since the burst of the bubble.

This aggressive monetary easing in the middle of 1995, apparently the one and only during the 1990s, achieved the greatest success. Certainly, both the drastic reduction in interest rates and the depreciation of the yen associated with it contributed to the recovery in 1996. However, two problems remained that became crucial enough to continue the stagnation of the Japanese economy. One problem was chronic deflation. As a result of the violent appreciation of the yen in 1995, Japan's inflation rate, specifically the increase in the CPI and the GDP deflator, dropped into the negative range. Therefore, the Japanese economy shifted from a phase of mere disinflation to that of genuine deflation. The other problem was the liquidity trap, in which injections of money into an economy by a central bank could no longer lower interest rates. Successive reductions of the policy interest rate in the middle of 1995 lowered it to 0.4 percent, which apparently made further reductions difficult. These two problems were, so to speak, the social burden resulting from the BOJ's failure to make preemptive monetary easing at the earlier stage.

The problems were obfuscated during 1996 and early 1997 when the economy was expanding. Then, successive economic shocks hit Japan, including an increase in the consumption tax rate in April 1997, the outbreak of the Asian financial crisis in July 1997, and the onset of multiple bankruptcies in major financial institutions in November 1994, which completely changed the circumstances. The economy returned to another recession, and the inflation rate slipped to below zero once again. At this stage, the Japanese economy was essentially troubled by a paralysis in monetary policy in the sense that little room remained for conventional means to reduce the policy interest rate during a recession. Japan's economy was falling into a "deflationary trap" in which deflation promoted a rising real interest rate and vice versa. In a situation in which the policy rate already hit or was hovering near zero, the central bank could not use its traditional instruments to manage the problem. Consequently, the deflationary environment further deepened and deflationary expectations intensified. Inevitably, one observed the increase in the real interest rate, which is defined as the nominal interest rate minus the expected rate of inflation. An increase in the real interest rate discourages consumer spending and corporate investments. Accordingly, the economy's shrinking total demand further worsened deflation. Japan's economy after the 1997 crisis was about to fall into this self-sustaining deflationary process.

Despite the deepening deflation, the BOJ, led by Masaru Hayami, who was appointed the governor in March 1998, tended to indulge in a "wait-and-see" attitude toward deflation. Some exceptions existed within the BOJ. In particular, Nobuyuki Nakahara, a member of the BOJ's Policy Board, vigorously advocated aggressive monetary easing policies. However, he was never able to win a majority on the BOJ board. On February 12, 1999, when the economy was already recovering from the recession, the BOJ decided to introduce a ZIRP after many twist and turns. However, the BOJ's adoption of the ZIRP was apparently rather unwilling. In fact, on various occasions, Governor Hayami overtly expressed his eagerness to depart from the "unusual" zero interest rate situation as quickly as possible. On August 11, 2000, the BOJ finally decided to suspend the ZIRP by increasing the policy interest rate from 0 to 0.25 percent. The BOJ did this and stated that deflationary concerns were already dispelled, although no concrete evidence actually existed to prove its statement. In reality, exactly at this moment the true threat of a "deflation spiral" for the Japanese economy appeared.

4.2 The rise and fall of the good deflation theory

The unusual macroeconomic situation in Japan's economy since the end of the 1990s—that is, deflation under a zero or near-zero interest rate—prompted various debates and arguments among related experts consisting of economists, journalists, and policy officials over deflation and how to manage it. Inevitably, the arguments accompanied two interrelated questions. The first question was the meaning of deflation, and the other question was the efficacy and inefficacy of unconventional monetary policies within a zero or near-zero interest rate environment. However, the nature of the arguments was distinctively different between the former and the latter. Naturally, debates over the efficacy and inefficacy of unconventional monetary policies were conducted primarily by economists and policy officials and not by journalists because the issue required expertise in economics and monetary policy. In this sphere, the premise that deflation is harmful to the economy and had to be overcome was generally accepted among the participants despite their different opinions of unconventional monetary policies.

However, note that this basic agreement on the harm from deflation only existed among a limited number of experts, and the agreement did not extend to the outside sphere, including the mass media. Indeed, at this stage, the negative effect of deflation and the necessity to overcome it were seldom discussed in the media destined for the general public. Instead, until 2002 or so, when deflation became more severe, popular discussions among journalistic circles were about identifying and praising good deflation. They explained the extent to which a deflationary economy benefits consumers by economizing distribution processes and using more efficient methods of production, and the extent to which a deflationary economy could alter Japan's high cost structure. According to them, deflation should be welcomed because it is the result of great competition within a global economy. Naturally, in such an atmosphere, economists who advocated an expansive monetary policy to break away from the deflationary economy were seen as promoting unhealthy inflationary policies and, thus, were criticized and even teased by mass media.

As a case study for examining how preconceived ideas that are predominant in the general public positively or negatively affect actual economic policies, Hamada and Noguchi (2005) conducted an extensive survey on editorial opinions in the three major Japanese national newspapers—*The Asahi*, *The Mainichi*, and *The Yomiuri*—from 2000 to 2003. As the survey showed, the stance of "pro-deflation" and "anti-expansionary monetary policy" was the most conspicuous in *The Mainichi*'s editorials among the three, and the faintest in *Yomiuri's*. Until the early half of 2001, the tone of *Asahi's* editorials was similar to that of *Mainichi's* but gradually changed thereafter.

The following editorial was a typical expression of the good deflation theory prevalent in journalistic opinions around the turn of the 2000s.[5]

> According to an inquiry by the Economic Planning Agency, prices in Japan remain high compared internationally. It is necessary for us to continue to make further efforts to dismiss competition-restrictive regulations and irrational business practices. In addition, it is necessary for consumers to play a role in monitoring prices ... Since the beginning of this year, the rate at which prices are falling has accelerated. Nevertheless, Japan's prices of goods for daily living are still high compared internationally. To transform the economy into one in which consumers are able to experience richness, further lowering prices is necessary. In other words, we should allow the "collapse in prices" to further proceed to guide the economy toward such a transformation because lowering prices is good deflation. In this regard, "inflation targeting" as a way to hike prices to a certain level to dispel deflationary concerns in the Japanese economy is incorrect.
>
> ("Editorial: Deflation—Allow the collapse in prices to continue," *The Mainichi*, July 8, 2000)

After the BOJ suspended the ZIRP on August 11, 2000, Japan's domestic economy began to decline again, partly because of the worldwide economic slowdown, and indicators of deflation became more serious. Under the circumstances, policy discussions focused on policy instruments resurfaced, including the introduction of an inflation target and the fight against deflation through depreciation of the yen. *The Mainichi* and *The Asahi* expressed their critical opinions concerning these policy measures.

> The Bank of Japan has dug in its heels, rebuffing pressure from the Liberal Democratic Party and economists to adopt inflation targets in order to stem deflation caused by insufficient demand. The most important task of a central bank is to maintain the value of the currency, and price stability is essential for carrying out this task.... It is important to realize that much of the price declines can be attributed to deregulation.... And once inflation is triggered, it is difficult to bring under control. Central banks can establish various policies to stabilize prices but cannot manipulate prices in accordance with their whim. And once inflation gets underway, it rapidly devalues assets held by citizens. Central bankers have an obligation to prevent this from happening. It was only 10 years ago that Japan underwent a period of abnormally steep asset inflation. Why are people already clamouring for a new round of inflation?
> ("Editorial: Inflation targeting is the wrong way round," *The Mainichi*, October 29, 2000)

> The Bank of Japan, taking pride in its role as the guardian of the value of the yen, has a basic philosophy of encouraging price stability, and it cannot—and should not—assume a policy of devaluing the yen. Experience has shown that once inflation runs free, it cannot be controlled easily. The bank was right to ignore calls to purposely trigger inflation.
> ("Editorial: Bank of Japan should resist external pressure on its policy," *The Asahi*, November 1, 2000)

When deflation was deepening and the recession was becoming obvious to the public, the government decided to change the definition of "deflation" to conform it to the universal use of the term. The government rephrased it from "an economic slowdown accompanied by decline in prices" to "a continuous downward trend in prices." Then, on March 16, 2001, the government went on to admit publicly for the first time since the end of World War II that "the current state of Japan's economy is in mild deflation." The following editorial pieces show the contrasting views of *The Mainichi* and *The Yomiuri* on this matter.

> The government's monthly economic report issued on Friday acknowledged that the economy is in a state of deflation. The continuing decline in consumer and wholesale prices, in other words, has been construed as being undesirable. The drop, though, is largely the result of burgeoning imports,

technological advances and the streamlining of distribution. Even services, long considered too costly compared to other countries, have been getting cheaper. The economy is shifting to a new pricing structure due to globalization and deregulation. The declaration of deflation was accompanied by a new definition of the term as "a state in which prices keep falling," deviating from the previous official description as "a state in which prices are falling while the economy is receding." Apparently it is a disguised demand to the Bank of Japan for further quantitative easing. It is an admission of the dearth of economic policy options left at the administration's disposal. There is no need to prop up prices; they should be allowed to drop further.

("Editorial: Proclamation of being in deflation. Don't stop the decline of prices," *The Mainichi*, March 17, 2001)

On Friday, the government revised its definition of deflation. It officially recognized that the Japanese economy is in a state of deflation. The erstwhile government view that Japan was not in a state of deflation did not convince the general public, even as a deflationary spiral—a maelstrom of falling prices and recession that represents a malignant, advanced form of deflation—was growing increasingly visible. The government can take a kudos for its revision of the definition of deflation and its recognition that deflation is happening in Japan—for now at least—as actions that provide an accurate grasp of reality of the domestic economy.... Recognition of deflation is meaningless unless actual policies reflect the sense of crisis. The introduction of "an inflation target rate" is one measure likely to be effective in braking the price plunges that consequently contract production and consumption activities.

("Editorial: Government in economic never-never land," *The Yomiuri*, March 17, 2001)

In these circumstances, on March 19, 2001, the BOJ decided to not only return to a ZIRP but also introduce a quantitative monetary easing policy that it previously did not adopt. Since then, as deflation and depression continued to worsen, the BOJ was obliged to strengthen the QE measure little by little and step by step. The situation did not improve despite the BOJ's effort and, again, the question of whether to adopt the inflation target measure became a subject of debate.

There are no proven formulas to fight deflation, however, and the Bank of Japan has already reached its limit on what it can do from the monetary side. This has prompted many to urge the central bank to announce a target for the rate of inflation and utilize all policy measures at its disposal to achieve such a target. Expectations of higher prices in the future would, it is reasoned, compel investors and consumers to spend more. Indeed, the BOJ decided last March to maintain its lax monetary policy until prices at least stopped falling. It has since been pouring money into commercial banks to trigger spending. There is nothing more it can realistically do. It is not possible, moreover, to willfully steer the exchange rate lower in order to boost Japan's exports and induce higher prices domestically. The exchange rate is determined by economic fundamentals, and tampering with it, as US Treasury Secretary Paul O'Neill recently noted, can only weaken one's own economy. Instead of fighting it, the declining prices should be regarded as good news for consumers, and ways to boost demand should accordingly be considered.... The government should focus on achieving a soft-landing to a new pricing structure and express a positive vision for the future, such as by boldly shifting budgetary appropriations around and encouraging companies and individuals to increase spending.

("Editorial: Inflation is no cure-all," *The Mainichi*, January 26, 2002)

The Asahi's argument was consistently critical of the inflation target, similar to *Mainichi*'s. Nevertheless, its tone changed over time. In the following editorial, *The Asahi* no longer advocated the good deflation theory, although it was still skeptical of unconventional monetary policies aimed at mild inflation.

We do not disagree with those who say that mild inflation in the course of pulling the economy out of deflation would not be a bad thing. The problem is how that can be achieved. There is no specific or sure cure. If the Bank of Japan were to buy up corporate shares and properties without restraint, the result could be inflation. Such an approach, however, would not only worsen the financial position of the central bank, but would diminish public trust in the economy, leading to a plunge in the price of government bonds. There is also a danger that the result would be runaway inflation. And if that happened, much of the value of what people have worked so hard to put into savings would be lost. Similar results could come from application of a policy that promotes inflation by diminishing the value of the yen.

("Editorial: Everyone must cooperate in the renewed effort," *The Asahi*, January 6, 2003)

As the previous survey shows, the good deflation theory enjoyed its heyday around 2000 when the Japanese economy was in a brief stage of economic recovery induced by the worldwide IT dot-com boom. At the time, the proliferation of IT technology made the theory appear plausible. The burst of the dot-com bubble and the subsequent recession drove the Japanese economy to the brink of a deflation spiral, and the recovery promptly faded. Although a similar argument appeared repeatedly in the journalism, thereafter it never obtained a meaningful influence on actual policy making.

In contrast, the good deflation theory had a crucial influence on actual policy making during its heyday around 2000. This influence especially prevailed in the first half of 2000 when the BOJ sought appropriate timing to suspend the ZIRP introduced in February 1999. However, despite the BOJ's eagerness to suspend the ZIRP, domestic spending in the private sector had yet to recover, and the threat of deflation remained pervasive. To pave the way for suspending the ZIRP, the impatient BOJ then presented two logical grounds for the policy. One was the "dam" theory, meaning that expanding corporate earnings would surely lead to private domestic spending sometime in the near future, as if collected water would surely flow over the dam. The other was the precisely good deflation theory, implying that deflation caused by technological advances was good deflation and, thus, should be welcomed.

In the spring of 2000, when the BOJ was just leaning forward to suspend the ZIRP, its executives and some members of the Policy Board began to mention repeatedly the good deflation theory as if competing with one another. The following statement from a speech by Governor Hayami on March 21, 2000, represents the most typical opinions.

> In view of current economic conditions and price developments, Japan's economy is judged not to be in the middle of deflation. What is frightening about deflation is that it induces a vicious circle called a deflationary spiral whereby price declines reduce corporate profits and wages which, in turn, leads to a slowdown in business activity and further price declines. These can be called "pernicious price declines." In fact, there was a very high risk of Japan's economy falling into a deflationary spiral up until around the spring of 1999, but concern over such risk materializing has greatly subsided in the past year. Both CPI and WPI have been almost level. Corporate profits have been increasing and economic activity gradually picking up. Though it is true that prices of a number of products have been declining, this is against the backdrop of various revolutionary changes including the so-called IT revolution, that is, the progress of technological innovation in information and telecommunications, as well as the revolution in distribution networks represented by the emergence of so-called "category killers." Such phenomena cannot necessarily be regarded as pernicious price declines.
>
> (Hayami, 2000)

Consequently, the BOJ suspended the ZIRP in August 2000 and neglected various voices of concern for the worsening deflation and by rejecting the government's formal opposition to do so. During the event, the BOJ might have felt the necessity to publicly explain its own understanding of deflation. Therefore, the BOJ published a report titled, "On Price Stability" in October 2000. The report reconfirmed the BOJ's existing policy stance that defining price stability in terms of a price index was not appropriate because "the conduct of monetary policy may change depending on whether price fluctuation is due to demand-side or supply-side factors" (BOJ, 2000).

Specifically, in March 2001, the good deflation theory ceased to have a meaningful influence on actual policies. On March 16, 2001, the government publicly proclaimed that Japan's economy was in a deflationary condition. On March 19, 2001, the BOJ decided to return to a ZIRP and introduced a quantitative monetary easing policy, virtually approving the failure of the good deflation theory. After these announcements, the BOJ was obliged to accomplish the formal policy in cooperation with the government unambiguously confined to "defeat deflation." Since then, the good deflation theory was never restored in the sphere of public policy.

4.3 Fallacies of the good deflation theory

The good deflation theory, popular among the media at a certain time and which once constituted the formal view of the BOJ, had four propositions.

1   Deflation is a good phenomenon.
2   Deflation is not a monetary phenomenon but a structural, that is, a micro-economic, phenomenon.
3   The causes of the current deflation are globalization, deregulation, and technological innovation.
4   Depreciation of the yen harms both Japan and the rest of the world.

Obviously, all the arguments oppose the standard economic theory. Concerning the first proposition, economists usually believe that the changes in nominal variables such as deflation and inflation may be neutral to the real economy in the "long run." However, as long as the rigidity in nominal variables remains, the changes in absolute prices affect the real variables. Therefore, if the nominal adjustment is inadequate, deflation can function as a primary cause to keep the economy below its potential level in the short run. Irrespective of the case, deflation is not a "good" factor for the real economy.[6] The good deflation theory simply obscures the absolute price change of goods and services with the relative price depreciation of a certain commodity as a result of innovation.

The second and third propositions are the core of the good deflation theory. The question here is not whether real factors might affect prices. As the identity equation of the quantity theory of money shows, if the quantity of money is constant, an increase in real income inevitably results in deflation. Moreover, the analysis of aggregate demand and aggregate supply in a macroeconomics text-book shows that "positive supply shocks," such as a reduction in the price of traded goods and a technical innovation would, by shifting the supply curve rightward, lead to a reduction in general prices. The analysis has no errors. The problem with the good deflation theory rests on the fact that it claims, beyond this type of analysis, that monetary factors cannot affect general price levels. This claim is clearly false because absolute prices or the general price level are the prices of a currency relative to goods and services. Therefore, prices definitely depend on the supply of money.

Furthermore, the good deflation theory advocates that the deflation caused by a positive supply shock is good. This contention is also wrong. Without a doubt, a positive supply shock itself is a favorable phenomenon for increasing real income, at least potentially. However, it does not follow that the deflation caused by a positive supply shock is also favorable. Preventing deflation using monetary policies is always possible, even though a positive supply shock occurs. In general, a combination of a rise in the potential growth rate, induced by positive supply shocks and the implementation of an adequate monetary policy, which prevents these shocks from leading to excessive disinflation or deflation, allows the actual growth rate to increase to the most desirable level.[7] The US economy during the 1990s, called the "fabulous decade" (Blinder and Yellen, 2001), might be a typical example of a successful result of this combination.

The problem with the fourth proposition is that it neglects the fact that Japan and the other developed countries are primarily under a floating exchange rate system. Under such a system, the exchange rate is an endogenous variable determined by various macroeconomic variables. According to the classical open economy model, the nominal exchange rate is determined mostly by monetary factors and the influence of nominal factors on the real economy is completely neutral. In a Keynesian open-economy model, such as the Mundell–Fleming model, a depreciation in the nominal exchange rate of one's currency caused by a monetary expansion increases external demand by depreciating the real exchange rate. Advocates of the good deflation theory often define the phenomenon as a beggar-thy-neighbor policy. This perspective is incorrect. Under a floating exchange rate system in which each country maintains autonomy over its monetary policy, each country also retains the freedom to implement similar measures of its own. With autonomy over monetary policy, each country can easily minimize the negative effects imposed by the depreciation of the exchange rate of another country's currency. This process mutually promotes growth and, thus, is irrelevant to the beggar-thy-neighbor policy.

5 Controversy regarding unconventional monetary policy under zero interest rates at the turn of the 2000s

5.1 A prelude to the controversy regarding unconventional monetary policy

The autumn of 1995 was the epoch period during which the Japanese economy nearly faced a liquidity trap situation in which further reductions in nominal interest rates were made difficult. During this period, Japan's policy interest rate was lowered to 0.4 percent to mitigate the rapid appreciation of the yen exchange rate proceeding at the time. However, the subsequent economic recovery after the action obscured the risk underlying the situation. This inability to perceive the underlying risk was most conspicuously shown in the hasty shift from fiscal expansion to contraction. Eventually, consumption tax was raised in April 1997, which triggered a breakdown of the recovery and led to the overall economic crisis. During that time, the Japanese economy was continuously troubled by the liquidity trap situation in which conventional monetary policies were paralyzed.

Among the debates developed domestically, Takahiro Miyao first highlighted the problem residing in the situation associated with the liquidity trap. Miyao (1996) was probably the first article that highlighted the concept of liquidity trap to describe the Japanese economy during late 1996. He analyzed that the Japanese economy was then in a liquidity trap in which even the near zero nominal interest rate could not stimulate economic activity because the real interest rate was kept high from ongoing deflation (Miyao, 1996, p. 71). In the article, Miyao also argued the following.

> Although Keynesian prescriptions are losing efficacy, they cannot be completely ignored. If they are actually ignored such that interest rates increase, fiscal expenditures decline or taxes increase, business conditions would definitely deteriorate. Note that macroeconomic policies actually play their roles adequately, even if at first sight they appear to become ineffective.
>
> Therefore, it is necessary to keep the interest rates as low as possible, to activate public investment although its content should be reexamined, and to postpone the tax increase as far as possible. Nevertheless, business will decline to return to zero growth during fiscal year 1997, and the Japanese economy will be trapped in a vicious cycle of an intensifying crisis of depression and rising real interest rates.
>
> (Miyao, 1996, p. 74)

Unfortunately, actual macroeconomic policies during the period shifted in a direction that contradicted Miyao's warnings, and the Japanese economy literally fell into a vicious cycle of deflation and depression, exactly as he feared. In this regard, Miyao (1996) provided the most illuminating analysis of that period in the sense that it successfully identified—not as ex-post commentary but as advance warning—the risks associated with the liquidity trap.

Japan's liquidity trap situation attracted worldwide attention when the Japanese economy was involved in an unprecedented economic and financial crisis from late 1997 to early 1998. In this regard, Krugman (1998) was one of the most influential papers, which triggered debates on monetary policies under or near zero interest rates both at home and abroad. In this paper, Krugman presented the dynamic macroeconomic model of the liquidity trap in which the zero bound on the nominal interest rate, together with an anticipation of decreasing real future income, could result in the current economy producing chronically below its potential. Moreover, he pointed out that the policy to escape from the liquidity trap as he defined it was to make the expected inflation rate considerably higher than the absolute value of the decreasing potential growth rate. If the equilibrium real interest rate could be assimilated with the potential growth rate, it must be below zero for decreasing potential growth. This negative equilibrium real interest rate is attainable under the zero bound on the nominal interest rate only if the expected inflation rate is higher than the decreasing potential growth rate. Although Krugman did not mention actual policy measures to increase the expected inflation rate, he successfully provided the foundation for subsequent debates and arguments.

In February 1999, the BOJ introduced a ZIRP, which it subsequently suspended in August 2000. The BOJ eventually introduced a quantitative monetary easing policy in March 2001. As reflecting these policy developments, the debate on an unconventional monetary policy was developing extensively and intensively both at home and abroad. Since that time, many books and collections on this subject were published in Japanese and in English, including Mikitani and Posen (eds.) (2000), Iwata (ed.) (2000), Bank of Japan (2001a), Komiya and Japan Center for Economic Research (eds.) (2002), and Ito, Patrick, and Weinstein (eds.) (2005), to mention a few. The controversy continued to develop in a broader scope in which many developed countries were forced to face a near ZIRP after the Lehman Shock.

5.2 The efficacy or inefficacy of quantitative easing

Mentioning all related subjects in the controversy is difficult because the controversy was gradually extended to include variously diversified issues. Thus, this summary is confined only to the following three crucial subjects in dispute that attracted special attention in the initial phase of the controversy that was developing at home. These three subjects are related to QE.

1   The effects of QE as an unconventional monetary policy.
2   The channels of transmission from QE to the economy.
3   The role of inflation targeting under QE.

As early as 1998, the period during which the Japanese economy was devastatingly troubled by the financial crisis, the possibility of QE began to be mentioned in some economic journals and newspapers. This occurrence was rather natural because the BOJ was already losing room to lower the policy interest rate during that period. The arguments began to take on an air of reality, particularly after the BOJ introduced the ZIRP in February 1999.

Actually, at that time, an unconcealed conflict existed within the BOJ Policy Board, a specialized panel in the BOJ supremely responsible for setting monetary policy, on whether or not QE should be adopted. Among the Board members, Nobuyuki Nakahara alone consistently prompted the introduction of QE as early as the beginning of 1999, to which the other members, including the executives, were either hesitant or overtly negative. At the time, several economists were already preaching the introduction of QE in economic journals and papers. Among these propositions, Nakahara's speech on November 1, 1999 was not only the most concrete policy prescription but also the most comprehensive. Nakahara presented his proposal for QE as follows.

> My proposal has already been outlined in the minutes of the Monetary Policy Meeting. It aims for an annual increase of 0.5 to 2.0 percent in the consumer price index (CPI) excluding perishables in two years' time, while increasing excess reserves by about 500 billion yen over one reserve maintenance period, and continuing to increase the amount thereafter to produce annual growth of about 10 percent in the monetary base. Inflation targeting

would be employed as a framework to achieve the objectives of monetary policy, with a certain growth rate of the monetary base as the intermediate target.

(Nakahara, 1999)

Nakahara then explained the following five channels of "the transmission mechanism of quantitative easing," which are "a decline in interest rates on term instruments with relatively long maturities," "financial institutions' changing their portfolios," "a rise in the expected inflation rate lowering real interest rates," "a weaker tendency in the value of the yen," and "a rise in stock prices." Nakahara presented a framework for QE in which excess reserves on demand deposit of the BOJ, annual growth in the monetary base, and annual increases in the CPI were assigned as the instrumental target, the intermediate target, and the policy goal, respectively. He further explained the transmission mechanism on how to operate this framework. During the period between February 1999, when the ZIRP was adopted, and March 2001, when the QE was finally adopted, Nakahara stubbornly continued to propose this QE framework—occasionally with added improvements—at every meeting of the Policy Board. On all of these occasions, the rest of the Policy Board members consistently rejected his proposal.

Although a few members seemed at least partially sympathetic to QE, the majority of them, particularly the BOJ's executives, were completely negative. Their critical stance on QE as well as on Nakahara's proposal was best shown in Governor Hayami's speech on July 9, 1999.

Up to last February when the Bank decided on the zero interest rate policy, the target for guiding the unsecured overnight call rate had already been as low as 0.25 percent, which had left hardly any room for further reduction. Under such circumstances, a view was expressed at the Monetary Policy Meeting on February 12 that for further monetary easing quantitative targeting might be more effective. The majority view, however, was that the demand for monetary base fluctuated widely depending on money market developments and that its relationship with the real economy was not stable. After thorough discussion, it was decided to make the maximum use of the remaining room for the further reduction of interest rates by eliminating the de facto floor for the call rate. Interest rates and the quantity of money are two sides of the same coin. A reduction of interest rates to zero accompanies simultaneous quantitative easing on a massive scale, which was expressed by the phrase "provide ample liquidity."

(Hayami, 1999)

In contrast, Nakahara proposed a framework of inflation targeting in which the policy aimed to attain in two years the situation that the CPI excluding perishables was increasing from 0.5 to 2.0 percent annually. The BOJ itself categorically rejected the virtue of inflation targeting at least while Hayami was governor. In a speech presented on March 21, 2000, Governor Hayami unfolded a comprehensive criticism of inflation targeting.

> Regarding inflation policy, first and foremost, I would like to point out that inflation is no solution to economic problems. Inflation policy assumes that moderate inflation will revitalize economic activity, alleviate the debt burden of firms as well as financial institutions, and relieve the fiscal deficit problem. Apparently those who advocate inflation policy argue, while taking due account of its negative effects, that the intended positive effects would be greater than the negative effects under the current situation. But, if we look more closely, the intended positive effects themselves would not likely be achieved.
>
> (Hayami, 2000)

Hayami then explained several reasons why the negative effects of the inflation policy would be greater than its positive effects. His understanding was that "inflation targeting was originally adopted as a policy framework geared toward price stability by those countries who were suffering from high inflation," a completely different situation from Japan. He cautioned that an artificial inflation policy in the name of inflation targeting might trigger uncontrollable inflation.

> Once inflationary expectations take a firm hold on society, they tend to proliferate. Workers would demand higher wage increases than would otherwise be the case. If wage costs rise, firms would try to pass them on to product prices. Such an economy has a built-in risk of increasing inflationary pressure.
>
> (Hayami, 2000)

Apparently, the BOJ's stance during the period was more cautious toward inflation than toward deflation. The BOJ's adoption of QE in March 2001 did not bring a simultaneous conversion of the doctrine in this regard. The governor, other executives, and some of the Policy Board members continued to strongly oppose the inflation targeting in their speeches and interviews even after the adoption of QE.

In parallel with the controversy provoked in the BOJ's Policy Board regarding the decision on national monetary policy, an essentially similar controversy was developed within economists' circles as well, occasionally in a fiercer manner. The confrontation was primarily between the economists calling for both adopting inflation targeting and extending QE more boldly and those defending the BOJ's existing stance. Kikuo Iwata, Koichi Hamada, and Takatoshi Ito represented the former, and Ryutaro Komiya, Kunio Okina, and Masaaki Shirakawa represented the latter.[8] Among the latter economists, Okina and Shirakawa belonged to the BOJ during the period. As mentioned in the previous section, Ryutaro Komiya was the leading opponent of the BOJ in the 1970s, whose criticism cast significant influence on the critical argument developed by

Kikuo Iwata in the first half of the 1990s. This time, Komiya was on the BOJ's side and, thus, confronted Iwata and the other economists who were critical of the BOJ.

The economists criticizing the BOJ at that time had a common core vision as to what the BOJ should do, although many differences in the details existed among them. First, they commonly advocated the adoption and expansion of QE through the BOJ's purchase of long-term government bonds and other assets. Second, they believed that QE would make various transmission channels effective by promoting financial and non-financial institutions' changing their portfolios even if short-term interest rates could not be lowered. These channels were declines in long-term interest rates, increases in asset prices, and depreciation in the yen exchange rate, which commonly contributed to stimulating aggregate demand and, thus, overcoming deflation. Third, they believed that inflation targeting was a prerequisite for QE to be effective, especially for reducing real interest rates. As Krugman (1998) suggested, increasing the expected inflation rate is the only way to reduce real interest rates when reducing nominal interest rates is not possible. They argued that the BOJ's announcement of its policy goal as reflected in the inflation rate and its commitment for accomplishing the goal—that is exactly what the inflation targeting means—would assist in forming an expectation of inflation that was relevant to the targeted inflation rate. This "expectation channel" or the transmission channel to lower real interest rates by reversing deflationary expectations that stubbornly settled in people's minds was highlighted in Iwata (2002). Throughout the controversy, Iwata and the other economists who emphasized the importance of realizing a regime change for monetary policy through the BOJ's adoption of inflation targeting were sometimes called "reflationists."

The controversy surrounding QE generated various derivations, among which was the debate on the relationship between QE and foreign exchange policy. The excessive appreciation of the yen exchange rate was apparently one of the crucial factors contributing to stagnation in the 1990s. When the appreciation of the yen seemed excessive, the MOF used to intervene in the foreign exchange market to contain the rising yen, which was the situation in the latter half of 1999. Experiencing a rapid appreciation of the yen when the Japanese economy did not sufficiently recover and the BOJ continued the ZIRP, the MOF intervened extensively in the foreign exchange market, as usual.

Hamada (1999) mentioned that the effect of such an intervention by the MOF to contain the rising yen was always weakened by the BOJ's sterilizing operations of offsetting the monetary base enlarged during the course of the MOF's intervention. Thus, Hamada argued that the BOJ should stop these sterilizing operations and leave the monetary base enlarged to make the MOF's intervention more effective. His argument was based on a standard open-economy macroeconomic model called the Mundell–Fleming model, which deduced the conclusion that monetary expansion in a flexible exchange rate system takes effect by promoting depreciation of the foreign exchange rate. Therefore, unsterilized intervention is supposed to be more effective than sterilized intervention because the former is more expansionary than the latter with respect to the size of the monetary base. This contention in Hamada (1999) invited prompt objections from Komiya (1999) and Okina and Shiratsuka (2000), in which they argued that the distinction between unsterilized intervention and sterilized intervention was meaningless under the ZIRP. According to them, unsterilized intervention has no additional expansionary effect because the monetary base is already completely expanded, resulting in the lowest policy interest rate regardless of intervention in the foreign exchange market. Hamada (2000) replied to them by contending that expansion of the monetary base was meaningful even under the ZIRP.

This debate revealed that whether or not unsterilized intervention under the ZIRP is meaningful depends ultimately on whether or not QE has an effective transmission channel for depreciating the foreign exchange rate because expansion of the monetary base under the ZIRP is nothing more than QE. Additionally, the debate revealed that unsterilized intervention is made possible only when foreign exchange market intervention operations are followed by simultaneous changes in the monetary target on the BOJ's side. Conversely, foreign exchange market intervention operations are automatically sterilized if the BOJ keeps its monetary target unchanged, which explained why intervening operations to date have been sterilized in principle. Although the debate on the relationship between QE and foreign exchange market intervention was not further developed, the understanding obtained influenced a later event in which massive foreign exchange market intervening operations from October 2003 to January 2004 were accompanied by an increase in the monetary target set by the BOJ.

Regarding the main controversy on QE, the economists defending the existing stance of the BOJ used to contend that the transmission channels from QE to the economy, specifically to the inflation rate, were either ineffective or unreliable. In addition, they tended to underestimate the benefits of QE and to empathize with its harmful side effects. The arguments in Fujiki, Okina, and Shiratsuka (2001) were typical in this regard. In this article, they specified the two types of QE commonly implemented by the outright purchase of long-term government bonds depending on whether QE aimed to promote (1) a decline in long-term interest rates primarily through portfolio rebalancing effects or (2) a change in private-sector expectations with respect to future inflation or asset price developments. They called type (1) and type (2) "mild" and "aggressive" versions of outright purchases of long-term government bonds, respectively (Fujiki *et al.*, 2001, p. 108). In case of mild QE, they contended that "the effects are extremely uncertain" because portfolio rebalancing could not be reliable given the malfunction of credit channels attributable to NPLs. Furthermore, they pointed out a possible risk that a long time lag between implementation of the operation and the materialization of the effects on prices and economic activity would deteriorate the BOJ's balance sheet position (Fujiki *et al.*, 2001, pp. 109–110). In case of aggressive QE that attempted to actively work on expectations and aimed to buoy the economy, they concluded that the effects were rather uncertain because the operations were not sure to affect expectations. Therefore, they stated, "aggressive operations should be regarded as a high-risk, high-return policy option verging on a high-stakes bet" (Fujiki *et al.*, 2001, p. 111).

It is quite natural that the economists on the BOJ's side were more dubious about inflation targeting than QE. They argued that for the BOJ to commit to bringing about mild inflation was meaningless because the transmission effects of QE on general prices were relatively uncertain. Thus, Komiya (2002, p. 296) stated that the inflation targeting theory was just "harassment" for the BOJ because the bank had no reliable option for getting the economy out of deflation. Reflecting on the proliferation of the good deflation theory around 2000, Shiratsuka (2000) also argued that the positive supply shocks such as deregulation and technological innovation could be another reason why the BOJ should not adopt inflation targeting under such structural deflation, since the desirable inflation rate might temporarily diverge from the inflation rate that should be committed to maintain in place for a long duration.

While empathizing with the unreliability of QE for overcoming deflation as such, they sometimes suggested that QE could bring about uncontrollable inflation that would disrupt rather than stimulate the economy.[9] Although the possibility that QE would create such vicious inflation or hyperinflation in the worst case was never a formal subject of the controversy within economists' circles, sympathy to the good inflation theory and associated antipathy to inflation targeting within journalistic circles apparently rested on this fear. Therefore, Takeshi Kimura, previously on the BOJ staff, became the media's favorite after he wrote a story cautioning that the Japanese economy would be ruined in the near future through a collapse of government bonds, capital freight, currency depreciation, and hyperinflation (Kimura, 2001).

The controversy surrounding the effectiveness of QE could not be reconciled in the end. However, note that advocates of QE had strong grounds for proving that QE could cause inflation eventually if extended further, although they seldom resorted to this notion in the formal controversy. Bernanke (2000, p. 158) first presented this concept.

> The general argument that the monetary authorities can increase aggregate demand and prices, even if the nominal interest rate is zero, is as follows: Money, unlike other forms of government debt, pays zero interest and has infinite maturity. The monetary authorities can issue as much money as they like. Hence, if the price level were truly independent of money issuance, then the monetary authorities could use the money they create to acquire indefinite quantities of goods and assets. This is manifestly impossible in equilibrium. Therefore money issuance must ultimately raise the price level, even if nominal interest rates are bounded at zero. This is an elementary argument, but, as we will see, it is quite corrosive of claims of monetary impotence.

In addition, Bernanke (2000, p. 162) used the same logic to refute the contention that the unsterilized foreign exchange intervention under the ZIRP cannot be effective.

To rebut this view, one can apply a reductio ad absurdum argument, based on my earlier observation that money issuance must affect prices, else printing money will create infinite purchasing power. Suppose the Bank of Japan prints yen and uses them to acquire foreign assets. If the yen did not depreciate as a result, and if there were no reciprocal demand for Japanese goods or assets (which would drive up domestic prices), what in principle would prevent the BOJ from acquiring infinite quantities of foreign assets, leaving foreigners nothing to hold but idle yen balances? Obviously this will not happen in equilibrium. One reason it will not happen is the principle of portfolio balance: Because yen balances are not perfect substitutes for all other types of real and financial assets, foreigners will not greatly increase their holdings of yen unless the yen depreciates, increasing the expected return (including the risk premium) on yen assets.

Bernanke proved that QE could ultimately affect prices using a reductio ad absurdum argument. Noguchi (2002, p. 57) first introduced this logic into Japan's journalistic circles. Thereafter, it became diffused, particularly through various Internet forums that argued over economic issues.

5.3 Influence of the controversy surrounding the policy

Evaluating the QE controversy at this moment is difficult because evaluation of QE itself has not yet been settled. Even when restricted to Japan's experience with QE, a number of papers and books on the topic have been published to date, and are being published. These studies have not yet provided sufficiently convincing evaluations on the entire topic. Therefore, the following note is confined only to summarizing briefly the noticeable influences of the controversy on actual policy developments.

On March 19, 2001, the BOJ decided to return to the ZIRP and to introduce QE. Considering that BOJ executives repeatedly expressed their negative views of QE, such a sudden change in policy beyond the mere restoration of the ZIRP was nothing short of a surprise. At that time, newspapers and economic journals interpreted that the BOJ was forced to do more than restore the ZIRP to avoid being blamed for making deflation worse after suspending the ZIRP in August 2000. It was a decision that went against the government's formal objection. The media frequently reported on the possible resignation of Governor Hayami thereafter, which did not occur. In April 2001, the Koizumi cabinet was installed and was enthusiastically welcomed by the media. The issue of Governor Hayami's responsibility was completely lost in the atmosphere.

The fact that the BOJ adopted QE meant that the bank's orthodoxy eventually surrendered to its inside heresy embodied by Nobuyuki Nakahara. However, note that the actual implementation of QE by the BOJ was largely different from Nakahara's original proposal. This difference explains why the economists who initially welcomed the BOJ's adoption of QE were disappointed as things proceeded. Nakahara's proposal precisely defined its final policy goal as the targeted inflation rate and its procedure to achieve that goal as "increasing excess reserves by about 500 billion yen over one reserve maintenance period, and continuing to increase the amount thereafter to produce annual growth of about 10 percent in the monetary base" (Nakahara, 1999). In the BOJ's implementation, the commitment was far weaker because it simply decided that "the new procedures for money market operations continue to be in place until the consumer price index (excluding perishables, on a nationwide statistics) registers stably a zero percent or an increase year on year," without any prescription for the final policy goal. Moreover, no provision was made on the procedure to extend QE, except that "for the time being, the balance outstanding at the Bank's current accounts be increased to around five trillion yen, or one trillion yen increase from the average outstanding of four trillion yen in February 2001" (BOJ, 2001b). Therefore, whether the BOJ actually extended QE to an efficient amount was left to its discretion. The situation continued as before even after the adoption of QE, and the BOJ decided to change its instrumental target reluctantly only when external demand became large enough. Only after March 2003, when Governor Hayami's official term expired and Toshihiko Fukui took his place, did the BOJ activate QE in a meaningful manner.

As described previously, the BOJ officially opposed inflation targeting by stating that it was inappropriate in times of deflation. However, after the adoption of QE, some members of the Policy Board began to maintain that the BOJ's commitment to continue QE until the core CPI registered stably a zero percent was similar to inflation targeting. This ambiguous evaluation of inflation targeting by the BOJ continued even after Fukui took office. On March 9, 2006, the BOJ under Governor Fukui announced "a new framework for the conduct of monetary policy" in which "an understanding of medium- to long-term price stability" was defined as "an approximate range between zero and two percent in the rate of year-on-year change in the consumer price index" (BOJ, 2006), which was similar to inflation targeting at its face. The ironic fact is that the framework was introduced to terminate QE.

The most noticeable policy development after Fukui's inauguration is that extensions of QE during its initial term, specifically those from October 2003 to January 2004, were obviously related to the MOF's massive foreign exchange market intervention called the Great Intervention, as described in Taylor (2006). This situation was particularly interesting because the unsterilized foreign exchange intervention under the ZIRP, which virtually indicated a combination of the MOF's intervention and the BOJ's simultaneous extension of QE, was the focal subject of the controversy. Alan Greenspan, then Chairman of the Federal Reserve, made the point clear in his speech on March 2, 2004.

Granted the level of intervention pursued by the Japanese monetary authorities has influenced the market value of the yen, but the size of the impact is difficult to judge. In any event, it must be presumed that the rate of accumulation of dollar assets by the Japanese government will have to slow at some point and eventually cease. For now, partially unsterilized intervention is perceived as a means of expanding the monetary base of Japan, a basic element of monetary policy. (The same effect, of course, is available through the purchase of domestic assets.) In time, however, as the present deflationary situation abates, the monetary consequences of continued intervention could become problematic. The current performance of the Japanese economy suggests that we are getting closer to the point where continued intervention at the present scale will no longer meet the monetary policy needs of Japan.

(Greenspan, 2004)

As anticipated by Greenspan, the trend in the movement of the foreign exchange rate began to reverse around mid-2004. The Great Intervention was terminated on March 16, 2004, and no foreign exchange market intervention occurred until September 2010. From 2004 to 2007, the Japanese economy enjoyed a moderate recovery supported by a depreciating yen and extended overseas demand.

6 The political economy of the unconventional monetary policy in Japan

The development of the controversy surrounding Japan's monetary policy after the burst of the bubble and the actual conduct of the policy might raise the question as to why the actual policies were always implemented too late and on too small a scale. The controversies in the period revealed that numerous advance suggestions were made related to how the BOJ should act to prevent the economy from falling into the difficult situation of persistent deflation and a liquidity trap. The BOJ always refused to accept these suggestions by over-emphasizing the risks and side effects that might accompany them and continued to justify conventional policies that were useless in the end. Given that no such risk was realized from the adoption of the ZIRP or QE, the BOJ's excessive conservatism appeared more problematic. The following remarks by Kazuo Ueda, then a member of the Policy Board, on October 20, 1999 were indicative of this mentality.

Hence, suggestions have been made to go beyond traditional tools of operations. The list is very long: long-term government bonds, stocks, consumer durables, real estate, foreign exchanges, and so on.... Whether central banks can systematically affect the prices of these assets is an old question to which no one has a satisfactory answer. Let us for the moment assume that they can. Then, surely central bank purchase of at least some of these assets will affect the economy.... Going back to outright purchases of non-traditional assets, I must say that they generate various types of costs for the central bank and for the economy, some of which we may not be aware of and most of which are not explicitly dealt with in formal models economists use. These costs certainly ought to be weighed against possible benefits of the operations before any decision is made. I hope we will not be the one to make such a risky decision.

(Ueda, 1999)

Posen (2000, p. 202) posed the question as to why the BOJ chose a deflationary monetary policy despite its apparent contradiction with its official mission of achieving macroeconomic stability. He then attributed the reason to ideological factors. Such an explanation is highly plausible considering that the BOJ tended to adhere to biased thinking that led to erroneous policy directions. The BOJ doctrine and the good deflation theory are typical examples of such thinking.

However, note that the BOJ may have chosen such odd theories because they were favorable to the bank. In other words, they suited the interests of the BOJ as a bureaucratic organization. Although a bureaucratic organization is not a profit-maximizing body, it certainly maximizes its benefits in various ways. An example of such maximizing behavior is minimizing the possibility of being criticized by minimizing its responsibilities. Actually, the BOJ doctrine and the good deflation theory were utilized to avoid being responsible for allowing inflation or deflation.

The common circumstance that a bureaucratic organization prefers conservative rather than activist policy making can be explained as minimizing behavior. A bureaucratic organization is usually hesitant to implement an unconventional policy to which it is not accustomed, and taking that step experiences more disincentive than incentive. An unconventional policy always accompanies a greater possibility of failing, thus a greater possibility of being criticized. Moreover, the success of such a policy is not always beneficial because of the resulting criticism that the policy should have been realized earlier. Therefore, it is a good strategy for a bureaucratic organization to maintain a conventional policy for as long as it can. A bureaucratic organization daring to adopt an unconventional policy may encounter a situation in which it can no longer conceal the inefficiencies related to conventional policies and, thus, cannot defend its conventional policy stance from external criticism. This precisely occurred in Japan with respect to its unconventional monetary policy when the country's economy faced the zero bound of the policy interest rate for the first time in the world since World War II.

Notes

1 Bernanke and Reinhart (2004) characterized and analyzed various options to the unconventional monetary policies.
2 The fact that the BOJ's policy of containing the bubble consequently resulted in persistent stagnation was grasped as evidence to support the so-called Fed view stating that monetary policy should not be aimed at preventing asset bubbles, thereby discrediting the so-called BIS (Bank for International Settlements) view that it should be. The literature representing the Fed view and the BIS view are Bernanke and Gertler (1999, 2001) and White (2006), respectively.
3 The sentences that Shimanaka actually cited were as follows:

> On the average, a change in the rate of monetary growth produces a change in the rate of growth of nominal income about six to nine months later. This is an average that does not hold in every individual case.
>
> The changed rate of growth of nominal income typically shows up first in output and hardly at all in prices. If the rate of monetary growth is reduced then about six to

nine months later, the rate of growth of nominal income and also of physical output will decline. However, the rate of price rise will be affected very little.

In the short run, which may be as much as five or ten years, monetary changes affect primarily output.

(Friedman, 1970, pp. 22–23)

4   The most famous manifestation of the situation is a statement that then Federal Reserve Board Chairman Alan Greenspan made at a July 1993 congressional testimony:

The historical relationships between money and income, and between money and the price level have largely broken down, depriving the aggregates of much of their usefulness as guides to policy. At least for the time being, M2 has been downgraded as a reliable indicator of financial conditions in the economy, and no single variable has yet been identified to take its place.

(Greenspan, 1993, pp. 9–10)

5   The most of the following editorial sentences were retrieved from a full text database LexisNexis Academic. The rest were from G-Search Classic, except "Editorial: Deflation—Allow the collapse in prices to continue," *The Mainichi*, July 8, 2000, which was translated by this author from the Japanese edition.

6   If an economic theory exists that can justify deflation, it might be Milton Friedman's "optimal rate of inflation" concept (Friedman, 1969). Because this optimal rate is given by a zero nominal interest rate, an optimal inflation rate becomes negative as long as an economy's real interest rate remains positive. Friedman argued that this zero nominal interest rate is ideal because households enjoy a maximum consumer surplus in money holding. (By definition, we have $\rho=r-\pi$, where ρ is the real interest rate, r is the nominal interest rate, and π is the rate of inflation. Therefore, we have $\pi=-\rho<0$ in case of $r=0$ and $\rho>0$.) However, note that this reasoning is applicable only in a hypothetical world in which nominal rigidities do not exist. In fact, no single central bank in the world has set a goal for negative inflation by following Friedman's rule.

7   In his critical view of the BOJ's report "On Price Stability" (BOJ, 2000), Takeo Hoshi (2001) pointed out the fallacy of the BOJ's contention that "the conduct of monetary policy may change depending on whether price fluctuation is due to demand-side or supply-side factors." Hoshi argued that allowing deflation during a positive supply shock has no merit because deflation generally arose from a deflationary GDP gap, which meant wasting of employment and other resources.

8   Their major contributions to the controversy were collected in Iwata (ed.) (2000) and Komiya and Japan Center for Economic Research (eds.) (2002).

9   Some economists critical of the BOJ ironically called this instability thesis of inflation dynamics the "rolling stone theory," implying that inflation cannot be contained once it begins, similar to a stone too heavy to move cannot stop rolling once it begins down a slope. As a criticism to the BOJ's interfering caution of spiraling inflation as a result of an anti-deflation policy, Posen (2000, p. 201) stated, "these assertions are directly contradicted by all the available econometric evidence on inflation dynamics, as well as the experience of preemptive monetary policy around the world."

References

Ahearne, A., J. Gagnon, J. Haltmaier, S. K. C. Erceg, J. Faust, L. Guerrini, C. Hemphill, L. Kole, J. Roush, J. Rogers, N. Sheets, and J. Wright (2002) "Preventing deflation: Lessons from Japan's experience in the 1990s," *International Finance Discussion Papers* 729, Board of Governors of the Federal Reserve System, USA.

Bank of Japan (2000) "On price stability," October 13, 2000 (www.boj.or.jp/en/announcements/release_2000/k001013a.htm/).

Bank of Japan (2001a) "The role of monetary policy under low inflation: Deflationary shocks and policy responses," *Monetary and Economic Studies*, Institute for Monetary and Economic Studies Vol. 19, No. S-1 (www.imes.boj.or.jp/english/publication/mes/mes01.html#me19-S1).

Bank of Japan (2001b) "New procedures for money market operations and monetary easing," March 19, 2001 (www.boj.or.jp/en/announcements/release_2001/k010319a.htm/).

Bank of Japan (2006) "The introduction of a new framework for the conduct of monetary policy," March 9, 2006 (www.boj.or.jp/en/announcements/release_2006/k060309b.htm/).

Bernanke, B. S. (2000) "Japanese monetary policy: Case for self-induced paralysis?" in R. Mikitani and A. Posen (eds.) *Japan's Financial Crisis and its Parallels to U. S. Experience*, Washington D. C.: Institute for International Economics, pp. 149–166.

Bernanke, B. S. and M. Gertler (1999) "Monetary policy and asset price volatility," in Federal Reserve Bank of Kansas City, *New Challenges for Monetary Policy*, pp. 77–128.

Bernanke, B. S. and M. Gertler (2001) "How should central banks respond to asset prices," *American Economic Review, Papers and Proceedings*, 91–2, pp. 253–257.

Bernanke, B. S. and V. R. Reinhart (2004) "Conducting monetary policy at very low short-term interest rates," *American Economic Review* 94–2, pp. 85–90.

Blinder, A. S. and J. L. Yellen (2001) *The Fabulous Decade: Macroeconomic Lessons from the 1990s—US*, New York: The Century Foundation Press.

Friedman, M. (1969) *The Optimal Quantity of Money and Other Essays*, Chicago: Aldine.

Friedman, M. (1970) *The Counter-Revolution in Monetary Theory: First Wincott Memorial Lecture, Delivered at Senate House, University of London, 16 September*, London: Transatlantic Arts.

Fujiki, H., K. Okina, and S. Shiratsuka (2001) "Monetary policy under zero interest rate: Viewpoints of central bank economists," *Monetary and Economic Studies*, Institute for Monetary and Economic Studies, Bank of Japan 19–1, pp. 89–130.

Greenspan, A. (1993) "Testimony," before the Subcommittee on Economic Growth and Credit Formation of the Committee on Banking, Finance and Urban Affairs, House of Representatives, July 20, 1993 (http://fraser.stlouisfed.org/docs/historical/greenspan/Greenspan_19930720.pdf).

Greenspan, A. (2004) "Current account," Remarks before the Economic Club of New York, March 2, 2004 (www.federalreserve.gov/boarddocs/speeches/2004/20040302/).

Hamada, K. (1999) "Nichigin no futaika seisaku wa machigatte iru (The Bank of Japan is wrong to take sterilized intervention)," *Shukan Toyo Keizai*, November 13, pp. 72–76 (in Japanese).

Hamada, K. (2000) "Zero kinri-ka no kin'yu seisaku nimo kaisei no shudan ari: Komiya-shi, Okina-shi heno sai-hanron (There is a measure of economic recovery by monetary policy under zero interest rate: Counterargument against Messrs. Komiya and Okina, again)," *Shukan Toyo Keizai*, March 11, pp. 80–84 (in Japanese).

Hamada, K. and A. Noguchi (2005) "The role of preconceived ideas in macroeconomic policy: Japan's experiences in the two deflationary periods," *International Economics and Economic Policy* Vol. 2, No. 2–3, pp. 101–126.

Harada, Y. (1992) "Ayamatta kin'yu seisaku siso wo tadase (Correct the misguided thought on monetary policy)," *Shukan Toyo Keizai*, November 7, pp. 74–80 (in Japanese).

Hayami, M. (1999) "On recent monetary policy," Speech given at the Japan National Press Club in Tokyo on June 22, 1999 (www.boj.or.jp/en/announcements/press/koen_1999/ko9907b.htm/).

Hayami, M. (2000) "Price stability and monetary policy," Speech given to the Research Institute of Japan in Tokyo on March 21, 2000 (www.boj.or.jp/en/announcements/press/koen_2000/ko0003b.htm/).

Hoshi, T. (2001) "'Bukka no antei' ni kansuru hokokusho wa machigai darakeda (The report 'On price stability' is full of mistakes)," *Ronso Toyo Keizai*, January, pp. 164–169 (in Japanese).

Ito, T., H. T. Patrick, and D. E. Weinstein (eds.) (2005) *Reviving Japan's Economy: Problems and Prescriptions*, Cambridge, Massachusetts: MIT Press.

Iwata, K. (1992) "'Nichigin riron' wo houki seyo (Abandon 'the Bank of Japan doctrine')," *Shukan Toyo Keizai*, September 12, pp. 124–128 (in Japanese).

Iwata, K. (1993) *Kin'yu Seisaku no Keizaigaku: "Nichigin Riron" no Kensho (The Economics of Monetary Policy: An Examination of "the Bank of Japan doctrine")*, Tokyo: Nihon Keizai Shinbunsha (in Japanese).

Iwata, K. (1994) "Naze Nichigin wa jisshitsu-teki 'hikishime' wo tsuzukeru noka (Why does the BOJ continue to make 'tightening' in real terms?)," *Ekonomisuto*, January 4, pp. 50–53 (in Japanese).

Iwata, K. (ed.) (2000) *Kin'yu Seisaku no Ronten (Discussion Points of Japan's Monetary Policy)*, Tokyo: Toyo Keizai Shinposha (in Japanese).

Iwata, K. (2002) "Yoso keisei ni hatarakikakeru kin'yu seisaku wo: Komiya ronbun hihan (1) (Monetary policy aiming for expectation formation is needed: A criticism to Komiya's article (1))," in R. Komiya and Japan Center for Economic Research (eds.) *Kin'yu Seisaku Rongi no Souten (Main Issues of Monetary Policy Debates)*, Tokyo: Nihon Keizai Shinbunsha, pp. 391–418 (in Japanese).

Jinushi, T., Y. Kuroki, and R. Miyao (2000) "Monetary policy in Japan since the late 1980s: Delayed policy actions and some explanations," in R. Mikitani and S. A. Posen (eds.) *Japan's Financial Crisis and its Parallels to U. S. Experience*, Washington, D. C.: Institute for International Economics, pp. 115–148.

Kaku, K. (1992) "Kyokyu-ryo, fusoku towa iezu (The supply is not supposed to be insufficient)," *Nihon Keizai Shinbun*, December 23, p. 21 (in Japanese).

Keynes, J. M. (1978) *The Collected Writing of John Maynard Keynes: Vol. 7, The General Theory of Interest, Interest and Money*, London: Macmillan.

Kimura, T. (2001) *Capital Freight: Yen ga Nihon wo sisuteru (Capital Fright: The Yen is Leaving Japan)*, Tokyo: Jitsugyo no Nihon Sha (in Japanese).

Komiya, R. (1976) "Showa 48–9 nen inflation no gen'in (The cause of the Showa 48–9 inflation)," *Keizaigaku Ronshu* (The University of Tokyo), 42–1, pp. 2–40 (in Japanese).

Komiya, R. (1999) "Hyakki yako no kawase kin'yu seisaku rongi wo tadasu (Straightening the weird debates on the foreign exchange and monetary policy)," *Shukan Toyo Keizai*, December 25, pp. 128–130 (in Japanese).

Komiya, R. (2002) "Nichigin hihan no ronten no kentou (Study of the points of criticism against the BOJ)," in R. Komiya and Japan Center for Economic Research (eds.) *Kin'yu Seisaku Rongi no Souten (Main Issues of Monetary Policy Debates)*, Tokyo: Nihon Keizai Shinbunsha, pp. 235–312 (in Japanese).

Komiya, R. and Japan Center for Economic Research (eds.) (2002) *Kin'yu Seisaku Rongi no Souten (Main Issues of Monetary Policy Debates)*, Tokyo: Nihon Keizai Shinbunsha (in Japanese).

Kosai, Y. (1992) "Tsuka no jyuyo to kyokyu (Demand and supply of money)," *Nihon Keizai Kenkyu Center Kaiho*, November 1, pp. 48–51 (in Japanese).

Krugman, P. (1998) "It's baaack: Japan's slump and the return of the liquidity trap," *Brookings Papers on Economic Activity* 2, pp. 137–187.

Mieno, Y. (1995) "Keiki teitai no choki-ka no haikei to seisaku taiou no arikata (Background of lengthening business stagnation and the way of policy responses)," Speech before the Kisaragi meeting on November 10, 1993, in Y. Mieno, *Nihon Keizai to Chuou Ginkou (The Japanese Economy and the Central Bank)*, Tokyo: Toyo Keizai Shinposha, pp. 129–148 (in Japanese).

Mikitani, R. and S. A. Posen (eds.) *Japan's Financial Crisis and its Parallels to U. S. Experience*, Washington, D. C., Institute for International Economics.

Miyao, T. (1992) "Fukyo akka no seisaku sekinin wo tou (Accusing the policy responsibility of making the depression worse)," *Shukan Toyo Keizai*, September 12, pp. 124–128 (in Japanese).

Miyao, T. (1993) "Shi ni itaru yamai 'Shinsei defure fukyo' no shindan to chiryohou (The diagnosis and the remedy for a decease to die 'the genuinely deflationary depression')," *Gekkan Asahi*, December, pp. 96–103 (in Japanese).

Miyao, T. (1996) "Keynes' 'ryudosei no wana' kara no dasshutu no michi (The way of escaping from Keynes' 'liquidity trap')," *Ekonomisuto*, December 24, pp. 71–74.

Nakahara, N. (1999) "Current economic conditions in Japan and challenges for monetary policy," Speech given at the Capital Market Research Institute in Tokyo on November 1, 1999 (www.boj.or.jp/en/announcements/press/koen_1999/ko9912b.htm/).

Noguchi, A. (2002) *Keizaigaku wo Shiranai Ekonomisuto Tachi (Economists Who Don't Know Economics)*, Tokyo: Nihon Hyoron Sha (in Japanese).

Okina, K. (1992) "'Nichigin Riron' wa machigatte inai ('The Bank of Japan doctrine' is not wrong)," *Shukan Toyo Keizai*, October 10, pp. 106–111 (in Japanese).

Okina, K. (1993a) "Dento-teki Monetarism shiso wa hokai (The traditional Monetarism thought has collapsed)," *Nihon Keizai Kenkyu Center Kaiho*, March 15, pp. 4–11 (in Japanese).

Okina, K. (1993b) *Kin'yu Seisaku: Chuou Ginkou no Shiten to Sentaku (Monetary Policy: Perspectives and Choices of the Central Bank)*, Tokyo: Toyo Keizai Shinposha (in Japanese).

Okina, K. and S. Shiratsuka (2000) "Hi-futaika kainyu no 'sakkaku' (The 'illusion' of unsterilized intervention)," *Shukan Toyo Keizai*, January 15, pp. 60–63 (in Japanese; English translation at www.imes.boj.or.jp/japanese/kouen/ki0001en.html).

Posen, S. A. (2000) "The political economy of deflationary monetary policy," in R. Mikitani and S. A. Posen (eds.) *Japan's Financial Crisis and its Parallels to U. S. Experience*, Washington, D. C.: Institute for International Economics, pp. 194–208.

Shimanaka, Y. (1991) "Money supply kyu-gensoku de 'tsuka fukyo' no kiki (The crisis of 'monetary depression' due to rapid contraction of money supply)," *Ekonomisuto*, June 14, pp. 30–33 (in Japanese).

Shimanaka, Y. (1992) "Sokoire wa 92 nen 7–9 gatsu daga, nibui kaifuku-ryoku (Bottoming out is July to September in 1992, but the recovery is slow)," *Toyo Keizai Rinji Zokan*, February 7, pp. 46–51 (in Japanese).

Shinpo, S. (1994) "Shisan defure kokufuku niwa kin'yu wo (Monetary policy is useful for overcoming the asset deflation)," *Nihon Keizai Kenkyu Center Kaiho*, April 1, pp. 11–17 (in Japanese).

Shiratsuka, S. (2000) "Inflation targeting wa jigi ni kanatta seisaku dewa nai (Inflation targeting isn't an appropriate policy proposal in this stage)," *Kin'yu Zaisei Jijyo*, November 13, pp. 26–30 (in Japanese).

Taylor, J. B. (2006) "Lessons from the recovery from the 'lost decade' in Japan: The case of the great intervention and money injection," ESRI international conference, Cabinet Office, Government of Japan, September 14 (www.stanford.edu/~johntayl/Onlinepaperscombinedbyyear/2006/Lessons_from_the_Recovery_from_the_Lost_Decade_in_ Japan-The_Case_of_the_Great_Intervention_and_Money_Injection.pdf).

Ueda, K. (1992) "Money supply doko no 'tadashii' mikata ('Correct' way of how to view the money supply trend)," *Shukan Toyo Keizai*, December 12, pp. 114–117 (in Japanese).

Ueda, K. (1999) "Remarks," at the Fed Conference on "Monetary Policy in a Low-Inflation Environment," in Woodstock, Vermont on October 20.

White, W. (2006) "Is price stability enough?" *BIS Working Papers* No. 205.

5 Is there any cultural difference in economics?

Keynesianism and monetarism in Japan[1]

Masazumi Wakatabe

1 Introduction: culture and economics

The current economic and financial crisis has provided us with an ample opportunity to reconsider our way of thinking about the economy and economics. One
prominent feature of the current crisis was more or less the same set of policy
responses: governments and central banks engaged in an expansionary fiscal and
monetary policy mix. However, there was also a certain variation in policy
responses: the US and the UK were more aggressive in their response, while the
Euro-area and Japan were less so. The Bank of Japan (BOJ) did not increase its
balance sheet as much as the Federal Reserve Board (FRB), Bank of England
(BOE), or European Central Bank (ECB) (Figure 5.1), so that the yen appreciated against the US dollar and the euro (Figure 5.2), which led to the severe
plunge in industrial production (Figure 5.3).[2]

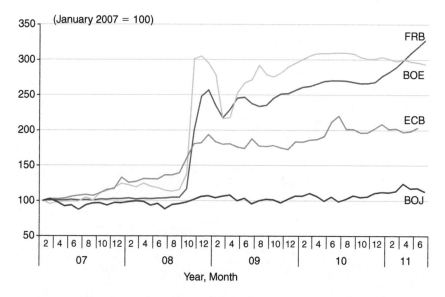

Figure 5.1 Changes in balance sheets of central banks (source: HP of central banks).

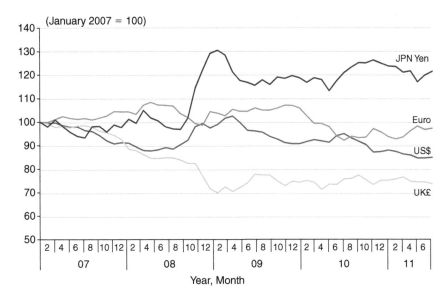

Figure 5.2 Changes in real effective exchange rate (source: BIS Statistics).

Needless to say, these policy responses are constrained as much, or even more, by political and institutional factors as by economic ideas: in the case of the Eurozone, monetary policy is conducted by the European Central Bank and constrained within the single currency euro. In the case of Japan, the government was and still is divided, with the opposition parties holding the majority of one of two diets, and there is no inflation-targeting framework despite the independence of the Bank of Japan. But there is also a concern among policy makers and even economists for inflationary policy even in the midst of deflation.

Here is a problem for the historians of economic thought who are interested in the extent to which economic ideas influence policy choice. One feature of Japanese academic economic discourse is the prevalence of hostility toward monetarism. True that there is still opposition to monetarism in the US, and the Keynesian–Monetarism debate is no longer in vogue, but the historical interpretation of the role of monetarism is starkly different between Japan and the US. For example, J. Bradford DeLong, economist with a new Keynesian bent, wrote an article entitled 'The Triumph of Monetarism?' in 2000 (DeLong 2000). Although he questioned the success and validity of what he termed 'Political Monetarism,' monetarists' specific proposal of k% rule, the overall assessment was rather sympathetic: monetarist 'insights survive, albeit under a different name than 'monetarism.' Perhaps the extent to which they are simply part of the air that modern macroeconomists today believe is a good index of their intellectual hegemony' (DeLong 2000, 92). On the other hand, Hiroshi Yoshikawa, a Yale-trained University of Tokyo Professor of Economics and a member of the

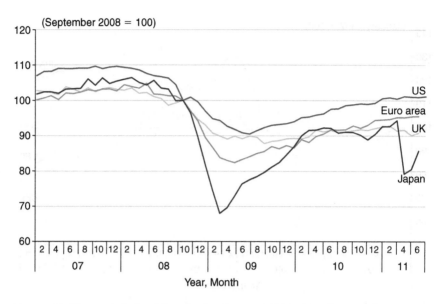

Figure 5.3 Changes in industrial production (source: METI, FRB, Eurostat, ONB).

Council on Economic and Fiscal Policy (2001–2005, 2008–2009) and numerous government committees, was quite negative toward monetarism. Although he regarded highly one of the contributions of DeLong which showed that more nominal variable flexibility would lead to more instability of the economy (DeLong and Summers 1986; Yoshikawa 2000, 48), he did not share DeLong's assessment of positive achievements of monetarism. Yoshikawa grouped Friedman and Lucas together, commenting that the relevance of their monetary shock model of the business cycle was lost during the 1980s because of the change in the major economic problems, from inflation of the 1970s to more real shocks of the 1980s. Curiously, Yoshikawa did not attribute the ending of the Great Inflation to any of the possible influences of monetarism, even though he accepted the conclusion of Komiya's (1976) paper that attributed the inflation to the failure of monetary policy (Yoshikawa 2000, 23–4).

In this chapter, I shall examine the extent to which 'culture' affects the reception of economic ideas, Keynesianism and monetarism in particular, across countries. The very concept of 'culture' is so elusive that self-proclaimed social scientists, economists who ascribe to the scientific method in particular, tend not to use it. However, with the resurgence of interest in the role of attitudes, beliefs, customs, identities, norms, trust, social capital, and religion in the economy, it is now becoming more legitimate to use it (Throsby 2001; Guiso *et al.* 2006; Klamer 2007; Fernández 2008). Culture is defined in two ways: 'a broadly anthropological or sociological framework to describe a set of attitudes, beliefs, mores, customs, values and practices which are common to or shared by any group. The group may be defined in terms of politics, geography, religion, ethnicity or some other characteristics,' or 'certain activities that are undertaken by people, and the products of those activities, which have to do with the intellectual, moral and artistic aspects of human life' (Throsby 2001, 3–4). I shall use the word culture in this paper mainly in the first sense, which is closely related to ideas: if attitudes and beliefs are culturally constrained, economic thought is to be culturally constrained. This is what Throsby suggests when he refers to the 'cultural context of economics.' Also the concept of culture does not mean something predetermined and unchangeable: on the contrary, culture evolves throughout time, but a different historical path of the same idea may be attributable to culture among other contingent factors.

I would argue that there are some cultural components to the reception of economic ideas. Particularly, I shall focus on economic ideas pertinent to economic policy, analyzing Keynesianism and monetarism in Japan in particular. Both ideas originated in areas other than Japan; therefore, comparison of ideas between the US, Europe, and Japan would reveal differences in their contents. It is, however, not a straightforward exercise to single out cultural components, since other factors are also at work in the reception. In the literature, there have been several attempts at comparative economic thought, or the systematic comparison of economic ideas across countries. One notable example is the reception of Keynesianism across countries headed by Peter A. Hall. Another example is the 'economists in government' project conceived and conducted by A. W. Coats (1981; Komiya and Yamamoto 1981). The third example is a larger institutionalization of economics project, again initiated by A. W. Coats, which has been published in many forms (e.g., Sugiyama and Mizuta 1988). With respect to the influence on policy ideas, the reception of Keynesianism is closely related to this chapter. Among them, Peter A. Hall offered an insightful survey, pointing out three factors affecting the reception of Keynesian ideas (Hall 1989), economic, administrative, and political viability. According to him, the adoption of a new economic theory as a policy would be affected by such factors as 'relationship to existing theories,' 'nature of the national economy,' 'collective associations with similar policies and their exponents,' and 'administrative biases.' His scheme is rather broad, but one could point out that the 'relationship,' 'nature,' 'associations,' and 'biases' could be analyzed in terms of 'culture.' In this sense, this chapter is an attempt at bringing 'culture' into the history of economic thought.

The adoption and reception of Keynesianism in Japan has been well-documented (Hamada 1986; Hadley 1989; Ikeo 2006, Chapter 6). There is even a book on the Keynes literature (Hayashida 1986; cf. Ikeo 2006, 181), counting 970 Japanese authors and listing 55 pages of bibliography up until the mid-1980s. On the other hand, the reception of monetarism in Japan—or lack thereof—has not yet been discussed: Tessa Morris-Suzuki (1989) has a section called 'Monetarism in Japan: Suzuki Yoshio and Shimpo Seiji' in Chapter 6, which is entitled 'Contemporary Japanese Economic Thought,' devoting two pages to explaining the contributions of two economists (165–6). There are several problems with her account, however. By concentrating on two economists, one working for the Bank of Japan (Suzuki Yoshio), and the other working for the Economic Planning Agency (Shimpo Seiji), she did not discuss the academic status of monetarism in relation to other academicians. Also she did not take into account the fact that Suzuki did not call himself a 'monetarist.' Other books on the history of Japanese economic thought do not deal with the reception of monetarism (Hayasaka and Masamura 1974; Sugihara and Tanaka 1998; Ikeo 2000).

The rest of this chapter is organized as follows. Section 2 examines the characteristics of Keynesianism in Japan. It will be argued that Keynesian economics in Japan was strongly influenced by Marxism and developmentalism, and remarkably diverse. Section 3 turns to the status of monetarism in Japan. Despite several attempts, monetarism remained not only a minority status but also a vilified one. Section 4 concludes the paper.

2   Keynesianism, Japanese style

The Japanese economists encountered the works of Keynes as a contemporary economist fairly quickly, but the outbreak of World War II slowed, if not stopped, the intellectual communications between Japan and the western world (Dimand and Wakatabe 2011). A brief description of post-World War II economic thought in Japan is due.

2.1 Marxism and developmentalism

Until the 1980s, the majority of academic economists were neither Keynesians nor neoclassicals: they were Marxians. Keynesian and/or neoclassical economics were called Kindai Keizaigaku (modern economics), and treated as a different type of economics.[3] Marxian economists dominated economics departments of Japanese universities for a long time, including the University of Tokyo, arguably the most prestigious and well-funded national university in Japan.[4] The situation gradually changed throughout the 1970s and 1980s, but the influence had been felt within media discourse throughout the period. Second, there was a strong tendency among the Japanese economists to view the positive role of the state to promote economic development: what was first coined as Japan as a 'developmental state,' and later called developmentalism, was found among some proponents of modern economics (Gao 1997; Noguchi 2000). Many academics took for granted the success of Japanese economic development as a state-driven one, the so-called industrial policy of the Ministry of International Trade and Industry (MITI) being a prime successful example of its characteristics. Martin Bronfenbrenner described it as 'schizophrenia,' since modern economists taught the merits of free trade in the classroom, while the same supported protectionist measures in a government committee. Third, we must note the diversity of Keynesianism in Japan in the post-World War II period. Here the strong presence of Marxian economics and the prevalence of developmentalism in the Japanese academic and media discourse played an important role. Keynes was accepted as someone who endorsed the role of government in the economy.

2.2 Shigeto Tsuru and his students

Bronfenbrenner noted and appreciated a change in attitude among the Japanese economists during the 1950s, finding a 'common ground' between Marxian and other economics (Bronfenbrenner 1956, 394–5): in this, a 'common ground movement,' the role of Eiichi Sugimoto (1901–1952) and Shigeto Tsuru (1912–2006) cannot be underestimated, since both attempted to integrate or at least bridge two economics. Eiichi Sugimoto, Professor of Economics at Hitotsubashi University, in his historical survey of economics, compared two economics in the hope of founding a unified economics (Sugimoto 1950). Sugimoto died early in 1952, but Tsuru remained active and successful for a long period in academia and media discourse. Tsuru was a very unique economist in Japan: he did not graduate from a Japanese university, because he was arrested by the 'thought police' when he was a high school student. With the help of his rich family, he went to the US, receiving his BA, *magna cum laude*, and PhD from Harvard University before the war broke out. There he befriended Joseph A. Schumpeter, John Kenneth Galbraith, Paul Samuelson, and Paul Sweezy. After he was deported to Japan at the outbreak of the war, he assumed the role of political and economic advisor to politicians, culminating in his post as Undersecretary of the Economic Stabilization Agency under the occupied Japan. After 1948, he became the Professor of Economics at the Institute of Economic Research at Tokyo College of Commerce (later Hitotsubashi University).[5] Tsuru's sympathy toward Marxian, Institutionalist, and even Schumpeterian economics showed up in his emphasis on the 'structural approach' to economic problems: the Japanese economists, Marxians or otherwise, saw one of the major problems of the Japanese economy as the 'dual structure of the economy,' inter-and-intra industrial disparities regarding wages and salaries. Marxian economists in turn tended to grasp the contemporary economy in terms of monopoly capitalism. This focus on the structure of the economy became blended with modern economics' analytical developments of imperfect and monopolistic competition developed by Joan Robinson and Edward Chamberlin during the 1930s.

Therefore it is no coincidence that the students of Shigeto Tsuru, including Yoshikazu Miyazaki (1919–1998), Mitsuharu Ito (1929–), and Yoshihiro Takasuka (1932–1991), focused on the monopolistic nature of the Japanese economy throughout their careers. Miyazaki received special attention from Morris-Suzuki (1989, 155–8). He wrote extensively about the significance of dominant Kigyo Shudan (corporate groups) in the Japanese economy.[6] Ito was originally a student of Sugimoto, becoming Tsuru's after Sugimoto's untimely death. Together they wrote a book of commentaries on Keynes' *General Theory* (Miyazaki and Ito 1964). The book, which came from their joint lectures and seminars, was a huge success, going through three editions and numerous reprints. It was characterized by three things: first, they sympathized more with the British, or

Cambridge, interpretation of Keynesianism, with an emphasis on not only multiplier and effective demand theory, but also with liquidity preference theory of money[7]; second, they referred to and compared with Marx quite often; third, this commentary on Keynes was infused with their analysis of contemporary capitalism. Ito had already published a short book entitled *Keynes* in 1962, which became an instant bestseller and a long seller; it still sells well (Ito 1962).

The third student of Tsuru's, Takasuka, became a Marxian of analytical and mathematical bent, but his first major work was on post-war inflation (Takasuka 1973). He offered a structural explanation of inflation, the so-called Seisansei Koujyo Kakusa Infure Riron (differential productivity improvement theory of inflation). This was his version of cost-push inflation, which was caused by structural problems. The key assumption was the 'dual structure' of the Japanese economy. There were two types of firms: monopolistic large corporations and competitive small firms. The corporations, so went the argument, succeeded in increasing productivity, earning a great deal of profits even though their prices were stable, while profits fed into an upward pressure on wages, which small competitive firms had no choice but to transfer to their prices.

It should be noted that British or Cambridge-type Keynesianism has an affinity with Marxian economics, and with the structuralist approach to economic problems. Although Cambridge economists were not entirely sympathetic to it, Joan Robinson thought that there were some positive things to learn from Marx (Robinson 1942). However, Japan not only had both types of Keynesianism, British and neoclassical synthetic, at the same time, but also British-like Keynesianism was homegrown: this version of Keynesianism was not a direct descendant of Cambridge Keynesians, such as Joan Robinson and Nicholas Kaldor, although the proponents, including Tsuru, Miyazaki, and Ito, displayed much sympathy toward them.[8]

There was a different type of Keynesianism in Japan. American Keynesianism was built around economists at the University of Tokyo. Here the effect of study networking had some influence. Studying abroad had been an important step for Japanese economists to gain respectable status. The destination has changed throughout history: in the prewar period, they went to European countries, while in the post-war period, the majority went to the US with the help of the Fulbright Scholarship. Japanese modern economists tended to go to East Coast Ivy League universities or the West Coast universities such as Stanford. Perhaps following Ryuichiro Tachi's (1921–2012) precedent, more and more University of Tokyo economists chose Yale University as their favorite destination. The prime example was Koichi Hamada (1936–), who received his PhD from Yale in 1965 under the supervision of James Tobin, and later became Professor of Economics at Yale University in 1986.[9]

2.3 Neoclassical synthesis in Japan

American-type, neoclassical synthetic Keynesians also took an interest in industrial structure, although their interests reflected the developments in US academia, such as industrial organization, a field developed by Joe S. Bain. The most vocal promoter of Keynesian or neoclassical synthesis economics in Japan was Ryutaro Komiya (1928–), who graduated from the University of Tokyo and worked there from 1955 to 1989. Komiya was unique in many respects. Komiya challenged implicit assumptions of the Japanese economic community. First, he challenged the pure theory-oriented nature of Japanese academia: when he studied at Harvard, he worked as an assistant for W. W. Leontief, learning the importance of empirical analysis; also he was deeply impressed by American economists' ability and willingness to apply mainstream economic tools to engage in real-world issues over lunch or during a seminar, so that he was deter-mined to apply mainstream economic tools, neoclassical synthesis, to real issues of the Japanese economy. He became a regular contributor to the column 'Yasashii Keizaigaku (Economics Made Easy),' which appeared in *Nihon Keizai Shimbun* (*Japan Economic Journal*), the Japanese equivalent of the *Wall Street Journal*, espousing basic concepts of modern economics. Furthermore, he made a presentation at the annual meeting of the Economic Theory and Econometrics Association of Japan (later the Japanese Economic Association) to the effect that there were too many Japanese economists whose research areas were either the methodology, the history of economic thought, pure theory, or mathematical theory. Without denying their significance, he advocated that more resources should be directed toward empirically oriented research based on the logic of economics (Komiya 1960).[10] Second, he challenged Japanese modern econo-mists' implicit cooperation with, and endorsement of, government policy. He was instrumental in promoting counter-measures against the government deci-sion to overrule the Fair Trade Commission's objection to the merger of two of the large steel companies. The two steel companies eventually became Nippon Steel in 1968. Komiya drafted a report against the anti-competitive merger: the report was co-signed by 90 economists. He also questioned a view which attrib-uted the success of Japanese economic growth to the positive role of industrial policy and planning. In July 1971, one month before Japan was forced to abandon the peg to the US dollar, Komiya, together with more than 35 econo-mists, proposed a gradual and piecemeal appreciation of the yen, 'crawling peg.' After a few skirmishes with bureaucrats, he determined not to be a member of the government committee. Third, he challenged the dominant Marxian eco-nomic thought in 1970: as he later recollected, there was a 'cold peace' or mutual non-interference pact between Marxian and modern economists within the Department of Economics at the University of Tokyo, which was quite natural at that time. His 40-page long article on contemporary capitalism became a frontal attack on the ambiguous and stagnant status of Marxian economics (Komiya 1970).

Naturally Komiya came to have disagreements with Tsuru on many points, although they remained good friends.[11] Tsuru and Komiya both appeared in the January 1, 1971 issue of *Nihon Keizai Shimbun*. In the 1970s, the issue of environmental pollution was becoming keenly felt among the general public, considered to be the direct consequence of the rapid economic growth of the preceding decade. There was a surge of anti-growth sentiment, which Tsuru strongly supported. In May 1970, the *Asahi Shimbun*, the second largest and most influential newspaper, launched an anti-growth campaign, which was called 'Kutabare GNP (Damn with the GNP),' to which Tsuru contributed one short article, 'In Place of Gross National Product' (Tsuru 1971). He thought that

> The concept like national income or GNP which essentially is specific to a particular economic system is bound to be affected by the evolution and changes of that system itself. On the other hand, social life of man can be described not only in terms of a set of concepts specific to a particular economic system that society has, but also with reference to what might be called 'the physical aspect' which transcends differences in economic systems.
>
> (Tsuru 1971, xxx)[12]

In his discussion with Komiya, Tsuru criticized 'wasteful goods' such as a laughing box distinct from 'basic needs' in a Galbraithian term, questioning further the appropriateness of economic growth. Komiya countered Tsuru arguing that all needs were socially determined and economic growth may not lead to human happiness, but no growth was even worse than growth. Komiya speculated later that Tsuru never adopted Keynesian macroeconomics and remained an old pre-Keynesian, since he never analyzed Japanese or international economic problems using macroeconomics (Komiya 2010, 291). But it is important to note that a part of Japanese Keynesianism was influenced by someone who was critical about Keynes.

As for inflation, Komiya and his associates were extremely critical toward Takasuka's approach. They could have agreed with the cost-push approach since the classification of inflation into the cost-push and the demand-pull was a staple during the 1960s and 1970s (Bronfenbrenner and Holzman 1963). Also Komiya and Hiroshi Niida (1931–) relied on a cost-push analysis during the 1960s, following a similar analysis by American economists (Kataoka and Wakatabe 2011). However, they were not satisfied with two features of Takasuka's theory: Takasuka's refusal to be grouped into a cost-push camp, and the validity of differential productivity improvement as the source of cost-push inflation (Niida 1963).

3 The minor monetarism

3.1 Friedman came to Japan

Friedman's work had already been known to Japanese academicians after he visited Japan for a substantial length of time in 1963.[13] His *Theory of Consumption Function* (1957) was translated into Japanese in 1961,[14] but the invitation did not come from academia: it came from an economic newspaper, *Nihon Kaizai Shimbun* (*Japan Economic Journal*), with the initiative of Jiro Enjoji, then its Executive Director, later the President. Friedman had a chance to give public lectures on free economy, and have a discussion with Saburo Okita: Chiaki Nishiyama chaired the occasion. Okita was a career economic bureaucrat. He graduated from the Faculty of Engineering at the Tokyo Imperial University, and served the Economic Planning Agency as a high-ranking official. He later became one of the foremost economic statesmen. Although he was not a Keynesian in any formal sense, the meeting revealed many differences between Okita, probably the best representative of contemporary Japanese economists, and Friedman. The discussion started with a definition of inflation, and seemingly both agreed on it, but Okita frequently referred to 'structural factors' behind inflation, to which Friedman countered vigorously. Lastly, they turned to the issue of 'planning.' When the meeting took place, Okita was a Director of Planning in General of the Economic Planning Agency, and had just received a Doctorate for his work on economic planning (Okita 1962). Okita explained the Japanese version of 'planning' as an indicative 'guidance'; Friedman welcomed this softer approach, but questioned the necessity of having 'planning' and government involvement, however they may be called.

3.2 A career BOJ economist and a lone academician

Friedman had a chance to talk to two economists from the Bank of Japan; one of them was Yoshio Suzuki. Upon the first encounter, Suzuki was impressed with Friedman, starting to take his analysis seriously. Yoshio Suzuki graduated from the University of Tokyo and worked for the Bank of Japan for a long time. Although he came to be considered the foremost proponent of monetarism in Japan, he did not consider himself a monetarist. He maintained a friendly relationship with the mainstream, mostly Keynesian academic economists, such as Komiya and Hamada. When Koichi Hamada came back to Japan, virtually smuggling James Tobin's then unpublished lecture notes on money and banking, which were later published (Tobin 1998), Suzuki was one of the first to digest their general equilibrium approach to assets markets, and to apply them to the Japanese economy (Suzuki 1994, 8–9). It is important to note that Suzuki studied works of Tobin and Friedman in tandem.

In Japanese academia, however, monetarists' status remained marginal. It was even claimed that 'there was no economists, academic or otherwise, who self-proclaim a monetarist in Japan, except Chiaki Nishiyama' (Saito 1981, 84). This was an exaggeration, since there were several more academic economists who were sympathetic to monetarist ideas. But it was not too far from the truth. Chiaki Nishiyama (1924–) attempted to first act as a catalyst between Friedman and the Japanese academia. He served as a moderator and/or translator whenever Friedman came to Japan. Nishiyama received his PhD from the Committee for Social Thought, University of Chicago, under the supervision of Friedrich von Hayek in 1960, came back to Japan, and became a Professor of Economics at Rikkyo University, a private university in Tokyo. His original research field was in the history of economic thought, but he was also quite active in propagating free-market and monetarist ideas, serving the President of the Mont Pelerin Society from 1980 to 1982.[15] His work on *Nihon Keizai no Kaheiteki Bunseki* (*Monetary Analysis of the Japanese Economy*) with colleagues such as Kokichi Asakura was meant to be the Japanese counterpart of Friedman and Schwartz (1963), as the title testified (Asakura and Nishiyama 1974). Also he wrote a short introductory book on economic liberalism for the general reader (Nishiyama 1974). His book *Monetarism* was a concise introduction to the topic, with 13 chapters describing the main tenets of monetarism and classical liberarism (Nishiyama 1976). Friedman's (1962) classic *Capitalism and Freedom* had already been translated into Japanese in 1975, along with Poole (1978) in 1981, Vane and Thompson (1979) in 1982, and Laidler (1982) in 1987, but Nishiyama (1976) was one of the first to introduce monetarist ideas in its entirety. Coinciding with Friedman's Nobel Prize, the book did sell well. Despite his efforts, however, Nishiyama remained almost a lone voice in Japanese economics academia. Asakura and Nishiyama (1974) did receive a prestigious Nikkei Economic Books Prize, awarded to four or five best economics and management books each year, sponsored by *Nihon Keizai Shimbun*, but still he remained a lone voice.[16]

3.3 Monetarism vindicated and/or vilified

As I have already documented elsewhere (Kataoka and Wakatabe 2011), the Great Inflation in Japan was suppressed rather quickly, more quickly than the American and British counterparts. It was not because the Bank of Japan learned from Friedman and monetarism, but at least the Bank of Japan used monetarist rhetoric in the late 1970s, preventing another round of inflation which the US and the UK experienced in 1979. Suzuki wrote a series of papers in line with monetarist ideas, while Komiya wrote a very influential paper in 1976, and another in 1977 together with Suzuki (Komiya and Suzuki 1977). The evaluation was in line with monetarist logic in that the Great Inflation was caused by an overly expansionary monetary policy of the Bank of Japan. The Economic Planning Agency, once Okita's homeground, employed monetarist economist Seiji Shimpo (1945–2004), whose *Gendai Nihon Keizai no Kaimei*, which analyzed the Great Inflation and Stagflation using a monetarist line, won the Nikkei Economic Book Prize in 1979 (Shimpo 1979).[17] Along with Friedman's Nobel Memorial Prize in Economics in 1976, the reputation of monetarism seemed to be cemented.

However, monetarism did not lack critics. Hirofumi Uzawa (1928–), once a colleague of Friedman at the University of Chicago, best known for his contributions to the theory of economic growth, came back to the University of Tokyo in 1968, having launched a series of attacks on Friedman and monetarism. With a great deal of sympathy toward the radical economics movement in the early 1970s, he did not hide his theoretical and ideological dislike of Friedman. On January 4, 1971, in *Nihon Keizai Shimbun*, three days after the aforementioned Tsuru and Komiya debate appeared, Uzawa wrote a piece entitled 'Modern

Economics in Disarray,' attacking mainstream economics. This was published before Joan Robinson's Richard T. Ely lecture at the annual meeting of the American Economic Association in December 1971. Indeed the similarities were striking. Both knew each other well, and Uzawa had been a promoter of Robinson's works: he translated Robinson (1971) in 1971 and Robinson and Eatwell (1973) in 1976. But the contemporary historians of economic thought detected in Uzawa's critique similarities with Marxian criticisms of mainstream economics (Hayasaka and Masamura 1974, 164).[18] In 1984, Uzawa wrote his own version of commentary on Keynes's *General Theory*, in commemoration of Keynes's one-hundredth birth (Uzawa 1984). The book was a line-by-line account, and as such not particularly informative or remarkable for a theorist of his stature, but it did not miss a chance to snipe at monetarism. From the viewpoint of a proponent of disequilibrium dynamics during the late 1970s and early 1980s, he attacked monetarism. But his criticisms had several peculiarities. First, he grouped Friedman, Becker, and Lucas together, calling monetarism the extreme extension of 'rational economics,' economics based on pure maximizing behavior of self-interested agents (Uzawa 1986/1994, Chapter 7). It is problematic, since as Laidler (1981) and Taniuchi (1982) had already argued, monetarism was not the same as the equilibrium macroeconomics of Lucas.[19] Ironically, a self-claimed disequilibrium theorist, Uzawa failed to see the difference. Second, he attacked monetarism on another theoretical ground in that the quantity theory of money on which monetarism based was flawed. His criticism was purely theoretical, and it is striking that he did not refer to any empirical validity which monetarism might have. Third, his own theory of inflation was structural. He considered inflation as a problem specific to the contemporary economy: in a well-advanced capitalist economy, the market mechanism is inherently, dynamically extremely unstable, and it is impossible to achieve full employment and a stable inflation rate. In particular, the constant money growth rate policy would lead to involuntary unemployment or hyperinflation if full employment was to be maintained (Uzawa 1987/1994, 28).[20]

Once again, Ryutaro Komiya stood up, this time against his colleague.[21] He had numerous discussions with Uzawa, but when Uzawa's translation appeared, he wrote a book-length criticism of Robinson and Eatwell (1973). He did not defend monetarist arguments, but rightly pointed out that they were becoming integrated into mainstream economics (Komiya 1979). On the other hand, Robinson and Eatwell were too skeptical about the potency of monetary policy, neglecting monetary forces in inflation and ignoring recent developments after the 1973–1974 inflation, focusing on the money growth rate. After much discussion, his conclusion was straightforward: 'The book is not worth reading at all; reading this book would be a waste of time not only for the beginners' (Komiya 1979, 243). Furthermore, when he referred to the 'publication of such an empty, crude, sloppy, and totally confused book,' its translation, and its favorable reviews as a symbol of 'confusion of economics, or economists, especially in Japan,' he must have had one particular Japanese economist in mind.[22]

The comparison with the US situation reveals several Japanese features. First, there was no monetarist of Milton Friedman's stature in Japan. Friedman was recognized and highly respected as a part of the economics community in the US: he received the John Bates Clark medal in 1951, worked at the University of Chicago from 1946 to 1976, served as a President of the American Economic Association in 1968, and received the Nobel Memorial Prize in Economics in 1976. The closest economist to Friedman we had was probably Komiya, but he did not consider himself a monetarist. Second, monetarist ideas gained support in a wider circle: students of Friedman, the Federal Bank of St. Louis, influential politicians such as presidential candidate Barry Goldwater, and business people. Although the Bank of Japan somewhat changed its stance, they tried to conceal this change. They began announcing a quasi-monetary growth rate target from 1978, but did not call it a target. There would be increased support for Friedman later among Japanese politicians and business people, especially after his book with his wife, *Free to Choose*, was translated into Japanese in 1980, published by *Nihon Keizai Shimbun*. The book became an instant success, but it was his free market belief which appealed to the Japanese most, not his macroeconomics.

4 Concluding comments

Roger Backhouse summarized the reception of monetarism as follows:

> It is probably correct to say that in the 1950s and for much of the 1960s, the dominant views in the economics profession were those of Samuelson, Arrow and Tobin. Friedman and Stigler were taken seriously, but Chicago was widely taken to represent an extreme view. Friedman's support of the quantity theory of money went against the dominant Keynesian consensus, and the Chicago faith in markets was considered mistaken. In the 1970s, the situation changed dramatically. The economic crisis of 1973, when oil prices quadrupled, involved rising unemployment and rising inflation that caused problems for conventional Keynesian models and convinced many economists that Friedman was right that there was no permanent trade-off between inflation and unemployment.
>
> (Backhouse 2010, 147–8)

This 'dramatic change' did not happen in Japan. Kindai Keizaigaku (modern economics) in Japan was formed as an amalgam of Keynesian macroeconomics and neoclassical microeconomics. But Keynesianism was also diverse, one being more influenced by Marxism. One might expect monetarism to be accepted, and certainly it was, but it did not penetrate into the mainstream Japanese academia. Why did monetarism not penetrate into Japanese economic academia? In a sense, it did remarkably well in terms of economic analysis and policy of a particular economic episode: Komiya's (1976) paper focused on the relationship between changes in the money stock and changes in the price level in his analysis of the Great Inflation in Japan in a, what one would argue, monetarist fashion; also in terms of monetary policy, the Bank of Japan implemented a contractionary monetary policy in a quasi-monetarist fashion. Although Komiya's paper was accepted as the definitive explanation of the Great Inflation in Japan, it did not lead to the acceptance of monetarism. One may point to several reasons why monetarism did not get accepted in Japan as in the United States. First, Komiya did not call himself a 'monetarist': his 1976 paper did not refer to any work by Friedman or monetarists, and did not use terms such as 'monetarism' or 'monetarists.' In one interview conducted in 1981, Komiya declared that he was not interested in labeling any economist, including himself, either as a Keynesian or monetarist. All that mattered for him was the content of economic analysis: economics is like a 'tool box' which includes not only Keynesian, but also monetarist tools, and it is up to the economists to choose which tool to use and when (Saito 1981, 126). Nor did Yoshio Suzuki identify himself as a monetarist, although he was considered one of the foremost monetarist economists.

Second, this 'intellectual smoothing' was the product of a particular interpretation of monetarism. Komiya and Suzuki did not have to be monetarists, since they had a general IS-LM framework as a proper macroeconomic model to which monetarist contributions could be incorporated. We may argue with the validity of this interpretation,[23] but this is what they understood monetarism to be. This interpretation was also suitable for Komiya and Suzuki, who had worked within neoclassical synthesis. More specifically, Komiya at least did not support rule-based monetary policy: despite the Bank of Japan's failure, he did not demand any institutional reform.

Third, Komiya distanced himself from the ideology of Friedman so that he had no reason to be aligned with him:

> We would like to comment on our policy stance. On various occasions we expressed our policy views, we have been criticized as a 'manifestation of nostalgia toward 19th century-type laissez-faire,' or 'neo-liberal tendency to go backward against the welfare state.' But such criticisms have missed our core policy stance completely. We regard highly the price mechanism as a means to allocate resources; probably there is no alternative to it as the basic principle of efficient and fair economic management.... At the same time, however, we think that it is indispensable to have a government which conducts discretionary fiscal and monetary policy to achieve full-employment, economic growth, and price stability, strengthens the public sector and redistributes income through the social security system and progressive taxation system, and exercise anti-monopoly policy to enable the smooth functioning of the price mechanism.... It is entirely clear that our policy stance is different from either classical liberalism or the Chicago School of Henry Simons and Milton Friedman.
>
> (Tachi and Komiya 1964, 5–6)

Komiya chose to remain in the worldview of neoclassical synthesis.

Turning back to the original question: why was there no widespread support for expansionary macroeconomic policy among the Japanese economists? Needless to say, the responses are diverse, yet I would suggest the following. A self-proclaimed Keynesian, Yoshikawa envisions a new macroeconomic theory which emphasizes 'real' factors such as real effective demand, trying to integrate insights of Keynes and Schumpeter. He believes that a 'structural reform' would foster technological change, in turn leading to an increased real effective demand, what the Japanese economy needs now. On the other hand, he is very critical toward the role of monetary policy during the recession, the criticism being directed toward Krugman's 1998 famous proposal for escaping from the liquidity trap by setting 4 percent inflation targeting. Without any concrete macroeconomic policy proposals on his part and his emphasis on 'real' factors, there is an implicit hesitancy or reluctance to support expansionary macroeconomic policy.[24]

Notes

1 This paper is based on the research project on 'Economic Crisis and Economics: The Case of Great Inflation of the 1970s Japan.' I would like to thank my collaborator, Goushi Kataoka of Mitsubishi UFJ Research and Consulting. The paper was read at the annual meeting of the History of Economics Society, Notre Dame University, Illinois, USA, and the first annual meeting of the Keynes Society Japan, Sophia University, Tokyo. I would also like to thank the Tokyo Center for Economic Research and the Japan Society for the Promotion of Science (Grant No. 22530199) for indispensable financial assistance.

2 For more quantitative evaluation of quantitative easing, see Bullard (2011) and Joyce, Mathew, and Wood (2011). They both found positive effects of QE on inflation expectation, stock price, exchange rate, and GDP.

3 The term had already been used in the prewar period and it was reputedly influenced by Oskar Lange (Lange 1935), who was in turn inspired by Kei Shibata (Shibata 1933). See also Bronfenbrenner (1956) and Dimand and Wakatabe (2011).

4 The division between two economics was so visible that the history of the Department of Economics at the University of Tokyo, in its commemoration of the fiftieth year of its founding, had two separate roundtable retrospective discussions, one for the Marxian economics oriented majority, and the other for the minority modern economics (Tokyo Daigaku Keizaigakubu 1976).

5 For the life and works of Tsuru, see Odaka and Nishizawa (2010). Tsuru organized a joint lecture with Bronfenbrenner in 1949 at the then Tokyo College of Commerce.

6 This view has recently been criticized. See Miwa and Ramseyer (2006).

7 They were aware that Franco Modigliani, Roy F. Harrod, Don Patinkin, and Harry Johnson pointed out the significance of liquidity preference theory. The one economist whom they regarded highly was a Canadian economist, Mabel Frances Timlin (Timlin 1942). For Timlin, see Dimand (2008). They traced the lineage of this interpretation to a Japanese economist and one of the earliest commentators of Keynes, Nisaburo Kito (Miyazaki and Ito 1964, 12).

8 Hitotsubashi University, with the probable initiative of Tsuru, invited Joan Robinson to Japan in 1955.

9 Tachi, an expert on monetary economics, was one of a few modern economists at the University of Tokyo during the early 1950s, who later headed the department and became a member of numerous government committees.

10 According to Komiya himself, this plea made quite a splash among his fellow economists (Komiya 2008, 14 December). Also see Hayasaka and Masamura (1974, 74).
Komiya's plea resonated with Tsuru's similar one a decade ago: when launching
Keizai Kenkyu, journal of the Institute of Economic Research, Tsuru as its Director
lamented that economics in Japan had devoted too much to the introduction, interpretation, and commentary of economics in foreign countries (Tsuru 1950).

11 It was Tsuru who took care of the family of Komiya's at Harvard, and recommended
Komiya to Leontief; Tsuru was a Visiting Professor at Harvard then.

12 The book is unusual for the Japanese general reader, since it has three papers in
English appended at the end of the book. This might be Tsuru's idea since the other
two papers were written by John Kenneth Galbraith and Jan Tinbergen, both of whom
Tsuru knew well. Tsuru was an advisor to the editorial board of the newspaper from
1975.

13 This was not his first visit: he came to Japan briefly in 1955 on his way to India
(Friedman and Friedman 1998, 257–9), and he was invited to dinner by Tsuru. He
recalled that 'I had no difficulty having a number of long and informative exchanges
with him. His American training meant that he had no hesitancy in disagreeing with
me. He had a distinguished career, at one point being mayor of Tokyo' (Friedman and
Friedman 1998, 324). Only the last sentence is wrong: Tsuru had repeatedly been
asked to run for the Governor of Tokyo Metropolitan Area by left-wing parties, but
declined stubbornly. According to Ito, Friedman, who wanted to have a discussion
with a Japanese Marxian economist, had difficulty finding a counterpart, but with the
help of Tsuru, eventually had one with Kazushi Nagasu, then Professor of Economics
at Yokohama National University; he was grateful for Tsuru's effort (Ito 2006).

14 Friedman's major works, such as Friedman (1960, 1962), were translated into Japanese, but not Friedman and Schwartz (1963), although Chapter 7 'The Great Contraction' was translated into Japanese in 2008.

15 The history of the Japanese side of the Mont Pelerin Society has not yet been written.

16 As far as the record shows, no Japanese academic association invited Friedman to
Japan. Tellingly, it was *Nihon Keizai Shimbun*, a commercial business paper, that
invited Friedman for the first time and for other numerous occasions.

17 Morris-Suzuki commented that the 'leading Japanese monetarists have in general
been concerned less with the pursuit of major theoretical innovations than with the
verification, adaptation, and modification of US monetarist theory in light of Japanese
experience' (Morris-Suzuki 1989, 165). This is misleading. First, they were government and central bank economists who should be primarily interested in applications
of theory to real economic issues. Second, monetarism also has such characteristics of
emphasizing empirics rather than theory.

18 Uzawa claimed that his two sector model of economic growth (Uzawa 1964) was the
mathematical reexamination of Karl Marx's capital accumulation espoused in Volume
II of *Das Kapital* (Uzawa 1988/1994, 147).

19 Mitsuru Taniuchi (1949–), another Economic Planning Agency economist, received
his PhD from Brown University, under the supervision of Herschell I. Grossman.
William Poole was also there. Taniuchi, whose book received the Nikkei Economic
Book Prize, referred to Laidler (1981).

20 Uzawa's criticisms of Friedman became more explicit and personal. He told of the
episode in which 'one prominent libertarian Professor' was refused by Chicago banks to
sell pounds short in 1967, the same episode reported in Friedman and Friedman (1998,
351). Uzawa did not reveal the identity of the Professor in question in 1977 (Uzawa
1977/1994, 13), although he criticized the self-interested behavior of the Professor. He
revealed the identity in 2000 (Uzawa 2000, 179–87) with a shifting emphasis. Uzawa
said that Frank Knight became so dissatisfied with Friedman that he wanted to dissociate
from him. Its authenticity aside, Uzawa used his experience as Professor of Economics
at the University of Chicago to give credibility to his anecdotes.

21 During the 1970s, at one conference in which both Uzawa and Komiya attended, Uzawa talked about something like 'The Second Crisis in Economics.' Komiya retorted: 'There is no such thing as the crisis of economics. There is, however, one economist in crisis in front of us' (Noguchi 2003).

22 He also thought that modern dynamic economic growth theory, to which Uzawa contributed most, was mere 'child's play' that offered no insights to real-world economic issues (Komiya 1979, 120–1).

23 Bordo and Schwartz (2004) trace the evolution of Friedman's intricate attitudes toward the IS-LM model.

24 Should we strive for a deeper cultural explanation? Interestingly, Komiya took a cultural approach to the question of whether economics was rooted in Japanese academic economists: he was pessimistic since he believed that economics was for the Anglo-Saxons and the Jewish (Saito 1981, 125). We may point out the eclectic nature of Japanese economics: at one point in time, we have diverse strands of thought existing at the same time. We may also point out the 'receptive' nature of Japanese scholarship: translation, commentary, and interpretation of foreign scholarship have been the focal point of learning in Japan. Furthermore, we may point out the hierarchical structure of Japanese academia: the University of Tokyo is at the top of the hierarchy, so there is not as much competition as the US has, say, between Harvard, Yale, and Chicago.

References

Asakura, K. and C. Nishiyama eds. (1974) *Nihon Keizai no Kaheiteki Bunseki, 1868–1970 (The Monetary Analysis of the Japanese Economy, 1868–1970)*, Tokyo: Sobunsya (in Japanese).

Backhouse, R. E. (2010) *The Puzzle of Modern Economics: Ideology or Science?*, Cambridge: Cambridge University Press.

Bordo, M. and A. Schwartz (2004) 'IS-LM and Monetarism,' in M. De Vroey and K. Hoover (eds.), *The IS-LM Model: Its Rise, Fall and Strange Persistence, Annual Supplement to Vol. 36 of History of Political Economy*, Durham, NC: Duke University Press, 217–39.

Bronfenbrenner, M. (1956) 'The State of Japanese Economics,' *American Economic Review*, 46: 389–98.

Bronfenbrenner, M. and F. D. Holzman (1963) 'A Survey of Inflation Theory,' in *Surveys of Economic Theory*, Vol. I, London: Macmillan, 46–107.

Bullard, J. (2011) 'QE2: An Assessment,' Quantitative Easing Conference, 30 June, St. Louis, 2011, http://research.stlouisfed.org/econ/bullard/pdf/Bullard_QE_Conference_June_30_2011_Final.pdf.

Coats, A. W. (ed.) (1981) 'Economists in Government,' *History of Political Economy*, 13–3: 341–694.

DeLong, J. B. (2000) 'The Triumph of Monetarism?' *Journal of Economic Perspectives*, 14: 83–94.

DeLong, J. B. and Lawrence H. Summers (1986) 'Is Increased Price Flexibility Stabilizing?' *American Economic Review*, 76: 1031–44.

Dimand, R. W. (2008) 'Timlin, Mabel Frances,' in Steven N. Durlauf and Lawrence E. Blume (eds.), *The New Palgrave Dictionary of Economics*, second edition, Basingstoke: Palgrave Macmillan, vol. 8, 301–2.

Dimand, R. W. and M. Wakatabe (2011) 'The *Kyoto University Economic Review* (1926–1944) as Importer and Exporter of Economic Ideas: Bringing Lausanne,

Cambridge, Vienna, and Marx to Japan,' in Heinz D. Kurz, Tamotsu Nishizawa, and Keith Tribe (eds.), *The Dissemination of Economic Ideas*, Cheltenham: Edward Elgar, 260–91.

Fernández, R. (2008) 'Culture and Economics,' in Steven N. Durlauf and Lawrence E. Blume (eds.), *The New Palgrave Dictionary of Economics*, second edition, Basingstoke: Palgrave Macmillan, 333–40.

Friedman, M. (1957) *A Theory of Consumption Function*, Princeton: Princeton University Press.

Friedman, M. (1960) *A Program for Monetary Stability*, Fordham: Fordham University Press.

Friedman, M. (1962) *Capitalism and Freedom*, Chicago: University of Chicago Press.

Friedman, M. and R. D. Friedman (1980) *Free to Choose: A Personal Statement*, New York: Harcourt Brace Jovanovich.

Friedman, M. and R. D. Friedman (1998) *Two Lucky People: Memoirs*, Chicago: University of Chicago Press.

Friedman, M. and A. J. Schwartz (1963) *A Monetary History of the United States, 1867–1960*, Princeton: Princeton University Press.

Gao, B. (1997) *Economic Ideology and Japanese Industrial Policy*, Cambridge: Cambridge University Press.

Guiso, L., P. Sapienza, and Luigi Zingales (2006) 'Does Culture Affect Economic Outcomes?' *Journal of Economic Perspectives*, 20: 23–48.

Hadley, E. M. (1989) 'The Diffusion of Keynesian Ideas in Japan,' in Peter Hall (ed.), *The Political Power of Economic Ideas: Keynesianism across Nations*, Princeton: Princeton University Press, 291–309.

Hall, P. A. (1989) 'Conclusion: The Politics of Keynesian Ideas,' in Peter A. Hall (ed.), *The Political Power of Economic Ideas: Keynesianism across Nations*, Princeton: Princeton University Press, 361–91.

Hamada, K. (1986) 'The Impact of the General Theory in Japan,' *Eastern Economic Journal*, 12: 451–66.

Hayasaka, T. and K. Masamura (1974) *Sengo Nihon no Keizaigaku (Economics in Post-War Japan)*, Tokyo: Nikkei Shinsyo (in Japanese).

Hayashida, M. (1986) *Keinzu Ippan Riron Kenkyu Gojinenshi: Wagakuni no Sho Kenkyu Seika to Godai Ronso (The Fifty Years of Research on Keynes' General Theory)*, Tokyo: Taga Shuppan (in Japanese).

Ikeo, A. (ed.) (2000) *Japanese Economics and Economists since 1945*, London and New York: Routledge.

Ikeo, I. (2006) *Nihon no Keizaigaku (Economics in Japan: The Internationalization of Economics in the Twentieth Century)*, Nagoya: Nagoya Daigaku Shuppan (in Japanese).

Ito, M. (1962) *Keynes: Atarashii Keizaigaku no Tanjo (Keynes: The Birth of New Economics)*, Tokyo: Iwanami Shoten (in Japanese).

Ito, M. (2006) 'Keizaigaku Nidai Kyojin no Oshie (Lessons from Two Giants of Economics),' *Ekonomisuto*, 84, December 19: 64–7 (in Japanese).

Joyce, M. A. S., R. T. Mathew, and R. Woods (2011) 'The Economic Impact of QE: Lessons from the UK,' Vox, November 1, 2011, www.voxeu.org/index.php?q=node/7192.

Kataoka, G. and M. Wakatabe (2011) 'The Great Inflation in Japan: How Economic Thought Interacted with Economic Policy,' TCER Working Paper, www.tcer.or.jp/wp/pdf/e36.pdf.

Klamer, A. (2007) *Speaking of Economics: How to Get in the Conversation*, London and New York: Routledge.

Komiya, R. (1960) 'Nihon ni okeru Keizaigakukenkyu ni tsuite (On the Research in Economics in Japan),' *Keizai Seminar*, January: 70–5 (in Japanese).

Komiya, R. (1970) 'Genndai Shihon Shugi no Tenkai–Marukusu-shugi he no Kaigi to Hihan (Development in Contemporary Capitalism: Skepticism and Criticism against Marxism),' *Ekonomisuto*, November 10 (in Japanese).

Komiya, R. (1976) 'Causes of the Inflation from 1973 to 1974,' *Keizaigaku Ronsyu*, 42 (in Japanese).

Komiya, R. (1979) *Joan Robinson Gendai Keizaigaku no Kaibo (The Anatomy of Joan Robinson's Introduction to Modern Economics)*, Tokyo: Nihon Keizai Shimbunsya (in Japanese).

Komiya, R. (2008) 'Watashi no Rirekisyo (My Memories),' *Nihon Keizai Shimbun (Japan Economic Journal)*, December, 1–31 (in Japanese).

Komiya, R. (2010) 'Tsuru-san's Kokorozashi (The Aspiration of Mr. Tsuru),' in Konosuke Odaka and Tamotsu Nishizawa (eds.), *Kaiso no Tsuru Shigeto (Tsuru Shigeto in Retrospect)*, Tokyo: Keiso Shobo (in Japanese), 271–308.

Komiya, R. and Y. Suzuki (1977), 'Inflation in Japan,' in L. B. Krause and W. S. Salant (eds.), *Worldwide Inflation: Theory and Recent Experience*, Washington, D. C.: The Brookings Institution, 303–48.

Komiya, R. and K. Yamamoto (1981) 'Japan: The Officer in Charge of Economic Affairs,' *History of Political Economy*, 13: 600–28.

Krugman, P. (1998) 'It's Baaack!: Japan's Slump and the Return of the Liquidity Trap,' *Brookings Papers on Economic Activity*, 2: 137–205.

Laidler, D. (1981) 'Monetarism: An Interpretation and an Assessment,' *Economic Journal*, 91: 1–28.

Laidler, D. (1982) *Monetarist Perspectives*, Oxford: P. Allan.

Lange, O. (1935) 'Marxian Economics and Modern Economic Theory,' *Review of Economic Studies*, 2: 189–201.

Miwa, Y. and M. Ramseyer (2006) *The Fable of the Keiretsu: Urban Legends of the Japanese Economy*, Chicago: University of Chicago Press.

Miyazaki, Y. and M. Ito (1964) *Commentar Keynes Ippan Riron (Commentaries on Keynes's General Theory)*, Tokyo: Nihon Hyoronsya (in Japanese).

Morris-Suzuki, T. (1989) *A History of Japanese Economic Thought*, London and New York: Routledge.

Niida, H. (1963) 'Kakaku Mondai (Price Problems),' in Ryutaro Komiya (ed.), *Sengo Nihon no Keizai Seicho* (*Economic Growth in Post-War Japan*), Tokyo: Iwanami Shoten, 50–70 (in Japanese).

Nishiyama, C. (1974) *Jiyu Keizai (Free Economy)*, Tokyo: Chuo Koron (in Japanese).

Nishiyama, C. (1976) *Monetarism*, Tokyo: Toyo Keizai Shimpo Sya (in Japanese).

Noguchi, A. (2000) 'External Liberalization and "Industrial Structural Policy",' in Ikeo, A. (ed.), *Japanese Economics and Economists since 1945*, London and New York: Routledge, 254–80.

Noguchi, A. (2003) *Keizai Ronsen (Debates on the Economic Problems)*, Tokyo: Toyo Keizai Shimpo Sya (in Japanese).

Odaka, K. and T. Nishizawa eds. (2010) *Kaiso no Tsuru Shigeto (Tsuru Shigeto in Retrospect)*, Tokyo: Keiso Shobo (in Japanese).

Okita, S. (1962) *Keizai Keikaku (Economic Planning)*, Tokyo: Shisei Do (in Japanese).

Poole, W. (1978) *Money and the Economy: A Monetarist View*, Addison-Wesley.

Robinson, J. (1942) *An Essay on Marxian Economics*, London: Macmillan.

Robinson, J. (1971) *Economic Heresies: Some Old Fashioned Questions in Economic Theory*, New York: Basic Books.

Robinson, J. and J. Eatwell (1973) *An Introduction to Modern Economics*, New York: McGraw-Hill.

Saito, S. (1981) *Keizaigaku ha Gendai wo Sukueruka (Can Economics Save the Present Time?)*, Tokyo: Bungei Shunjyu (in Japanese).

Shibata, K. (1933) 'Marx's Analysis of Capitalism and the General Equilibrium Theory of the Lausanne School,' *Kyoto University Economic Review*, 8–1: 107–36.

Shimpo, S. (1979) *Gendai Nihon Keizai no Kaimei (Analyzing Contemporary Japanese Economy)*, Tokyo: Toyo Keizai Shimpo Sya (in Japanese).

Sugihara, S. and T. Tanaka eds. (1998) *Economic Thought and Modernization in Japan*, Cheltenham: Edward Elgar.

Sugimoto, E. (1950) *Kindai Keizaigaku no Kaimei (Modern Economics Examined)*, Tokyo: Hyoron sha (in Japanese).

Sugiyama, C. and H. Mizuta eds. (1988) *Enlightenment and Beyond: Political Economy Comes to Japan*, Tokyo: University of Tokyo Press.

Suzuki, Y. (1994) *The Collected Writings of Suzuki Yoshio*, Tokyo: NTT Shuppan (in Japanese).

Tachi, R. and R. Komiya (1964) *Keizai Seisaku no Riron (Theory of Economic Policy)*, Tokyo: Keiso Shobo (in Japanese).

Takasuka, Y. (1973) *Gendai Nihon no Bukka Mondai (The Price Problems of Contemporary Japan)*, Tokyo: Shin Hyoron (in Japanese).

Taniuchi, M. (1982) *Atarashii Monetarism no Keizaigaku (New Economics of Monetarism)*, Tokyo: Toyo Keizai Shimpo Sya (in Japanese).

Throsby, D. (2001) *Economics and Culture*, Cambridge: Cambridge University Press.

Timlin, M. F. (1942) *Keynesian Economics*, Toronto: University of Toronto Press.

Tobin, J. with the collaboration of S. S. Golub (1998) *Money, Credit, and Capital*, Boston, MA: Irwin/McGraw-Hill.

Tokyo Daigaku Keizaigakubu ed. (1976) *Tokyo Daigaku Keizaigakubu Gojunenshi (The Fifty Years of the Department of Economics, University of Tokyo)*, Tokyo: University of Tokyo Press (in Japanese).

Tsuru, S. (1950) 'Sokan no Kotoba (A Preface in its Founding),' *Keizai Kenkyu*, 1 (in Japanese).

Tsuru, S. (1971) 'In Place of Gross National Product,' in Asahi Shimbun Keizaibu (ed.), *Kutabare GNP*, Tokyo: Asahi Shimbun, xxi–xxxii.

Uzawa, H. (1964) 'Optimal Growth in a Two-Sector Model of Capital Accumulation,' *Review of Economic Studies*, 31: 1–24.

Uzawa, H. (1971) 'Kindai Keizagaku Konmei no Kadai,' *Nihon Keizai Shimbun*, January 4.

Uzawa, H. (1977/1994) *Kindai Keizaigaku no Saikento: Hihanteki Tembo (Modern Economics Reexamined: A Critical Review)*, in his *Collected Works*, Vol. II, Tokyo: Iwanami Shoten (in Japanese).

Uzawa, H. (1984) *Keynes Ippan Riron wo Yomu (Reading Keynes's General Theory)*, Tokyo: Iwanami Shoten (in Japanese).

Uzawa, H. (1986/1994) *Kindai Keizaigaku no Tenkan (Transforming Modern Economics)*, in his *Collected Works*, Vol. IV, Tokyo: Iwanami Shoten (in Japanese).

Uzawa, H. (1987/1994) *Gendai Nihon Keizai Hihan (Critique of Contemporary Japanese Economy)*, in his *Collected Works*, Vol. VII, Tokyo: Iwanami Shoten (in Japanese).

Uzawa, H. (1988/1994) *Kokyo Keizaigaku no Saikochiku (The Reconstruction of Public Economics)*, in his *Collected Works*, Vol. VIII, Tokyo: Iwanami Shoten (in Japanese).
Uzawa, H. (2000) *Veblen*, Tokyo: Iwanami Shoten (in Japanese).
Vane, H. R. and J. L. Thompson (1979) *Monetarism: Theory, Evidence and Policy*, Oxford: Martin Robertson.
Yoshikawa, H. (2000) *Gendai Marcro Keizaigaku (Macroeconomics)*, Tokyo: Sobunsha (in Japanese).

6 Macrodynamics of deflationary depression

A Japanese perspective

Toichiro Asada

1 Introduction: the paradoxical facts of the Japanese economy

The purpose of this chapter is to present a formal macrodynamic model that can contribute to the theoretical interpretation of the 'deflationary depression' of the Japanese economy in the 1990s and the 2000s during such a long period of twenty years, called the 'lost twenty years', and to present a theoretical foundation of the proper policy prescription based on the policy mix of the fiscal and monetary policies. We hope that the model that is presented in this chapter will provide some insight to the theoretical interpretation and the policy prescription of the recent economic crises of other countries, such as the USA and European countries, as well as Japan.

Before constructing the theoretical model, we shall consider the main macroeconomic data of the Japanese economy during the period from the 1980s to the 2000s, which seem quite paradoxical at first glance. In fact, Figures 6.1–6.5 summarize the empirical 'stylized facts' of the Japanese economy.

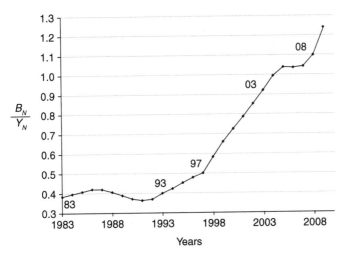

Figure 6.1 Ratio of gross nominal balance of national debt (B_N) to nominal GDP (Y_N) in Japan (source: Mitsuhashi, Uchida and Ikeda 2010, chap. 5).

We can observe the following five 'stylized facts' from these five figures.

1   Figure 6.1 shows the following facts. In the prosperity period of the 1980s, 'the national debt–income ratio' (ratio of the gross nominal balance of the national debt to the nominal GDP) B_N/Y_N was stabilized at relatively low levels, but it began to increase continuously from 1993, and the speed of the increase of this ratio has accelerated since 1997.

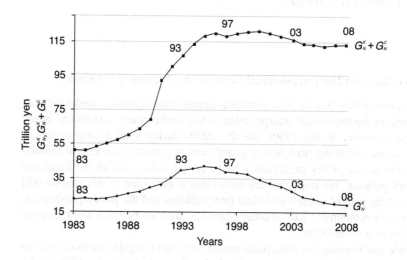

Figure 6.2 Nominal government investment on productive capital (G_N^K) and nominal government consumption expenditure (G_N^C) in Japan (sources: Mitsuhashi, Uchida and Ikeda 2010, chap. 5, and Miwa and Hara 2010, Part I).

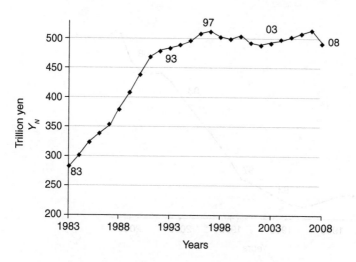

Figure 6.3 Nominal GDP (Y_N) in Japan (sources: Mitsuhashi, Uchida and Ikeda 2010, chap. 5, and Asada 2005, chap. 1).

2 Figure 6.2 shows the following facts. The 'nominal government investment expenditure' on productive capital formation G_N^K continued to increase steadily up to 1993, but it decreased rapidly from 1997. In fact, G_N^K in 2008, which is less than that in 1983, is less than half of that in 1993. Since 1993, the 'nominal government consumption expenditure' G_N^C had the tendency to

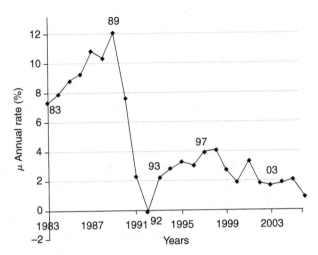

Figure 6.4 μ=growth rate of nominal money supply (M_2+CD) in Japan (source: Miwa and Hara 2010, Part I).

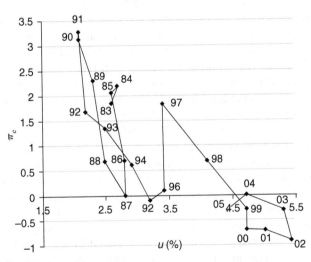

Figure 6.5 Phillips curve in Japan (1983–2005) (source: Miwa and Hara 2010, Part I and Part II).

Notes
u=(completely) unemployment rate.
π_c=rate of inflation of consumer price index.

increase, but the 'total nominal government expenditure' $G_N = G_N^K + G_N^C$ has not increased since 1997, but it had the tendency to decrease in the 2000s, because the speed of the decrease of G_N^K was too rapid.

3   Figures 6.2 and 6.3 show the following facts. The movement of the 'nominal GDP' Y_N is quite similar to the movement of the 'nominal government expenditure' G_N. That is to say, Y_N increased rapidly up to 1993, but it became stagnant after 1997. This means that the traditional Keynesian 'multiplier effect' seems to work quite well in the Japanese economy in this period. Y_N in 2008, which is immediately after the 'subprime mortgage crises' in USA and three years *before* the Great East Japan Earthquake, was less than that in 1997.

4   Figure 6.4 shows the following facts. The 'annual growth rate of money supply' μ increased rapidly in the period of prosperity of the 1980s, which is called the 'bubble period', but it decreased quite rapidly during the period from 1989 to 1992 due to the monetary policy of BOJ (the Bank of Japan) that intentionally caused the crash of the 'bubble'. During the period from 1993 to 1997 it increased mildly, but it had the tendency to decrease after 1997. In the 1990s and the 2000s, μ is only about 2 percent on average, while it was about 10 percent on average in the 1980s. Apparently, the 'structural change' of the monetary policy of BOJ occurred after 1989. It may be interesting to note that BOJ got the excessive independency from the Japanese government after the problematical amendment of the BOJ law in 1997.

5   Figure 6.5 shows the following facts. This figure reveals that the traditional negatively sloping 'Phillips curve' is quite well suited to the Japanese economy from the 1980s to the 2000s. In the 1980s, during which the growth rate of the nominal government expenditure and that of the nominal money supply were relatively high, the combination of the quite low 'completely unemployment rate' (about 2 percent on average) and the relatively high (but not excessively high) rate of inflation (about 2 percent annual rate on average) was attained. On the other hand, since the 1990s, in particular in the 2000s, during which both the growth rate of the nominal government expenditure and that of the nominal money supply were quite low, the economy stuck into the 'deflationary depression' that entails a mildly negative rate of inflation (about -1 percent annual rate on average) and the high 'completely unemployment rate' (about 5 percent in average). Incidentally, it is worth pointing out two facts. First, the 'completely unemployment rate' in Japan has a bias to estimate the 'rate of unemployment' much smaller than that in the western countries such as the USA and European countries. Roughly speaking, double the 'completely unemployment rate' in Japan may be equivalent to the 'rate of unemployment' that is measured in reference to the western standard. Second, the annual rate of inflation of the consumer price index temporally increased about 2 percent from 1996 to 1997. This phenomenon is due to the fact that the Japanese government raised the 'consumption tax rate' (value added tax rate) from 3 percent to 5 percent in 1997, which seemed to make worse the subsequent deflationary depression.

The above 'stylized facts' reveal the seemingly paradoxical fact that the combination of the *increase* of the tax rate, the *decrease* of the government expenditure and the *tight* monetary policy of the central bank entails the *increase* rather than decrease of the ratio of the gross nominal balance of the national debt to the nominal GDP. Table 6.1 summarizes such an apparent paradox.[1]

At this stage of analysis, we shall introduce some mathematical formulae. The budget constraint of the 'consolidated government' including the central bank can be written as

$$pT + \dot{B} + \dot{H} = pG + rB,$$

where p=price level, T=real tax, B=stock of nominal *net* national debt,[2] H=stock of nominal high-powered money issued by the central bank, G=real government expenditure, and r=nominal interest rate of long-term national debt. Next, differentiating the definitional equation $d=B/(pY)$ with respect to time, we have

$$\dot{d}/d = \dot{B}/B - \dot{p}/p - \dot{Y}/Y = \dot{B}/B - \pi - z,$$

where d=net national debt–GDP ratio (the ratio of the stock of the nominal *net* national debt to the nominal GDP), Y=real GDP, pY=nominal GDP, $\pi=\dot{p}/p$=rate of price inflation, $z=\dot{Y}/Y$=growth rate of real GDP and $z_N=\pi+z$=growth rate of nominal GDP.

From these two equations, we obtain the following dynamic equation that describes the movement of the variable d.

$$\dot{d} = (G/Y) - (T/Y) - (\dot{H}/pY) + (r - \pi - z)d \qquad (*)$$

We can see from this equation that in case of $r-\pi-z<0$, the *increase* of d induces the *decrease* of $\dot{d}$, which is a *stabilizing* negative feedback mechanism. On the other hand, in case of $r-\pi-z>0$, the *increase* of d induces the *increase* of $\dot{d}$, which is a *destabilizing* positive feedback mechanism. That is to say, the inequality

nominal interest rate of long-term national debt$=r<\pi+z=z_N$=growth rate of nominal GDP $\qquad (**)$

Table 6.1 Movements of B_N/Y_N, Y_N and $G_N^K + G_N^C$ in Japan

Years	B_N/Y_N	Y_N	$G_N^K + G_N^C$
1983–1993	1.05 times	1.71 times	2.06 times
1993–2003	2.31 times	1.02 times	1.09 times
1993–2008	2.76 times	1.02 times	1.06 times

Sources: Mitsuhashi, Uchida and Ikeda (2010, chap. 5), Miwa and Hara (2010, Part I) and Asada (2005, chap. 1).

or equivalently

> real interest rate of long-term national debt $=r-\pi<z=$ growth rate of real
> GDP   (***)

has a *stabilizing* effect, and the opposite inequality has a *destabilizing* effect. Although these inequalities are only the partial conditions for the dynamic stability/instability of the system, they provide us some important insights for the dynamic stability/instability of the macroeconomic system. The (partial) stability condition (**) or (***) is called the 'Domar condition' after Domar (1957).

We can interpret the 'paradox of national debt accumulation' in Japan by using the equation (*) as follows. The *direct* effect of the decrease of G and the increase of the consumption tax rate will be to *suppress* the increase of d. However, such a policy mix will induce the decrease of Y and the resulting decrease of T/Y through the decreases of the income tax and the corporate tax. All of such *indirect* effects are to *accelerate* rather than suppress the increase of d. The tight monetary policy will also cause the *increase* of d through the decrease of $\dot{H}/(pY)$. Moreover, in such a situation, it is likely that the *destabilizing* 'anti-Domar condition' $(r>\pi+z=z_N)$ is satisfied, because the induced deflationary depression may result in the *negative* growth rate of nominal GDP $(z_N=\pi+z)$, but the nominal interest rate of the long-term national debt (r) cannot be negative.

In fact, in the Japanese economy in the 1990s and the 2000s, the above scenario applied. In 1997, the Japanese government raised the consumption tax rate from 3 percent to 5 percent. The Japanese nominal GDP in 1997 was about 520 trillion yen. However, since then, the Japanese economy stuck into the deflationary depression, and in 2010, which is a year *before* the Great East Japan Earthquake, the Japanese nominal GDP was only 480 trillion yen. As a result, the total tax revenue of the Japanese government in 2010 decreased about 15 trillion yen compared with that in 1997. During the process of the deflationary depression, all of r, π and z declined, but since 2000, the destabilizing 'anti-Domar condition' is continuing to be satisfied, because $z_N=\pi+z$ became mildly negative but r was between $+1$ percent and $+2$ percent in this period. The result is the rapid increase of d, which is consistent with our theoretical reasoning.

At this stage, we have already used some simple mathematical formulae to interpret the macroeconomic performance of the Japanese economy. The remaining part of this chapter is devoted to constructing a more elaborated formal macrodynamic model that can give some insight into the analysis and the policy prescription of the practical macroeconomic problems that have been explained in this section. The analyses in this paper are based on the 'high-dimensional Keynesian macrodynamic model' that has been developed by Asada (2006a, 2006b), Asada, Chiarella, Flaschel and Franke (2003, 2010), Asada, Flaschel, Mouakil and Proaño (2011), Asada and Ouchi (2009), etc. The high-dimensional macrodynamic model means the macrodynamic model with many (at least three) endogenous variables.

Sections 2 and 3 are devoted to the formulation of the model. Formally, our model consists of twenty independent (static and dynamic) equations with twenty endogenous variables. However, it is shown in section 3 that our model can be reduced to a system of the five-dimensional nonlinear differential equations with five endogenous variables. Sections 4 and 5 are devoted to the mathematical analysis and the economic interpretation of the model. In section 6, we review the mainstream 'New Keynesian' dynamic model critically in contrast to our modeling strategy that is based on the rather traditional 'Old Keynesian' method. In section 7, we provide some concluding remarks. The complicated mathematical proofs and the interpretation of some complicated topics are relegated to the appendices.

We do not agree with the conventional dichotomy which says that the under-employment Keynesian model is the 'short run' model with fixed prices without capital accumulation, and the full employment neoclassical model is the 'long run' model with flexible prices and capital accumulation. In fact, our model is the 'long run' model with variable prices and capital accumulation. The steady solution (long run equilibrium) of our model has the 'classical' features that the rate of (un)employment and the rate of capital accumulation are at their 'natural' levels. However, the long run equilibrium point is not necessarily dynamically stable in our model. In other words, the economy may perpetually fluctuate in the 'out-of-equilibrium' region unless the proper policy mix of the fiscal and monetary policies is adopted.[3] Incidentally, in our model the 'natural' as well as the 'actual' rate of growth fluctuates endogenously depending on the endogenous fluctuations of the effective demand. In this sense, our model is a Keynesian endogenous growth model without full employment in contrast to the neoclassical endogenous growth models with full employment that are represented by Barro and Sala-i-Martin (2004) and Romer (2006, chap. 3).[4]

2 Basic system of equations

Our model consists of the following system of equations.[5]

$$y = c + i + g; \quad y = \frac{Y}{K}, c = \frac{C}{K}, i = \frac{I}{K} = \frac{\dot{K}}{K}, g = \frac{G}{K} \tag{1}$$

$$c = \delta(y + rb - t) + c_0; \quad 0 < \delta < 1, c_0 > 0, b = \frac{B}{pK}, t = \frac{T}{K} \tag{2}$$

$$t = \tau(y + rb) - t_0; \quad 0 < \tau < 1, t_0 > 0 \tag{3}$$

$$i = i(r - \pi^e); \quad i_{r-\pi^e} = \frac{\partial i}{\partial(r - \pi^e)} < 0 \tag{4}$$

$$m(r)h = \varphi(r)y; \quad m_r = \frac{dm}{dr} > 0, \varphi_r = \frac{d\varphi}{dr} < 0, h = \frac{H}{pK} \tag{5}$$

$$T + \frac{\dot{B}}{p} + \frac{\dot{H}}{p} = G + \frac{rB}{p} \tag{6}$$

$$\pi = \varepsilon(e - \bar{e}) + \pi^e; \quad \varepsilon > 0, \ 0 < \bar{e} < 1 \tag{7}$$

$$\pi = \frac{\dot{p}}{p} \tag{8}$$

$$\frac{\dot{e}}{e} = \frac{\dot{y}}{y} + i(r - \pi^e) - n(e); \quad n_e = \frac{dn}{de} \geq 0 \tag{9}$$

The meanings of the symbols in these equations are as follows. Y=real national income. C=real private consumption expenditure. I=real private investment expenditure. G=real government expenditure. K=real capital stock. T=real income tax. B=stock of nominal net public debt.[6] r=nominal rate of interest. H=stock of nominal high-powered money. p=price level. π=rate of price inflation. π^e=expected rate of price inflation. $r - \pi^e$=expected real rate of interest. N=labor employment. N^s=labor supply. $e = N/N^s$=rate of employment=$1 -$rate of unemployment. $\bar{e}$='natural' rate of employment. $a = Y/N$= average labor productivity. $n_1 = \dot{N}^s/N^s$ = growth rate of labor supply. $n_2 = \dot{a}/a$=rate of technical progress (growth rate of labor productivity). $n = n_1 + n_2$='natural' rate of growth.

Eq. (1) is the equilibrium condition in the goods market—that is, the IS equation.[7] Eq. (2) is the Keynesian consumption function that explicitly considers the consumption out of the interest income on public debt. Equations (3) and (4) are quite standard tax function and Keynesian investment function, respectively. Eq. (5) is the LM equation that describes the equilibrium condition of the money market. The right-hand side of this equation is the Keynesian money demand function, and its left-hand side is the real money supply. That is, $M = m(r)H$ is nominal money supply and $m(r)$ is money multiplier.[8] Eq. (6) is the budget constraint of the 'consolidated government' including the central bank, which means that the government expenditure including the interest payment on the government bond (public debt) must be financed through taxation, newly issued government bond (bond financing) or high-powered money newly issued by the central bank (money financing).[9] Eq. (7) represents a standard type of the expectations-augmented price Phillips curve. In this formulation, $\bar{e}$ is the level of 'natural rate of employment'. Eq. (8) is the definition of the rate of price inflation.

We can derive Eq. (9) as follows. Differentiating the definitional relationship

$$e = N/N^s = \frac{(Y/K)K}{(Y/N)N^s} = \frac{yK}{aN^s} \tag{10}$$

with respect to time, we have

$$\dot{e}/e = \dot{y}/y + \dot{K}/K - (\dot{a}/a + \dot{N}^s/N^s) = \dot{y}/y + \dot{K}/K - (n_1 + n_2). \tag{11}$$

Substituting $\dot{K}/K = i(r - \pi^e)$ and $n_1 + n_2 = n = n(e)$; $n_e = dn/de \geq 0$ into Eq. (11), we obtain Eq. (9).[10]

The system of equations (1)–(9) consists of seventeen independent equations including the definitional equations, while there are twenty endogenous variables $(Y, C, I, G, T, B, H, K, y, c, i, g, t, b, h, r, e, p, \pi, \pi^e)$. This means that there remains three degrees of freedom in this system. To close the system, we must specify (1) government's fiscal policy, (2) central bank's monetary policy, and (3) process of public's inflation expectations formation. In this chapter, we adopt the following specifications.

$$\dot{g} = \alpha\{\theta(\bar{e} - e) + (1 - \theta)(\bar{b} - b)\}; \quad \alpha > 0, 0 < \theta < 1, \bar{b} > 0 \tag{12}$$

$$\dot{r} = \begin{cases} \beta_1(\pi - \bar{\pi}) + \beta_2(e - \bar{e}) & \text{if} \quad r > 0 \\ \max[0, \beta_1(\pi - \bar{\pi}) + \beta_2(e - \bar{e})] & \text{if} \quad r = 0 \end{cases}; \quad \beta_1 > 0, \beta_2 > 0 \tag{13}$$

$$\dot{\pi}^e = \gamma[\xi(\bar{\pi} - \pi^e) + (1 - \xi)(\pi - \pi^e)]; \quad \gamma > 0, 0 \leq \xi \leq 1 \tag{14}$$

Eq. (12) is a formalization of the fiscal policy rule that considers both employment and outstanding stock of public debt, where $\bar{b}$ is the target value of the stock of public debt-capital ratio that is set by the government. Eq. (13) is a formalization of a kind of central bank's interest rate monetary policy rule (Taylor rule) that is called the 'flexible inflation targeting', which considers both rate of inflation and employment, where $\bar{\pi}$ is the 'target rate of inflation' that is set and announced by the central bank. In this formulation, the 'natural' nonlinearity that is based on the 'nonnegative constraint', which means that the nominal interest rate of public debt cannot be negative, is explicitly considered.[11] These fiscal and monetary policy rules are practical 'rules of thumb' in the environment with imperfect knowledge and imperfect information. In such an environment, the fiscal and monetary authorities must resort to some practical policy rules even if they do not know what policy is truly 'optimal'.

Eq. (14) is a formalization of the public's inflation expectations formation process, which is the mixture of the 'forward looking' and the 'backward looking' or 'adaptive' expectations. If $\xi = 0$, this equation is reduced to $\dot{\pi}^e = \gamma(\pi - \pi^e)$, which is nothing but purely 'backward looking' or 'adaptive' expectation formation process. If $\xi = 1$, it is reduced to $\dot{\pi}^e = \gamma(\bar{\pi} - \pi^e)$, which means that the expected rate of inflation gravitates toward the target rate of inflation that is announced by the central bank. We can consider that the parameter ξ reflects the 'degree of credibility' of the central bank's inflation targeting. The more credible the central bank's announcement for the public, the larger the value of ξ will be.

The system of equations (1)–(9) together with (12)–(14) constitutes a complete system with twenty endogenous variables that were referred to previously.

3 Derivation of a system of fundamental dynamic equations

In this section, we shall derive a more compact system of 'fundamental dynamic equations' from a system of equations that was formulated in the previous section. First, substituting equations (2)–(4) into Eq. (1) and solving with respect to y, we have the following 'IS equation', which is the equilibrium condition of the goods market.

$$y = \frac{1}{1-\delta(1-\tau)}\{\delta(1-\tau)rb+\delta t_0 + c_0 + i(r-\pi^e) + g\} = y(r,\pi^e,b,g);$$

$$y_r = \frac{\partial y}{\partial r} = \frac{\delta(1-\tau)b + \underset{(-)}{i_{r-\pi^e}}}{1-\delta(1-\tau)},$$

$$y_{\pi^e} = \frac{\partial y}{\partial \pi^e} = \frac{-\underset{(-)}{i_{r-\pi^e}}}{1-\delta(1-\tau)} > 0,$$

$$y_b = \frac{\partial y}{\partial b} = \frac{\delta(1-\tau)r}{1-\delta(1-\tau)} > 0,$$

$$y_g = \frac{\partial y}{\partial g} = \frac{1}{1-\delta(1-\tau)} > 1 > 0 \tag{15}$$

Next, we can rewrite the 'LM equation' (5) as follows.

$$h \equiv \frac{H}{pK} = \psi(r)y; \quad \psi(r) = \frac{\varphi(r)}{m(r)}, \psi'(r) < 0 \tag{16}$$

Substituting Eq. (15) into Eq. (16), we have

$$h = \psi(r)y(r,\pi^e,b,g). \tag{17}$$

Differentiating the definitional equation $h=H/(pK)$ with respect to time, we have

$$\dot{H}/(pK) = (\pi + \dot{K}/K)h + \dot{h} = \{\pi + i(r-\pi^e)\}h + \dot{h}. \tag{18}$$

Differentiating Eq. (17) with respect to time and substituting it into Eq. (18), we obtain

$$\frac{\dot{H}}{pK} = \{\pi + i(r-\pi^e)\}\psi(r)y + \psi'(r)y\dot{r} + \psi(r)\dot{y} \tag{19}$$

$$= \{\pi + i(r-\pi^e)\}\psi(r)y + \{\psi'(r)y + \psi(r)y_r\}\dot{r} + \psi(r)\{y_{\pi^e}\dot{\pi}^e + y_b\dot{b} + y_g\dot{g}\}.$$

Equations (17) and (19) imply that the dynamic path of the high-powered money H is determined endogenously when the central bank adopts a kind of 'Taylor rule' type interest rate monetary policy rule that is described by Eq. (13).

Differentiating the definitional equation $b = B/(pK)$ with respect to time, we have

$$\dot{B}/(pK) = (\pi + \dot{K}/K)b + \dot{b} = \{\pi + i(r - \pi^e)\}b + \dot{b}. \tag{20}$$

On the other hand, dividing both sides of Eq. (6) by K, we obtain the following equation.

$$t + \dot{B}/(pK) + \dot{H}/(pK) = g + rb \tag{21}$$

Substituting equations (3), (19) and (20) into Eq. (21), we can derive the following equation, which describes the dynamic of the public debt–capital ratio (b).

$$\dot{b} = \left[\frac{1}{1+\psi(r)y_b}\right]\left[\begin{array}{l} g - ty(r,\pi^e,b,g) + t_0 + \{r(1-\tau) - \pi - i(r - \pi^e)\}b \\ -\{\pi + i(r - \pi^e)\}\psi(r)y(r,\pi^e,b,g) \\ -\{\psi'(r)y(r,\pi^e,b,g) + \psi(r)y_r\}\dot{r} - \psi(r)(y_{\pi^e}\dot{\pi}^e + y_g\dot{g}) \end{array}\right] \tag{22}$$

At last, we can derive the following system of five-dimensional nonlinear differential equations from equations (7), (9), (12), (13), (14), (15) and (22).

i $\dot{g} = f_1(b,e) = a\{\theta(\bar{e} - e) + (1-\theta)(\bar{b} - b)\}$

ii $\dot{r} = f_2(\pi^e,e) = \begin{cases} (\beta_1\varepsilon + \beta_2)(e - \bar{e}) + \beta_1(\pi^e - \pi) & \text{if} \quad r > 0 \\ \max[0, (\beta_1\varepsilon + \beta_2)(e - \bar{e}) + \beta_1(\pi^e - \pi)] & \text{if} \quad r = 0 \end{cases}$

iii $\dot{\pi}^e = f_3(\pi^e,e) = \gamma[\xi(\bar{\pi} - \pi^e) + (1-\xi)\varepsilon(e - \bar{e})]$

iv $\dot{b} = f_4(g,r,\pi^e,b,e)$

$$= \left[\frac{1}{1+\psi(r)y_b}\right]\left[\begin{array}{l} g - ty(r,\pi^e,b,g) + t_0 + \{r(1-\tau) - \varepsilon(e - \bar{e}) - \pi^e - i(r - \pi^e)\}b \\ -\{\varepsilon(e - \bar{e}) + \pi^e + i(r - \pi^e)\}\psi(r)y(r,\pi^e,b,g) \\ -\{\psi'(r)y(r,\pi^e,b,g) + \psi(r)y_r\}f_2(\pi^e,e) \\ -\psi(r)\{y_{\pi^e}f_3(\pi^e,e) + y_g f_1(b,e)\} \end{array}\right]$$

v $\dot{e} = f_5(g,r,\pi^e,b,e)$

$$= e\left[\left\{\frac{1}{y(r,\pi^e,b,g)}\right\}\{y_r f_2(\pi^e,e) + y_{\pi^e}f_3(\pi^e,e) + y_b f_4(g,r,\pi^e,b,e) + y_g f_1(b,e)\} \\ + i(r - \pi^e) - n(e)\right] \tag{23}$$

We can consider that Eq. (23) is a system of 'fundamental dynamic equations' in our model.

4 Nature of the solution of a system of fundamental dynamic equations

Now, let us consider the mathematical properties of the solution of a system of fundamental dynamic equations (23) and their economic implications. First, we shall study the long run equilibrium solution $(g^*, r^*, \pi^{e*}, b^*, e^*)$ of this system such that $\dot{g} = \dot{r} = \dot{\pi}^e = \dot{b} = \dot{e} = 0$, $e = \bar{e}$. An economically meaningful equilibrium solution satisfies the following relationships.

i $e^* = \bar{e}, b^* = \bar{b}, \pi^{e*} = \pi^* = \bar{\pi}$

ii $i(r^* - \bar{\pi}) = n(\bar{e})$

iii $g^* - \{\tau + (\bar{\pi} + n(\bar{e}))\psi(r^*)\} y(r^*, \bar{\pi}, \bar{b}, g^*) + t_0 + \{r^*(1 - \tau) - \bar{\pi} - n(\bar{e})\}\bar{b} = 0$ (24)

Eq. (24)(i) implies that the 'natural' rate of employment, the government's target value of public debt–capital ratio, and the central bank's target rate of price inflation are realized at the long run equilibrium point.

Eq. (24)(ii) means that the 'natural' rate of growth is realized at the long run equilibrium point. We can determine the equilibrium nominal rate of interest (r^*) by solving Eq. (24)(ii). First, the equilibrium real rate of interest (ρ^*) is determined by the equation $i(\rho^*) = n(\bar{e})$, and then r^* is determined by

$$r^* = \rho^* + \bar{\pi}. \tag{25}$$

It follows from this equation that we have $r^* > 0$ *if and only if* the inequality

$$\bar{\pi} > -\rho^* \tag{26}$$

is satisfied. Needless to say, this inequality is automatically satisfied if both of ρ^* and $\bar{\pi}$ are positive. We *assume* that the inequality (26) is in fact satisfied in this model.

Substituting Eq. (25) into Eq. (24)(iii), we have the equilibrium value g^* by solving the following equation with single unknown (g).

$$\begin{aligned}
F(g) &\equiv g - \{\tau + (\bar{\pi} + n(\bar{e}))\psi(\rho^* + \bar{\pi})\} y(\rho^* + \bar{\pi}, \bar{\pi}, \bar{b}, g) \\
&\quad + t_0 + \{\rho^*(1 - \tau) - \tau\bar{\pi} - n(\bar{e})\}\bar{b} \\
&= 0
\end{aligned} \tag{27}$$

At this stage of the analysis, let us introduce the following assumption.

Assumption 1

1    $(1 - \delta)(1 - \tau) > \{\bar{\pi} + n(\bar{e})\}\psi(\rho^* + \bar{\pi})$.
2    $\rho^*(1 - \tau) - \tau\bar{\pi} < n(\bar{e})$.
3   t_0 is sufficiently small.

We can show that the right-hand side of the inequality (1) in this assumption is the ratio $\dot{H}/(pY)$ at the equilibrium point.[12] Therefore, **Assumption 1** (1) means that the ratio $\dot{H}/(pY)$ is not extremely large at the equilibrium point. On the other hand, **Assumption 1** (2) means that the 'Domar condition' is satisfied at the equilibrium point (for 'Domar condition', see section 1 of this chapter).

Under **Assumption 1**, we have the following properties.

$$F(0) = -\{\tau + (\bar{\pi} + n(\bar{e}))\psi(\rho^* + \bar{\pi})\}y(\rho^* + \bar{\pi}, \bar{\pi}, \bar{b}, 0) + t_0$$
$$+ \{\rho^*(1-\tau) - \tau\bar{\pi} - n(\bar{e})\}\bar{b} < 0 \tag{28}$$

$$F'(g) = \frac{(1-\delta)(1-\tau) - \{\bar{\pi} + n(\bar{e})\}\psi(\rho^* + \bar{\pi})}{1 - \delta(1-\tau)} > 0 \tag{29}$$

It follows from these inequalities and continuity of the functions that there exists the *unique* long run equilibrium solution $g^* > 0$.

From Eq. (16) we can see that at the equilibrium point $h = H/(pK)$ becomes constant. It follows from this fact and the relationship $M = m(r)H$ that we can obtain the following result at the long run equilibrium point.

$$\frac{\dot{M}}{M} = \frac{\dot{H}}{H} = \bar{\pi} + n(\bar{e}) \tag{30}$$

Incidentally, it is worth noting that the long run equilibrium solution is *independent of* the parameter values ε, α, θ, β_1, β_2, γ and ξ, although these parameter values may influence the *out of equilibrium* dynamics of the system.

Next, let us study the local stability/instability of the equilibrium point of the dynamic system (23). We suppose that the initial conditions of the endogenous variables ($y(0)$, $r(0)$, $\pi^e(0)$, $b(0)$, $e(0)$) are pre-determined historically. This means that we adopt the traditional concept of dynamic stability—that is, the equilibrium point of this system is locally stable *if and only if* all of the characteristic roots of this system at the equilibrium point have *negative real parts*.

The Jacobian matrix of this system *at the equilibrium point* becomes as follows.

$$J = \begin{bmatrix} 0 & 0 & 0 & -\alpha(1-\theta) & -\alpha\theta \\ 0 & 0 & \beta_1 & 0 & \beta_1\varepsilon + \beta_2 \\ 0 & 0 & -\gamma\xi & 0 & \gamma(1-\xi)\varepsilon \\ f_{41} & f_{42} & f_{43} & f_{44} & f_{45} \\ f_{51} & f_{52} & f_{53} & f_{54} & f_{55} \end{bmatrix} \tag{31}$$

The detailed expressions of partial derivatives f_{ij} are contained in **Appendix A**. We can write the characteristic equation of this system as

$$\Delta(\lambda) \equiv |\lambda I - J| = \lambda^5 + a_1\lambda^4 + a_2\lambda^3 + a_3\lambda^2 + a_4\lambda + a_5 = 0, \tag{32}$$

where

$$a_1 = -\text{trace } J, \tag{33}$$

$$a_j = (-1)^j(\text{sum of all principal } j\text{-th order minors of } J) \ (j=2, 3, 4), \tag{34}$$

$$a_5 = -\det J. \tag{35}$$

It is worth noting that a set of conditions

$$a_j > 0 \text{ for all } j \in \{1, 2, 3, 4, 5\} \tag{36}$$

is a set of necessary (but not sufficient) conditions for the local stability of the equilibrium point of the dynamic system (23).[13] In other words, the equilibrium point of this system becomes dynamically unstable if we have $a_j < 0$ for at least one of $j \in \{1, 2, 3, 4, 5\}$.

Now, let us introduce the following additional assumption.

Assumptio 2

$$\left| i_{r-\pi^e} \right| > \delta(1-\tau)\bar{b} \text{ at the equilibrium point.}$$

This assumption implies the inequality $y_r < 0$ so that the inequality $f_{42} = \partial \dot{b}/\partial r > 0$ at the equilibrium point, but it does not determine the sign of f_{52}. However, we have the inequality $f_{52} = \partial \dot{e}/\partial r < 0$ at the equilibrium point if the following further assumption is added.

Assumption 3

$$y_b \underset{(+)}{f_{42}} < \left| i_{r-\pi^e} \right| y \text{ at the equilibrium point.}$$

It follows from equations (A5) and (A10) in **Appendix A** that the coefficient f_{55} becomes a linear decreasing function of the parameter values β_1 and β_2 if the value of y_b is sufficiently small. We assume that this condition is in fact satisfied.

Assumption 4

The value of y_b is so small that the coefficient f_{55} becomes a linear decreasing function of the parameter values β_1 and β_2.

Now, we can prove the following two propositions.[14]

Proposition 1 (Instability Proposition)

Suppose that the following conditions (1)–(4) are satisfied.

1　The parameter value θ, which is the weight of employment consideration in the government's fiscal policy, is sufficiently small (close to zero).

2   The parameter values β_1 and β_2 that characterize the central bank's monetary policy are sufficiently small (close to zero).
3   The parameter value ξ that characterizes the 'credibility' of the central bank's inflation targeting is sufficiently small (close to zero). In other words, the public's inflation expectation formation is highly adaptive.
4   The parameter value α that characterizes the government's fiscal policy is sufficiently large.

Then, the equilibrium point of the dynamic system (23) becomes *locally unstable*.

Proof. See **Appendix B.**

Proposition 2 (Stability Proposition)

Suppose that the following conditions (1)–(3) are satisfied.

1   The fiscal policy parameter value θ is less than 1, but it is sufficiently close to 1.
2   Either of the monetary policy parameters β_1 or β_2 is sufficiently large.
3   The central bank's credibility parameter value ξ is close to 1 (including the case of $\xi = 1$).

Then, the equilibrium point of the dynamic system (23) becomes *locally stable* under **Assumptions 1–4**.

Proof. See **Appendix C.**
    Now, let us characterize the 'permissible' and 'impermissible' policy mixes of the fiscal and monetary policies as follows.

Definition

The policy mix of fiscal and monetary policies that can stabilize the macroeconomic system is called 'permissible' policy mix. On the other hand, the policy mix that cannot stabilize the macroeconomic system is called 'impermissible' policy mix.
    In view of this definition, **Proposition 1** characterizes the 'impermissible' policy mix. This proposition says that the long run equilibrium growth path tends to be *dynamically unstable* if (1) the government's fiscal policy responds to the public debt rather than the employment, (2) the central bank's monetary policy is relatively inactive, (3) the central bank does not propose the reliable anchor such as 'credible' inflation target to the public so that the public tends to form the inflation expectation adaptively (backward-lookingly), and (4) the government's fiscal policy strongly responds to the wrong target (public debt). On the other hand, **Proposition 2** characterizes the 'permissible' policy mix. This proposition says that the long run equilibrium growth path tends to be *dynamically stable* if (1) the

government's fiscal policy responds to the employment rather than the public debt, (2) the central bank's monetary policy is relatively active, and (3) the public can form the inflation expectation forward-lookingly based on the reliable and 'credible' inflation target that is set by the central bank. Unfortunately, the data which are presented in section 1 of this chapter seem to suggest that the conditions for 'impermissible' policy mix in **Proposition 1** were in fact satisfied during the 'lost twenty years' (the 1990s and the 2000s) in the Japanese economy.

Next, we shall try to interpret the mechanisms which are implicit in these two propositions intuitively.

If the government expenditure responds to the employment rather than the public debt, the *stabilizing* negative feedback mechanism such as

$$y\downarrow \Rightarrow g\uparrow \Rightarrow (c+i+g)\uparrow \Rightarrow y\uparrow \tag{F1}$$

will work. On the other hand, the *destabilizing* positive feedback mechanisms such as

$$y\downarrow \Rightarrow t\downarrow \Rightarrow b\uparrow \Rightarrow g\downarrow \Rightarrow (c+i+g)\downarrow \Rightarrow y\downarrow \tag{F2}$$

and

$$b\uparrow \Rightarrow g\downarrow \Rightarrow (y\downarrow, t\downarrow, h\downarrow) \Rightarrow b\uparrow \tag{F3}$$

will work if the government's expenditure strongly responds to the public debt rather than employment.

If the public forms the inflation expectation adaptively, the *destabilizing* positive feedback mechanism such as

$$y\downarrow \Rightarrow \pi\downarrow \Rightarrow \pi^e\downarrow \Rightarrow (r-\pi^e)\uparrow \Rightarrow i\downarrow \Rightarrow (c+i+g)\downarrow \Rightarrow y\downarrow \tag{F4}$$

will work because of the 'Mundell effect', which means the positive correlation between the expected rate of inflation and the investment expenditure through the effect on the real rate of interest. On the other hand, the stabilizing feedback mechanism such as

$$\bar{\pi} > \pi^e \Rightarrow \pi^e\uparrow \Rightarrow (r-\pi^e)\downarrow \Rightarrow i\uparrow \Rightarrow y\uparrow \tag{F5}$$

will work if the central bank's inflation targeting is sufficiently credible, even if the initial decrease of y induces the temporal decrease of π^e.

It is needless to say that the central bank's active monetary policy through large values of β_1 and β_2 will have a stabilizing effect because of the central bank's quick response to the changes of the economic environment.

The data on the Japanese economy in the 1990s and the 2000s suggest that the Japanese economy in this period suffered from the 'deflationary depression' with the 'liquidity trap' in which the nominal rate of interest is stuck to its nearly lower bound during such a long period of twenty years, because of the inactive monetary policy by BOJ without any commitment to the credible inflation targeting, which is described by the 'too late too small hypothesis' (see Asada 2010). This BOJ's inactive monetary policy in such a long period contrasts markedly with the quite active and aggressive monetary policies by FRB and the Bank of England after the 'subprime mortgage crisis' that was initiated in the USA in 2008 and rapidly propagated into the world outside the USA (see Hamada and Okada 2009 and Takahashi 2010).

The analysis in this section suggests the following results.

1   The *increase* of the parameter θ that is the weight of the employment consideration in the fiscal policy has a *stabilizing* effect.
2   The *increases* of the monetary policy parameters β_1 and β_2 have *stabilizing* effects.
3   The increase of the credibility parameter of the central bank's inflation targeting ξ has a *stabilizing* effect.

The increases of these parameter values may change the 'unstable' system into the 'stable' system. In this case, there exists at least one 'bifurcation point' at which the real part of at least one root becomes zero. On the other hand, from Eq. (32) and the inequality (C16) in **Appendix C** it follows that

$$\Delta(0) = a_5 > 0 \tag{37}$$

as long as $0 \le \theta < 1, \beta_1 > 0, \beta > 0 \le \xi \le 1$.

The inequality (37) means that the characteristic equation (32) does not have the real root such that $\lambda = 0$ In other words, at the bifurcation point a pair of pure imaginary roots exists, which means that the bifurcation of this system becomes 'Hopf bifurcation' type, and the Hopf bifurcation theorem ensures that the closed orbits exist at some parameter values that are near from such a bifurcation point.[15] In other words, the endogenous cyclical fluctuations occur at some intermediate ranges of the parameter values.

5 Two-dimensional model as a special case

The feedback mechanism (F3) in the previous section suggests that the *decrease* of the government expenditure per capital stock g coexists with the *increase* of the public debt–capital ratio b when the system is dynamically unstable. This observation is quite consistent with the empirical fact of the Japanese economy in the 1990s and the 2000s that is reported in section 1 of this chapter. In this section, we shall show that in fact this can occur in our model by using a simplified two-dimensional version of the model of the previous section.

Let us consider the special case of $\varepsilon = \gamma = 0$. In this case, we have $\pi = \pi^e =$ constant from equations (8) and (14). Now, we shall consider the further special case such as

$$\pi = \pi^e = \bar{\pi} = 0. \tag{38}$$

In this case, we can simplify a system of 'fundamental dynamic equations' (23) as follows.

i $\dot{g} = \tilde{f}_1(b,e) = \alpha\{\theta(\bar{e}-e)+(1-\theta)(\bar{b}-b)\}$

ii $\dot{r} = \tilde{f}_2(e) = \begin{cases} \beta_2(e-\bar{e}) & \text{if } r > 0 \\ \max[0, \beta_2(e-\bar{e})] & \text{if } r = 0 \end{cases}$

iii

$\dot{b} = \tilde{f}_3(g,r,b,e)$

$= \left[\dfrac{1}{1+\psi(r)y_b}\right]\left[\begin{array}{l} g - \tau y(r,b,g) + t_0 + \{r(1-\tau)-i(r)\}b - i(r)\psi(r)y(r,b,g) \\ -\{\psi'(r)y(r,b,g)+\psi(r)y_r\}\tilde{f}_2(e)-\psi(r)y_g\tilde{f}_1(b,e) \end{array}\right]$

iv

$\dot{e} = \tilde{f}_4(g,r,b,e)$

$= e\left[\left\{\dfrac{1}{y(r,b,g)}\right\}\{y_r\tilde{f}_2(e)+y_b\tilde{f}_3(g,r,b,e)+y_g\tilde{f}_1(b,e)\}+i(r)-n(e)\right]$ (39)

In this simplified four-dimensional version, the instability that is caused by the 'Mundell effect' on investment expenditure and the adaptive inflation expectation formation is excluded *by assumption*. Nevertheless, we can show that the equilibrium point of this system becomes dynamically unstable if the fiscal and monetary policy parameters θ and β_2 are sufficiently small under some additional conditions. To simplify the exposition, let us consider an extreme case in which the condition

$$\theta = \beta_2 = 0 \tag{40}$$

is satisfied. In this case, the government's fiscal policy does not respond to the employment condition but it only responds to the public debt condition, and the nominal rate of interest is fixed to some level by the central bank ($r=\bar{r}$). In such a case, the system (39) is reduced to the following system.

i $\dot{g} = F_1(b) = \alpha(\bar{b}-b)$

ii

$\dot{b} = F_2(g,b)$

$= \left[\dfrac{1}{1+\psi(\bar{r})y_b}\right]\left[\begin{array}{l} g - \tau y(\bar{r},b,g) + t_0 + \{\bar{r}(1-\tau)-i(\bar{r})\}b \\ -i(\bar{r})\psi(\bar{r})y(\bar{r},b,g) - \psi(\bar{r})y_g F_1(b) \end{array}\right]$

iii

$\dot{e} = F_3(g,b,e)$

$= e\left[\left\{\dfrac{1}{y(\bar{r},b,g)}\right\}\{y_b F_2(g,b)+y_g F_1(b)\}+i(\bar{r})-n(e)\right]$ (41)

Formally this is a three-dimensional system of differential equations. However, this is a *decomposable* system and the subsystem (i) and (ii) constitutes a two-dimensional closed system.

The equilibrium solution (g^*, b^*, e^*) of the system (41) is determined by the following system of equations.

$$b^* = \bar{b} \tag{42}$$

$$g^* - \{\tau + i(\bar{r})\psi(\bar{r})\} y(\bar{r}, \bar{b}, g^*) + t_0 + \{\bar{r}(1-\tau) - i(\bar{r})\}\bar{b} = 0 \tag{43}$$

$$i(\bar{r}) = n(e^*) \tag{44}$$

Let us write the left-hand side of Eq. (43) as $\Phi(g)$. Then, we have

$$\Phi(0) = -\{\tau + i(\bar{r})\psi(\bar{r})\} y(\bar{r}, \bar{b}, 0) + t_0 + \{\bar{r}(1-\tau) - i(\bar{r})\}\bar{b}, \tag{45}$$

$$\Phi'(g) = 1 - \{\tau + i(\bar{r})\psi(\bar{r})\} y_g = \frac{(1-\delta)(1-\tau) - i(\bar{r})\psi(\bar{r})}{1 - \delta(1-\tau)}. \tag{46}$$

Now, let us assume as follows.

Assumption 5

1   $(1-\delta)(1-\delta) > i(\bar{r})\psi(\bar{r})$.

2   $\{\tau + i(\bar{r})\psi(\bar{r})\} y(\bar{r}, \bar{b}, 0) > t_0 + \{\bar{r}(1-\tau) - i(\bar{r})\}\bar{b}$.

Under **Assumption 5**, we have

$$\Phi(0) < 0, \Phi'(g) > 0, \lim_{g \to +\infty} \Phi(g) = +\infty. \tag{47}$$

In this case, the existence of the *unique* equilibrium value $g^* > 0$ is ensured by continuity.

The remaining part of this section will be devoted to the analysis of the dynamic properties of the two-dimensional subsystem (41) (i), (ii). The Jacobian matrix of this two-dimensional system *at the equilibrium point* $(\tilde{J})$ becomes as follows.

$$\tilde{J} = \begin{bmatrix} 0 & -\alpha \\ F_{21} & F_{22} \end{bmatrix} \tag{48}$$

where

$$F_{21} = \left[\frac{1}{1+\psi(\bar{r})y_b}\right]\left[1-\{\tau+i(\bar{r})\psi(\bar{r})\}\,y_g\right]$$

$$= \frac{(1-\delta)(1-\tau)-i(\bar{r})\psi(\bar{r})}{\{1+\psi(\bar{r})y_b\}\{1-\delta(1-\tau)\}} > 0,$$

$$\text{(49)}$$

$$F_{22} = \left[\frac{1}{1+\psi(\bar{r})y_b}\right]\left[-\{\tau+i(\bar{r})\}\,y_b+\{\bar{r}(1-\tau)-i(\bar{r})\}+\alpha\psi(\bar{r})y_g\right]$$

$$= \frac{\alpha\psi(\bar{r})+\{\bar{r}(1-\tau)-i(\bar{r})\}\{1-\delta(1-\tau)\}-\{\tau+i(\bar{r})\psi(\bar{r})\}\delta(1-\tau)\bar{r}}{\{1+\psi(\bar{r})y_b\}\{1-\delta(1-\tau)\}}.$$

$$\text{(50)}$$

The characteristic equation of this two-dimensional subsystem *at the equilibrium point* becomes

$$\Delta_2(\lambda) \equiv \left|\lambda I - \tilde{J}\right| = \lambda^2 + d_1\lambda + d_2 = 0,$$

$$\text{(51)}$$

where

$$d_1 = -(\lambda_1 + \lambda_2) = -\operatorname{trace}\tilde{J} = -F_{22},$$

$$\text{(52)}$$

$$d_2 = \lambda_1\lambda_2 = \det\tilde{J} = \alpha F_{21} > 0$$

$$\text{(53)}$$

and λ_j $(j = 1, 2)$ are two roots of Eq. (51).

Proposition 3

1　Suppose that the inequality

$$\alpha\psi(\bar{r})+\{\bar{r}-i(\bar{r})\}\{1-\delta(1-\tau)\} < \{\tau+i(\bar{r})\psi(\bar{r})\}\delta(1-\tau)\bar{r}$$

$$\text{(54)}$$

is satisfied. Then, the equilibrium point of the subsystem (41) (i), (ii) is locally stable.

2　Suppose that the inequality

$$\alpha\psi(\bar{r})+\{\bar{r}(1-\tau)-i(\bar{r})\}\{1-\delta(1-\tau)\} > \{\tau+i(\bar{r})\psi(\bar{r})\}\delta(1-\tau)\bar{r}$$

$$\text{(55)}$$

is satisfied. Then, the equilibrium point of the subsystem (41) (i), (ii) is locally *totally* unstable.

Proof

1　In this case, we have $F_{22} < 0$ so that we obtain $d_1 = -(\lambda_1 + \lambda_2) > 0$ and $d_2 = \lambda_1\lambda_2 > 0$. These inequalities mean that the characteristic equation (51) has two roots with negative real parts. This implies the local stability of the equilibrium point.

2   In this case, we have $F_{22}>0$ so that we obtain $d_1=-(\lambda_1+\lambda_2)<0$ and $d_2=\lambda_1\lambda_2>0$. These inequalities mean that the characteristic equation (51) has two roots with positive real parts. This implies the local *total* instability of the equilibrium point.

This proposition implies that the equilibrium point of the two-dimensional sub-system (41) (i), (ii) becomes locally *totally unstable* whenever the fiscal policy parameter α is sufficiently large. In other words, the increase of α has a *destabilizing* effect. This proposition also implies that the 'Domar condition' $(\bar{r}(1-\tau)<i(\bar{r}))$ is a stabilizing factor and the 'anti-Domar condition' $(\bar{r}(1-\tau)>i(\bar{r}))$ is a *destabilizing* factor, although the 'Domar condition' is neither a sufficient nor a necessary condition for local stability.

Figures 6.6 and 6.7 are two possible phase diagrams of this system in which the 'instability condition' (55) is satisfied. Figure 6.6 describes the case in which the characteristic equation (51) has two positive real roots. Figure 6.7 describes the case in which the characteristic equation has a set of conjugate complex roots with positive real part.[16]

In the regions I and III in these figures, the variables g and b move to the same directions, but they move to the opposite directions in the regions II and IV. In the example that is described by Figure 6.6, the solution paths ultimately enter into the region II or the region IV. In the example that is described by Figure 6.7, the solution paths spend much time in the regions II and IV. These observations are consistent with the co-movement of the variables g and b in the Japanese economy in the 'lost twenty years' (the 1990s and the 2000s) that are reported in section 1 of this chapter.

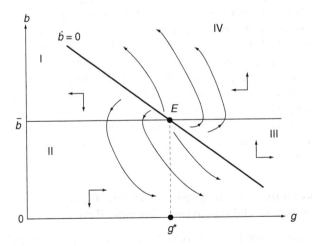

Figure 6.6 Instability case (1).

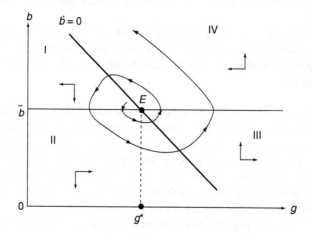

Figure 6.7 Instability case (2).

Incidentally, from Eq. (43) we obtain

$$\frac{\partial g^*}{\partial \tau} = \frac{\left[\underbrace{\left\{ \tau + i(\bar{r})\psi(\bar{r}) \right\} y_\tau}_{(-)} \right]}{\left[\underbrace{1 - \left\{ \tau + i(\bar{r})\psi(\bar{r}) \right\} y_g}_{(+)} \right]} < 0, \tag{56}$$

where $y_\tau = \partial y / \partial \tau < 0$. Eq. (56) implies that the increase of the marginal tax rate (τ) induces the decrease of the equilibrium value g^* which means that the increase of τ induces the leftward shifts of the $\dot{b} = 0$ curves in Figures 6.6 and 6.7. This observation provides us the following interesting result in case of instability.

Suppose that the initial combination of the variables (g, b) is at the equilibrium point (E) in Figure 6.6. Suppose, then, that the marginal tax rate (τ) is increased. The increase of τ induces the leftward shift of the $\dot{b} = 0$ curve, so that the point E is no longer the equilibrium point after the increase of τ. Then, the unstable disequilibrium dynamic process begins to activate, and paradoxically enough, the *increase* of the tax rate (τ) induces the *increase* of the debt–capital ratio (b) that is accompanied by the *decrease* of the government expenditure–capital ratio (g). This theoretical scenario is quite consistent with the empirical fact of the Japanese economy in the 1990s and the 2000s that is reported in section 1 of this chapter.

6 Critical remarks on the 'New Keynesian' dynamic theory in contrast to the traditional 'Old Keynesian' dynamic theory

At first glance, our model that has been developed in this chapter somewhat resembles the so-called 'New Keynesian' dynamic model that was developed by

Woodford (2003), Galí (2008) and others, which is at present the mainstream approach to macrodynamic modeling. For example, both models use some kind of IS curve, Phillips curve, and the 'Taylor rule' type interest rate monetary policy rule. However, there are important differences in these models. In particular, the macrodynamic model in the previous sections, which is based on the rather 'Old Keynesian' tradition in the sense of Tobin (1994), is immune from the anomalous dynamic behavior that is peculiar to the 'New Keynesian' dynamic model. In this section, we shall consider the prototype 'New Keynesian' dynamic model critically in comparison to the alternative 'Old Keynesian' dynamic model.

6.1 Formulation of the prototype 'New Keynesian' dynamic model

The simplest prototype version of the 'New Keynesian' dynamic model can be formulated as the following set of stochastic or deterministic difference equations.[17]

$$\pi_t = \pi_{t+1}^e + \varepsilon(y_t - \bar{y}) + \eta_t \tag{57}$$

$$y_t = y_{t+1}^e - \sigma(r_t - \pi_{t+1}^e - \rho_0) + \zeta_t \tag{58}$$

$$r_t = \rho_0 + \bar{\pi} + \beta_1(\pi_t - \bar{\pi}) + \beta_2(y_t - \bar{y}) \tag{59}$$

$$\pi_{t+1}^e = E_t \pi_{t+1}, \ y_{t+1}^e = E_t y_{t+1} \tag{60}$$

where the meanings of the symbols are as follows. π_t=rate of price inflation at the period t. π_{t+1}^e=rate of price inflation at the period $t+1$ that is expected at the period t (expected rate of price inflation). Y_t=real national income at the period t. $y_t = \log Y_t$. Y_{t+1}^e=real national income at the period $t+1$ that is expected at the period t (expected real national income). $y_{t+1}^e = \log Y_{t+1}^e$. r_t=nominal rate of interest at the period t. $r_t - \pi_{t+1}^e$=expected real rate of interest at the period t. ρ_0=equilibrium value of the real rate of interest (constant). $\bar{y}$=equilibrium value of y (constant). $\bar{\pi}$=target rate of price inflation that is set by the central bank (constant). All of the parameters ε, σ, β_1, and β_2 are positive, and the terms η_t and ζ_t are the stochastic or deterministic exogenous disturbances.

Equations (57) and (58) represent the 'New Keynesian Phillips curve' and the 'New Keynesian IS curve' respectively. Eq. (57) is usually derived from the optimal pricing strategy of the imperfectly competitive firms that allows for the cost of the price changes. Eq. (58) is usually derived from the optimizing behavior of the representative consumers, that is to say, this equation is in fact the log linear approximation of the representative consumers' 'Euler equation'.[18] Eq. (59) is a formalization of the 'Taylor rule' type interest rate monetary policy rule.[19] Eq. (60) represents the 'rational expectation' hypothesis. The symbol E_t represents the mathematical 'expected value' operator.

In the 'New Keynesian' literature, such a system with stochastic disturbances is called DSGE (Dynamic Stochastic General Equilibrium) model, but the similar system without stochastic disturbance is called DGE (Dynamic General Equilibrium) model.

If we assume that there is no exogenous disturbance in this model, that is,

$$\eta_t = \zeta_t = 0, \tag{61}$$

Eq. (60) becomes the following 'perfect foresight expectation' hypothesis.

$$\pi_{t+1}^e = \pi_{t+1}, \ y_{t+1}^e = y_{t+1}. \tag{62}$$

In this case, equations (57) and (58) become as follows.

$$\Delta \pi_t = \pi_{t+1} - \pi_t = \varepsilon(\bar{y} - y_t); \ \varepsilon > 0 \tag{63}$$

$$\Delta y_t = y_{t+1} - y_t = \sigma(r_t - \pi_{t+1} - \rho_0); \ \sigma > 0 \tag{64}$$

Substituting equations (59) and (63) into Eq. (64), we obtain the following two-dimensional system of difference equations.

i $\quad \Delta \pi_t = \pi_{t+1} - \pi_t = \varepsilon(\bar{y} - y_t) = \tilde{F}_1(y_t)$

ii $\quad \Delta y_t = y_{t+1} - y_t = \sigma\{(\beta_1 - 1)(\pi_t - \bar{\pi}) + (\varepsilon + \beta_2)(y_t - \bar{y})\} = \tilde{F}_2(\pi_t, y_t) \tag{65}$

Following the procedures by Asada, Chiarella, Flaschel and Proaño (2007) and Flaschel, Franke and Proaño (2008), let us approximate this system of difference equations by the following system of differential equations.

i $\quad \dot{\pi} = \varepsilon(\bar{y} - y) = \tilde{F}_1(y)$

ii $\quad \dot{y} = \sigma\{(\beta_1 - 1)(\pi - \bar{\pi}) + (\varepsilon + \beta_2)(y - \bar{y})\} = \tilde{F}_2(\pi, y) \tag{66}$

The equilibrium solution of this system (π^*, y^*) that satisfies $\dot{\pi} = \dot{y} = 0$ becomes

$$\pi^* = \bar{\pi}, \ y^* = \bar{y}, \tag{67}$$

and the Jacobian matrix of this system becomes

$$J^* = \begin{bmatrix} 0 & -\varepsilon \\ \sigma(\beta_1 - 1) & \sigma(\varepsilon + \beta_2) \end{bmatrix}. \tag{68}$$

Then, the characteristic equation becomes as follows.

$$\Gamma(\lambda) = |\lambda I - J^*| = \lambda^2 + v_1 \lambda + v_2 = 0 \tag{69}$$

where

$$v_1 = -\text{trace } J^* = -(\lambda_1 + \lambda_2) = -\sigma(\varepsilon + \beta_2) < 0, \tag{70}$$

$$v_2 = \det J^* = \lambda_1 \lambda_2 = \varepsilon\sigma(\beta_1 - 1), \tag{71}$$

$$D = v_1^2 - 4v_2 = \sigma\{\sigma(\varepsilon + \beta_2)^2 - 4\varepsilon(\beta_1 - 1)\}, \tag{72}$$

$\lambda_j (j = 1, 2)$ are two characteristic roots and D is the discriminant of this system.

The inequality (70) implies that this system has at least one characteristic root with positive real part. This means that the equilibrium point of this system is *always unstable* in the sense of the traditional stability/instability concept. More accurately, we have the following results.

Proposition 4

1 Suppose that $0 < \beta_1 < 1$. Then, the characteristic equation (69) has one positive real root and one negative real root. Namely, the equilibrium point of the system (66) becomes a saddle point.

2 Suppose that $1 < \beta_1 \leq 1 + \dfrac{\sigma(\varepsilon + \beta_2)^2}{4\varepsilon}$. Then, the characteristic equation (69) has two positive real roots. Namely, the equilibrium point of the system (66) becomes totally unstable, and any solution path that does not depart from the equilibrium point diverges monotonically.

3 Suppose that $1 + \dfrac{\sigma(\varepsilon + \beta_2)^2}{4\varepsilon} < \beta_1$. Then, the characteristic equation (69) has a set of complex roots with positive real part. Namely, the equilibrium point of the system (66) becomes totally unstable, and any solution path that does not depart from the equilibrium point diverges cyclically.

Proof

1 In this case, we have $\lambda_1 + \lambda_2 > 0$ and $\lambda_1 \lambda_2 < 0$ in view of the relationships (70) and (71). This means that the characteristic equation has a positive real root and a negative real root.

2 In this case, we have $\lambda_1 + \lambda_2 > 0$, $\lambda_1 \lambda_2 > 0$, and $D \geq 0$ in view of the relationships (70), (71), and (72). This means that the characteristic equation has two positive real roots.

3 In this case, we have $\lambda_1 + \lambda_2 > 0$, $\lambda_1 \lambda_2 > 0$, and $D < 0$ in view of the relationships (70), (71), and (72). This means that the characteristic equation has a set of complex roots with positive real part.

Figures 6.8–6.10 illustrate the phase diagrams in the cases (1)–(3) in this proposition.

6.2 The paradoxical characteristics of the prototype 'New Keynesian' dynamic model

In fact, there are several strange and paradoxical characteristics in the above-mentioned prototype 'New Keynesian' dynamic model, although they are not necessarily well understood among the economists. In this subsection, we shall comment on this problem briefly.

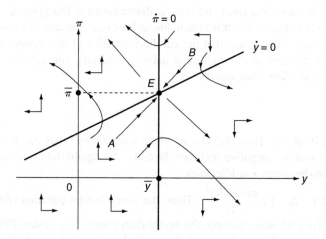

Figure 6.8 The case of $0<\beta_1<1$.

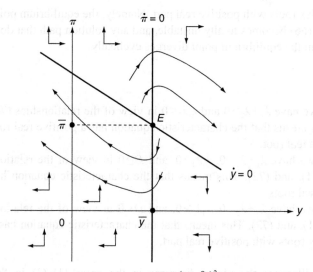

Figure 6.9 The case of $1<\beta_1<1+\dfrac{\sigma(\varepsilon+\beta_2)^2}{4\varepsilon}$.

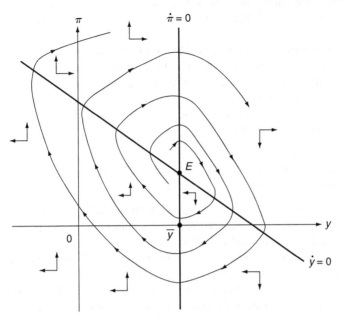

Figure 6.10 The case of $1+\dfrac{\sigma(\varepsilon+\beta_2)^2}{4\varepsilon}<\beta_1$.

6.2.1 'Sign-reversal' problems of the 'New Keynesian Phillips curve' and the 'New Keynesian IS curve'

Eq. (63) implies that the rate of inflation (π_t) continues to *accelerate* whenever the actual real output level (y_t) is *below* the 'natural' output level ($\bar{y}$), and π_t continues to *decelerate* whenever the level of y_t is *above* the level $\bar{y}$. This is the notorious 'sign reversal' problem of the 'New Keynesian Phillips curve' that was pointed out by Mankiw (2001) at the earlier stage of the development of the 'New Keynesian' dynamic theory (see also Flaschel and Schlicit 2006; Franke 2007; Asada *et al.* 2010). He writes as follows.

> Although the New Keynesian Phillips curve has many virtues, it also has one striking vice: It is completely at odds with the facts. In particular, it cannot come even close to explaining the dynamic effects of monetary policy on inflation and unemployment. This harsh conclusion shows up several places in the recent literature, but judging from the continued popularity of this model, I think that it is fair to say that its fundamental inconsistency with the facts is not very appreciated.
>
> (Mankiw 2001, p. C52)

Eq. (64) shows another type of 'sign reversal', that is to say, the real output (y_t) continues to *increase* whenever the actual (and expected) real rate of interest

$(r_t - \pi_{t+1})$ is *above* the equilibrium real rate of interest (ρ_0), and y_t continues to decrease whenever $r_t - \pi_{t+1}$ is below ρ_0. This is also unconvincing paradoxical behavior.

Anomalous dynamics that are produced by the combination of the 'New Keynesian Phillips curve' and the 'New Keynesian IS curve' are shown in Figures 6.8–6.10. These dynamics cause the 'deflationary boom' that is accompanied by the *increase* of the real output and the *decrease* of the rate of inflation or the 'inflationary depression' that is accompanied by the *decrease* of the real output and the *increase* of the rate of inflation.

6.2.2 Introduction of the 'jump variables' technique resolves the 'sign reversal' problems but it causes other paradoxes

In the traditional economic dynamic models, such as the model that was considered in the previous sections in this chapter, the initial values of all endogenous variables are the 'pre-determined variables' which are historically given. In this case, it is considered that the equilibrium point is locally 'stable' *if and only if* all characteristic roots of the system at the equilibrium point have negative real parts, and it is 'unstable' if *at least* one characteristic root has positive real part. **Proposition 4** means that the equilibrium point of the prototype 'New Keynesian' dynamic model is always 'unstable' in this traditional sense, and the anomalous behaviors of the main variables emerge in the process of the 'out of equilibrium' dynamics. However, the 'New Keynesian' economists could successfully conceal this anomalous dynamics by adopting the so called 'jump variables' technique.

Usually, in the 'New Keynesian' models both of two endogenous variables π and y are treated as the not-pre-determined 'jump variables' which can be freely 'chosen' by the economic agents in the model economy. Furthermore, it is supposed that only the initial values of the 'jump variables' that ensure the convergence to the equilibrium point are chosen by the economic agents.[20] Under this supposition, the equilibrium point becomes always 'stable' unlike the traditional interpretation. Instead, the system is called 'determinate' if the initial condition of the 'jump variables' that ensures the convergence to the equilibrium point is uniquely determined, and it is called 'indeterminate' if there exist the multiple combinations of the initial conditions of the 'jump variables' that ensure the convergence to the equilibrium point.[21]

In case of Figure 6.8, the system is 'stable' but 'indeterminate' in the 'New Keynesian' sense. Namely, any combination of the initial conditions in the 'saddle path' (path AE and BE) ensures the convergence to the equilibrium point. On the other hand, in the cases of Figure 6.9 and Figure 6.10, the system is 'stable' and 'determinate' in the 'New Keynesian' sense. Namely, the combination of the initial conditions that ensures the convergence to the equilibrium point is uniquely determined. In fact, in this case only the combination at the point E (the equilibrium point) can be chosen as the 'proper' set of initial conditions, and the combination (π, y) continues to stay at the equilibrium point indefinitely unless there is (stochastic or deterministic) exogenous disturbance.

Is the above 'New Keynesian' solution to the problem of instability by means of the 'jump variables' technique persuasive? We do not think so because of the following reasons. First, as Mankiw (2001) correctly pointed out, the rate of inflation (π) in the actual data in many countries is not the 'jump variable' that can jump conveniently, but it is the 'state variable' that moves continuously and slowly. He writes as follows: 'In these models of staggered price adjustment, the price level adjusts slowly, but the inflation rate can jump quickly. Unfortunately for the model, that is not what we see in data' (Mankiw 2001, p. C54).

A possible method to resolve this problem is to introduce the backward-looking 'expectation inertia' as well as the forward-looking 'rational' expectation. The typical approach is to replace the 'New Keynesian' Phillips curve (57) with the following equation (see, for example, Fuhler 1997 and Romer 2006, chap. 6, as well as the critical remark by Franke 2007).

$$\pi_t = \theta\pi_{t+1}^e + (1-\theta)\pi_{t-1} + \varepsilon(y_t - \overline{y}) + \eta_t; \quad 0 < \theta < 1 \tag{73}$$

This modified equation is somewhat similar to the 'Old Keynesian' treatment of the inflation expectation such as Eq. (14) in this chapter, but it is not clear whether this modification is consistent with the 'New Keynesian' hypothesis of 'rational' agents.

Second, as already noted, in the 'New Keynesian' setting of the 'jump variables', the endogenous fluctuation never occurs. In particular, the solution of the system sticks to the equilibrium point indefinitely unless there are the (stochastic or deterministic) exogenous disturbances in the case of 'determinacy' ($\beta_1 > 1$). In other words, the apparent 'dynamic' model is in fact reduced to the 'static' model in case of 'determinacy'. This means that the (stochastic or deterministic) exogenous disturbances are *indispensable* to cause some motion in this setting.[22]

6.2.3 The limit of the rationally behaved 'representative agent' approach

Some authors such as Kirman (1992) and Asada *et al.* (2010) criticize the methodology of the 'representative agent approach' that is adopted by the mainstream economic theorists, including the New Keynesians, which tries to explain the macroeconomic performance by the behavior of the single or homogeneous rational and omniscient 'representative agent(s)'. They assert that the macroeconomic phenomena should be interpreted as the result of the interaction of the bounded-rationally behaved heterogeneous agents. The spirit of the 'Old Keynesian' approach that was adopted in the previous sections of this chapter is consistent with this view. According to this view, we cannot rationalize the 'jump variables' technique as the instrument to describe the real-world macroeconomic behavior as the result of the interaction of the bounded-rationally behaved heterogeneous economic agents.[23] Let us quote from Kirman (1992) and Asada *et al.* (2010).

A tentative conclusion, at this point, would be that the representative agent approach is fatally flawed because it attempts to impose order on the economy through the concept of an omniscient individual. In reality, individuals operate in very small subsets of the economy and interact with those with whom they have dealings. It may well be that out of this local but interacting activity emerges some sort of self organization which provides regularity at the macroeconomic level. Cycles and fluctuations emerge not as the result of some substantial exogenous shock and the reaction to it of one individual, but as a natural result of interaction, together with occasional small change or 'mutations' in the behavior of some individual.

(Kirman 1992, pp. 232–233)

While the *microfoundation* of economic behavior is per se an important desideratum to be reflected also by behaviorally oriented macrodynamics, the use of 'representative' consumers and firms for the explanation of macroeconomic phenomena is too simplistic and also too narrow to allow for a proper treatment of what is *really* interesting on the economic behavior of economic agents—the interaction of heterogeneous agents—and it is also not detailed enough to discuss the various feedback channels present in the real world.... Indeed, agents are heterogeneous, form heterogeneous expectations along other lines than suggested by the rational expectations theory, and have different short-and long term views about the economy.

(Asada *et al.* 2010, pp. 205–206)

We can consider that the inflation expectation hypothesis that is expressed by Eq. (14) of this chapter is the simplest formalization of the heterogeneous expectation hypothesis that was suggested by Asada *et al.* (2010). In fact, they also adopted the similar expectation hypothesis in their book.

7 Concluding remarks

In this chapter, we presented a formal dynamic model in a Keynesian setting that is designed to interpret the Japanese long-term deflationary depression theoretically. We hope that this model is useful for the theoretical interpretation of the macroeconomic performance of other countries as well as Japan. We also provided a critical consideration of the mainstream 'New Keynesian' approach in contrast to our 'Old Keynesian' approach. Before closing this chapter, we shall remark on the following two topics.

7.1 On an extension to the open economy macrodynamic model

We cannot neglect the international aspect of the long-term deflationary depression of the Japanese economy. For example, Hamada and Okada (2009) pointed out that the excessively passive and inactive monetary policy of BOJ compared to the monetary policies of the central banks of other main countries caused the rapid appreciation of the Japanese yen, which aggravated the Japanese deflationary depression. To analyze such a problem formally, we must construct the 'open economy macrodynamic model' incorporating the dynamics of exchange rate, international trade and the international capital movement into the model. We can construct such a model by using the analytical framework that was developed by Asada *et al.* (2003). The dimension of the dynamic system will become at least six, even if we restrict to the relatively tractable 'small country' model, although such a model is still workable and computable.

7.2 On the 'dynamic optimization' approach to fiscal and monetary policies

In this chapter, we have *deliberately* avoided the 'dynamic optimization' approach to fiscal and monetary policies. A typical example of such an approach may be formulated as follows.

Suppose that the 'consolidated government', including the central bank, tries to control the dynamic paths of fiscal and monetary policy variables such as g, τ and r in order to minimize the following 'loss functional' subject to the static and dynamic constraints which are described by the equations (1)–(9) and (14).

$$L = \int_0^\infty \{\omega_1(\pi - \bar{\pi})^2 + \omega_2(e - \bar{e})^2 + \omega_3(b - \bar{b})^2\}e^{-vt}dt;$$

$$0 < \omega_j < 1 \ (j = 1,2,3), \ \sum_{j=1}^{3}\omega_j = 1, v > 0 \tag{74}$$

'Pontryagin's maximum principle' is applicable to solve such a kind of problem (see Gandolfo 2009; Dockner *et al.* 2000).

A variant of such an approach assumes that the government and the central bank have different objective functionals. Suppose, for example, the government tries to minimize

$$L_G = \int_0^\infty \{\theta_1(e - \bar{e})^2 + (1 - \theta_1)(b - \bar{b})^2\}e^{-v_1 t}dt; 0 < \theta_1 < 1, v_1 > 0 \tag{75}$$

and the central bank tries to minimize

$$L_{CB} = \int_0^\infty \{\theta_2(\pi - \bar{\pi})^2 + (1 - \theta_2)(e - \bar{e})^2\}e^{-v_2 t}dt; 0 < \theta_2 < 1, v_2 > 0 \tag{76}$$

Furthermore, suppose that the government controls the dynamic paths of g and τ, and the central bank controls the dynamic path of r. Also in this case, both the government and the central bank are subject to the constraints which are described by the equations (1)–(9) and (14). This is a typical situation in which the theory of differential game is applicable (see Dockner *et al.* 2000).

In typical situations of both models, the solution paths will converge to the 'long run equilibrium position' such that $\pi = \bar{\pi}$, $e = \bar{e}$, and $b = \bar{b}$. In these situations, the deflationary depression will not occur if the target rate of inflation $\bar{\pi}$ is sufficiently large.

It is important to note that both of the above-mentioned models require that the government and the central bank have omniscient power with the accurate knowledge of the macroeconomic structure. In fact, however, they do not have such an omniscient power. For example, in Japan, the deflationary depression *did* occur in the 1990s and the 2000s, which means that the Japanese government and BOJ as well as the Japanese public did not have such an omniscient power.

It is not practical to stick to the 'optimality' criterion to evaluate the performance of the fiscal and monetary policies because of the following two reasons. First, it is in fact impossible that the government and the central bank know the correct parameter values and the correct functional forms that characterize the macroeconomic structure. Unless they know the accurate information of such parameter values and functional forms, they cannot design the 'optimal' policies. Second, the former 'optimal' policy will be no longer optimal even if only the slight changes of the parameter values are caused. In this sense, the 'optimal' criterion is not robust and such a criterion is actually unreliable. Instead, in section 4 of this chapter, we used another, more practical criterion of policy evaluation—that is, the 'permissibility' criterion.

The 'permissibility' criterion, which is described under **Definition** in section 4 of this chapter, is more generous to the policy makers than the 'optimality' criterion because there are many non-optimal but permissible policies. Furthermore, the 'permissibility' criterion is more robust than the 'optimality' criterion because a policy mix of the fiscal and monetary policies can be 'permissible' in a wide range of combinations of the parameter values. Nevertheless, as already noted in section 4 of this chapter, we must say that the Japanese fiscal and monetary policies in the 1990s and the 2000s were 'impermissible' even if we use our rather generous criterion.

Acknowledgment

This chapter is based on a thoroughly developed and extended version of the materials which are contained in Asada (2011). In particular, the mathematical proofs in this chapter are absent in Asada (2011). This research was financially supported by the Japan Society for the Promotion of Science (Grant-in-Aid for Scientific Research (C) 25380238) and Chuo University Grant for Special Research. Needless to say, only the author is responsible for possible remaining errors.

Appendices

Appendix A: Partial derivatives

All of the following partial derivatives are evaluated *at the equilibrium point.*

$$f_{41} = \frac{\partial f_4}{\partial g} = \left[\frac{1}{1 + \psi(r) \, y_b} \right] \left[\frac{(1 - \delta)(1 - \tau) - \{\overline{\pi} + n(\overline{e})\}\psi(r)}{1 - \delta(1 - \tau)} \right] > 0. \tag{A1}$$

$$f_{42} = \frac{\partial f_4}{\partial r} = \left[\frac{1}{1 + \psi(r) \, y_b} \right] \left[\begin{array}{c} -\tau y_r + (1 - i_{r - \pi^e})\overline{b} - i_{r - \pi^e} \psi(r) y \\ -\{\overline{\pi} + n(\overline{e})\}\psi(r) y_r \end{array} \right]. \tag{A2}$$

$$f_{43} = \frac{\partial f_4}{\partial \pi^e}$$

$$= \left[\frac{1}{1 + \psi(r) \, y_b} \right] \left[\begin{array}{c} -\tau y_{\pi^e} - \overline{b} - \psi(r) y + i_{r - \pi^e} \{\overline{b} + \psi(r)y\} \\ -\{\psi'(r) y + \psi(r) y_r\} \beta_1 + \psi(r) y_{\pi^e} \gamma \xi \end{array} \right]. \tag{A3}$$

$$f_{44} = \frac{\partial f_4}{\partial b}$$

$$= \left[\frac{1}{1 + \psi(r) \, y_b} \right] \left[\begin{array}{c} -\tau y_b + \{\rho * (1 - \tau) - \tau \overline{\pi} - n(\overline{e})\} \\ -\{\overline{\pi} + n(\overline{e})\}\psi(r) y_b + \psi(r) y_g \, \alpha(1 - \theta) \end{array} \right]. \tag{A4}$$

$$f_{45} = \frac{\partial f_4}{\partial e}$$

$$= \left[\frac{1}{1 + \psi(r) \, y_g} \right] \left[\begin{array}{c} -\varepsilon\{\overline{b} + \psi(r)y\} - \{\psi'(r) y + \psi(r) y_r\}(\beta_1 \varepsilon + \beta_2) \\ + \psi(r)\{-y_{\pi^e} \gamma(1 - \xi)\varepsilon + y_g \, \alpha\theta\} \end{array} \right]. \tag{A5}$$

$$f_{51} = \frac{\partial f_5}{\partial g} = \frac{\overline{e}}{y} y_b f_{41} > 0. \tag{A6}$$

$$f_{52} = \frac{\partial f_5}{\partial r} = \overline{e}\left[\frac{1}{y} y_b f_{42} + i_{r - \pi^e} \right]. \tag{A7}$$

$$f_{53} = \frac{\partial f_5}{\partial \pi^e} = \overline{e}\left[\frac{1}{y}(y_r \beta_1 - y_{\pi^e} \gamma \varepsilon + y_b f_{43}) - i_{r - \pi^e} \right]. \tag{A8}$$

$$f_{54} = \frac{\partial f_5}{\partial b} = \frac{\bar{e}}{y}\left[\underset{(+)}{y_b f_{44}} - \underset{(+)}{y_g \alpha(1-\theta)}\right]. \tag{A9}$$

$$f_{55} = \frac{\partial f_5}{\partial e} = \bar{e}\left[\frac{1}{y}\left\{\underset{(+)}{y_r(\beta_1\varepsilon+\beta_2)} + \underset{(+)}{y_g \gamma(1-\zeta)\varepsilon} + \underset{(+)}{y_b f_{45}} - y_g \alpha\theta\right\} - \underset{(+\text{ or }0)}{n_e}\right]. \tag{A10}$$

Appendix B: Proof of Proposition 1

Suppose that $\theta=\beta_1=\beta_2=\zeta=0$. Then, we have the following relationships in view of equations (A4), (A5) and (A10), where f_{45} is *independent of* the parameter value α.

$$a_1 = -f_{44} - f_{55}$$

$$= \left[\underset{(+)}{\frac{1}{1+\psi(r)y_b}}\right]\left[\underset{(+)}{\tau y_b} + \{n(\bar{e})-p^*\} + \{\bar{\pi}+n(\bar{e})\}\underset{(+)}{\psi(r)y_b} - \underset{(+)}{\psi(r)y_g\alpha}\right]$$

$$+ \bar{e}\left[\frac{1}{y}\left\{-\underset{(+)}{y_g\gamma\varepsilon} - \underset{(+)}{y_b f_{45}}\right\} + \underset{(+\text{ or }0)}{n_e}\right] \tag{B1}$$

Eq. (B1) means that we have $a_1<0$ for all sufficiently large values of $\alpha>0$ in case of $\theta=\beta_1=\beta_2=\zeta=0$, which violates one of a set of the necessary conditions for local stability (36). By continuity of the value a_1 with respect to the parameter values, we have $a_1<0$ for all sufficiently large values of $a>0$ even if the parameter values θ, β_1, β_2 and ζ are positive, as long as these parameter values are sufficiently small.

Appendix C: Proof of Proposition 2

Step 1

Assume **Assumptions 1–4**, and suppose that $\theta=\zeta=1$. Then, the Jacobian matrix (31) becomes as follows.

$$J = \begin{bmatrix} 0 & 0 & 0 & 0 & -\alpha \\ 0 & 0 & \beta_1 & 0 & \beta_1\varepsilon+\beta_2 \\ 0 & 0 & -\gamma & 0 & 0 \\ f_{41} & f_{42} & f_{43} & f_{44} & f_{45} \\ f_{51} & f_{52} & f_{53} & f_{54} & f_{55} \end{bmatrix} \tag{C1}$$

In this case, we can write the characteristic equation (32) as

$$\Delta(\lambda) \equiv |\lambda I - J| = |\lambda I - J_4|(\lambda+\gamma) = 0, \tag{C2}$$

where

$$J_4 = \begin{bmatrix} 0 & 0 & 0 & -\alpha \\ 0 & 0 & 0 & \beta_1\varepsilon+\beta_2 \\ f_{41} & f_{42} & f_{44} & f_{45}(\beta_1,\beta_2) \\ f_{51} & f_{52} & f_{54} & f_{55}(\beta_1,\beta_2) \end{bmatrix}. \tag{C3}$$

Under **Assumptions 1–4** and $\theta=1$, we have the following set of inequalities in view of **Appendix A**.

$$f_{41}>0, f_{42}>0, f_{44}<0, f_{51}>0, f_{52}<0, f_{54}<0 \tag{C4}$$

The characteristic equation (C2) has a negative real root $\lambda_5=-\gamma$, and other four roots are determined by the following equation.

$$\Delta_4(\lambda) \equiv |\lambda I - J_4| = \lambda^4 + b_1\lambda^3 + b_2\lambda^2 + b_3\lambda + b_4 = 0, \tag{C5}$$

where

$$b_1 = -\text{trace}\, J_4 = \underset{(-)}{- f_{44} - f_{55}(\beta_1,\beta_2)}, \tag{C6}$$

b_2 = sum of all principal second-order minors of J_4

$$= \begin{vmatrix} 0 & 0 \\ 0 & 0 \end{vmatrix} + \begin{vmatrix} 0 & 0 \\ f_{41} & f_{44} \end{vmatrix} + \begin{vmatrix} 0 & -\alpha \\ f_{51} & f_{55} \end{vmatrix} + \begin{vmatrix} 0 & 0 \\ f_{42} & f_{44} \end{vmatrix} + \begin{vmatrix} 0 & \beta_1\varepsilon+\beta_2 \\ f_{52} & f_{55} \end{vmatrix} + \begin{vmatrix} f_{44} & f_{45} \\ f_{54} & f_{55} \end{vmatrix}$$

$$= \underset{(+)}{\alpha f_{51}} \underset{(-)\ (-)}{- (\beta_1\varepsilon+\beta_2) f_{52} + f_{44}f_{55}(\beta_1,\beta_2)} \underset{(-)}{- f_{45}(\beta_1,\beta_2) f_{54}}, \tag{C7}$$

b_3 = −(sum of all principal third-order minors of J_4)

$$= - \begin{vmatrix} 0 & 0 & \beta_1\varepsilon+\beta_2 \\ f_{42} & f_{44} & f_{45} \\ f_{52} & f_{54} & f_{55} \end{vmatrix} - \begin{vmatrix} 0 & 0 & -\alpha \\ f_{41} & f_{44} & f_{45} \\ f_{51} & f_{54} & f_{55} \end{vmatrix} -$$

$$\begin{vmatrix} 0 & 0 & -\alpha \\ 0 & 0 & \beta_1\varepsilon+\beta_2 \\ f_{51} & f_{52} & f_{55} \end{vmatrix} - \begin{vmatrix} 0 & 0 & 0 \\ 0 & 0 & 0 \\ f_{41} & f_{42} & f_{44} \end{vmatrix} \tag{C8}$$

$$= -(\beta_1\varepsilon+\beta_2) \begin{vmatrix} f_{42} & f_{44} \\ f_{52} & f_{54} \end{vmatrix} + \alpha \begin{vmatrix} f_{41} & f_{44} \\ f_{51} & f_{54} \end{vmatrix}$$

$$= (\beta_1\varepsilon+\beta_2)\underset{(+)\ (-)}{(- f_{42}f_{54})} + \alpha(\underset{(+)\ (-)}{f_{41}f_{54}} \underset{(-)\ (+)}{- f_{44}f_{51}}),$$

$$b_4 = \det J_4 = \alpha \begin{vmatrix} 0 & 0 & 0 \\ f_{41} & f_{42} & f_{44} \\ f_{51} & f_{52} & f_{54} \end{vmatrix} = 0. \tag{C9}$$

Step 2

Substituting Eq. (C9) into Eq. (C5), we obtain

$$\Delta_4(\lambda) = (\lambda^3 + b_1\lambda^2 + b_2\lambda + b_3)\lambda = 0. \tag{C10}$$

This means that the characteristic equation (C10) has a real root $\lambda_4 = 0$ and other three roots are determined by the following equation.

$$\Delta_3(\lambda) \equiv \lambda^3 + b_1\lambda^2 + b_2\lambda + b_3 = 0 \tag{C11}$$

Suppose that either of the monetary policy parameter values β_1 or β_2 is sufficiently large. In this case, we have $f_{45}(\beta_1, \beta_2) > 0$ and $f_{55}(\beta_1, \beta_2) < 0$ in view of equations (A5), (A10) and **Assumption 4**. Then, we have the following set of inequalities if either of β_1 or β_2 is sufficiently large.

$$b_j > 0 \quad (j = 1, 2, 3) \tag{C12}$$

On the other hand, we can write $b_1 b_2 - b_3$ as

$$b_1 b_2 - b_3 = A_1(\beta_1\varepsilon + \beta_2)^2 + A_2(\beta_1\varepsilon + \beta_2) + A_3; \ A_1 > 0, \tag{C13}$$

where A_j ($j = 1, 2, 3$) are *independent of* the parameters β_1 and β_2. Therefore, we have a set of the Routh–Hurwitz conditions

$$b_j > 0 \ (j = 1, 2, 3), \ b_1 b_2 - b_3 > 0 \tag{C14}$$

if either of the parameter values β_1 or β_2 is sufficiently large. This means that the characteristic equation (C11) has three roots with negative real parts if either of β_1 or β_2 is sufficiently large (see Gandolfo 2009, chap. 16, for the Routh-Hurwitz conditions). In this case, the characteristic equation (32) in the text has four roots with negative real parts $(\lambda_1, \lambda_2, \lambda_3, \lambda_5)$ and a real root $\lambda_4 = 0$ if $\theta = \xi = 1$ and either of β_1 or β_2 is sufficiently large.

It follows from the continuity that the real parts of *at least* four roots of Eq. (32) are negative when either of β_1 or β_2 is sufficiently large even if $0 < \theta < 1$ and $0 < \xi \le 1$, as long as θ and ξ are sufficiently close to 1.

Step 3

Eq. (35) in the text becomes as follows in view of equations (31) and (32).

$$a_5 = -\prod_{j=1}^{5} \lambda_j = -\det J = \alpha\gamma \begin{vmatrix} 0 & 0 & 0 & 1-\theta & \theta \\ 0 & 0 & \beta_1 & 0 & \beta_1\varepsilon + \beta_2 \\ 0 & 0 & -\xi & 0 & (1-\xi)\varepsilon \\ f_{41} & f_{42} & f_{43} & f_{44} & f_{45} \\ f_{51} & f_{52} & f_{53} & f_{54} & f_{55} \end{vmatrix}$$

$$= \alpha\gamma\left\{-(1-\theta)\begin{vmatrix} 0 & 0 & \beta_1 & \beta_1\varepsilon + \beta_2 \\ 0 & 0 & -\xi & (1-\xi)\varepsilon \\ f_{41} & f_{42} & f_{43} & f_{45} \\ f_{51} & f_{52} & f_{53} & f_{55} \end{vmatrix} + \theta\begin{vmatrix} 0 & 0 & \beta_1 & 0 \\ 0 & 0 & -\xi & 0 \\ f_{41} & f_{42} & f_{43} & f_{44} \\ f_{51} & f_{52} & f_{53} & f_{54} \end{vmatrix}\right\} \quad (C15)$$

$$= \alpha\gamma(1-\theta)\left\{-\beta_1\begin{vmatrix} 0 & 0 & (1-\xi)\varepsilon \\ f_{41} & f_{42} & f_{45} \\ f_{51} & f_{52} & f_{55} \end{vmatrix} + (\beta_1\varepsilon + \beta_2)\begin{vmatrix} 0 & 0 & -\xi \\ f_{41} & f_{42} & f_{43} \\ f_{51} & f_{52} & f_{53} \end{vmatrix}\right\}$$

$$= -\alpha\gamma(1-\theta)\left\{\beta_1(1-\xi)\varepsilon + (\beta_1\varepsilon + \beta_2)\xi\right\}\begin{vmatrix} f_{41} & f_{42} \\ f_{51} & f_{52} \end{vmatrix}$$

$$= \alpha\gamma(1-\theta)\left\{\beta_1(1-\xi)\varepsilon + (\beta_1\varepsilon + \beta_2)\xi\right\}(-f_{41}f_{52} + f_{42}f_{51})$$

$$= -\alpha(1-\theta)\left\{\beta_1(1-\xi)\varepsilon + (\beta_1\varepsilon + \beta_2)\xi\right\}\overline{e}\underset{(+)}{f_{41}}\underset{(-)}{i_{r-\pi^e}}$$

This means that we always have

$$a_5 = -\prod_{j=1}^{5} \lambda_j > 0 \qquad (C16)$$

as long as $0 \leq \theta < 1$, $\beta_1 > 0$, $\beta_2 > 0$, and $0 \leq \xi \leq 1$.

From this fact and the conclusion of **Step 2**, it follows that all five roots of the characteristic equation (32) in the text have negative real parts under **Assumptions 1–4** if the conditions (1)–(3) in **Proposition 2** are satisfied. This proves **Proposition 2**.

Appendix D: On the concepts of stability, instability, determinacy and indeterminacy in dynamic economic models

In this appendix, we explain the concepts of stability, instability, determinacy and indeterminacy, mainly referring to Blanchard and Kahn (1980). These concepts play crucial roles in the recent mainstream macrodynamic theory such as 'New Keynesian' theory, although these concepts are rarely correctly understood even by the economists who are not deeply committing to these problems. Blanchard and Kahn (1980) use a system of difference equations in their explanation. But, in this appendix, we use a system of differential equations, which is more appropriate for the models in this chapter.

Let us consider the following system of linear differential equations.[24]

$$\dot{x} = Ax + b \tag{D1}$$

where A is $(n \times n)$ matrix, b is $(n \times 1)$ vector, and x is $(n \times 1)$ vector of the endogenous variables. We can write the characteristic equation of this system as follows.

$$\varphi(\lambda) \equiv |\lambda I - A| = \lambda^n + a_1 \lambda^{n-1} + \cdots + a_{n-1} \lambda + a_n = 0 \tag{D2}$$

Definition D1

The root of the characteristic equation (D2) that has positive real part is called 'unstable root', and the root of (D2) that has negative real part is called 'stable root'.[25]

Assumption D1

The characteristic equation (D2) has u unstable roots and $(n - u)$ stable roots, where $0 \leq u \leq n$.

Assumption D1 implies that the characteristic equation (D2) does not have the real root such that $\lambda = 0$. In this case, we have $\varphi(0) = |-A| = (-1)^n |A| \neq 0$, which means that $|A| \neq 0$ so that the inverse matrix A^{-1} exists. Then, the system (D1) has the *unique* equilibrium point x^* such that

$$x^* = -A^{-1}b. \tag{D3}$$

In the traditional dynamic economic models such as the 'Old Keynesian' dynamic model, the initial conditions of all endogenous variables $x(0)$ are fixed. In this case, the equilibrium point of the system is considered to be 'stable' *if and only if* $u = 0$, and it is considered to be 'unstable' if $u \geq 1$. However, in the recent mainstream dynamic economic models such as the 'New Keynesian' dynamic model, it is considered that some of the endogenous variables are 'jump variables', the initial conditions of which can be freely chosen by the economic agents.

Definition D2

If the initial condition of some variable is pre-fixed, such a variable is called the 'pre-determined variable' or the 'state variable'. If the initial condition of some variable is not pre-fixed but it can be freely chosen, such a variable is called the 'not-pre-determined variable' or the 'jump variable'.

Definition D3

1 Suppose that the solution path of the system (D1) converges to the equilibrium point if the initial conditions of the 'jump variables' are appropriately chosen. Then, the equilibrium point of this system is said to be 'stable'.

Suppose that the solution path of the system (D1) cannot converge to the equilibrium point irrespective of the initial conditions of the 'jump variables'. Then, the equilibrium point of this system is said to be 'unstable'.

2 Suppose that the equilibrium point of the system (D1) is 'stable' in the sense of **Definition D3** (1), and that there exists a *unique* set of the initial conditions of the 'jump variables' that ensures the convergence to the equilibrium point. Then, this system is said to be 'determinate'.

3 Suppose that the equilibrium point of the system (D1) is 'stable' in the sense of **Definition D3** (1), and that there exist *multiple* sets of the initial conditions of the 'jump variables' that ensure the convergence to the equilibrium point. Then, this system is said to be 'indeterminate'.

Blanchard and Kahn (1980) proved the following results under **Assumption D1**.[26]

Theorem D1

Let the number of the 'jump variables' of the system (D1) be j $(0 \leq j \leq n)$. Then, we have the following results (1)–(3).

1 Suppose that $j = u$. In this case, the equilibrium point of this system is 'stable' and this system is 'determinate'.

2 Suppose that $j > u$. In this case, the equilibrium point of this system is 'stable' and this system is 'indeterminate'.

3 Suppose that $j < u$. In this case, the equilibrium point of this system is 'unstable'.

In the traditional dynamic economic models such as 'Old Keynesian' dynamic models, it is supposed that $j = 0$. In this case, the equilibrium point of the system becomes 'stable' and the system becomes 'determinate' *if and only if* $u = 0$. The equilibrium point of this system becomes 'unstable' whenever $u > 0$. The system cannot be 'indeterminate' in case of $j = 0$. However, the possibility of the 'indeterminacy' arises in case of $j > 0$. Figures D1–D3 illustrate each possibility in the case of $n = 2$.

First, let us consider the case of $j = 0$. In this case, (1) the equilibrium point is 'stable' and the system is 'determinate' in the examples of Figure D1, and (2) the equilibrium point is 'unstable' in the examples of Figures D2 and D3. In this case, the system cannot be 'indeterminate'. This case corresponds to the traditional dynamic economic models.

Next, let us consider the case of $j = 1$. In this case, (1) the equilibrium point is 'stable' and the system is 'indeterminate' in the examples of Figure D1, (2) the

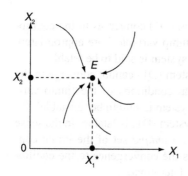

(a) Two negative real roots

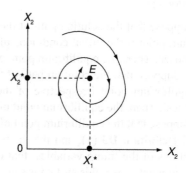

(b) A set of complex roots with negative real part

Figure D1 The case of $u=0$.

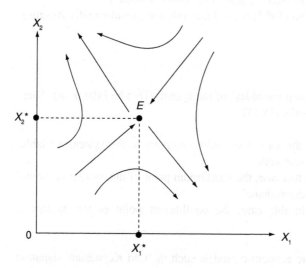

Figure D2 The case of $u=1$ (one positive real root and one negative real root).

equilibrium point is 'stable' and the system is 'determinate' in the example of Figure D2, and (3) the equilibrium point is 'unstable' in the examples of Figure D3.

Finally, let us consider the case of $j=2$. In this case, (1) the equilibrium point is 'stable' and the system is 'indeterminate' in the examples of Figures D1 and D2, and (2) the equilibrium point is 'stable' and 'determinate' in the examples of Figure D3. In this case, the equilibrium point cannot be 'unstable'. In fact, in this case the combination of the endogenous variables that is always stuck to the equilibrium point (the point E) is chosen as the 'solution' of the system in case of 'determinacy'. This case corresponds to the 'New Keynesian' dynamic model that was explained in section 6 of this chapter.

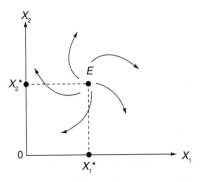

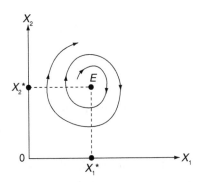

(a) Two positive real roots

(b) A set of complex roots with positive real part

Figure D3 The case of $u=2$.

Incidentally, in the two-dimensional dynamic system that was formulated in section 5 of this chapter, we have $u=2$ if the fiscal policy parameter α is sufficiently large. In this model, it is supposed that $j=0$ following the 'Old Keynesian' tradition. Therefore, the equilibrium point of this system is 'unstable' in the sense of **Definition D3** (1). What will occur, however, if we allow for the existence of the 'jump variable' like the 'New Keynesian' dynamic model? The endogenous variables in this system are the government expenditure–capital ratio (g), which is the ratio of a flow variable relative to a stock variable, and the public debt–capital ratio (b), which is the ratio of a stock variable relative to another stock variable. Following the mainstream method of economic modeling, the flow variable can be a 'jump variable', but the stock variable is considered to be a pre-determined variable that cannot jump. Therefore, in this model we have $0\leq j\leq 1$ even if the possibility of the existence of the 'jump variable' is allowed for, because b cannot jump. This means that the equilibrium point of this system is 'unstable' even if we allow for the possibility of the existence of the 'jump variable'.

Appendix E: An analysis of the motion that is caused by the exogenous disturbances in the 'New Keynesian' setting

Suppose that the term η_t in Eq. (57) is absent but the term ζ_t in Eq. (58) exists. Furthermore, suppose that the term ζ_t does not represent the stochastic disturbance but it represents the deterministic disturbance. If we adopt the continuous time version, we must replace Eq. (66) with the following system of equations.

i $\quad \dot{\pi} = \varepsilon(\bar{y} - y)$

ii $\quad \dot{y} = \sigma\{(\beta_1 - 1)(\pi - \bar{\pi}) + (\varepsilon + \beta_2)(y - \bar{y})\} - \zeta$ $\qquad$ (E1)

Now, let us assume

$$\pi(t) = \bar{\pi}, \ y(t) = \bar{y} \text{ for } t \in [0, t_0) \tag{E2}$$

and

$$\zeta(t) = \begin{cases} 0 & \text{for } t \in [0, t_0), \\ \zeta(t_0) = \text{given} \neq 0 & \text{at } t = t_0, \\ \zeta(t_0) e^{-\kappa(t-t_0)} & \text{for } t \in (t_0, +\infty), \end{cases} \tag{E3}$$

where $\kappa > 0$. This means that the equilibrium point is attained without disturbance up to the time $t = t_0$, the abrupt exogenous disturbance on the output occurs at $t = t_0$, and the disturbance continues to exist but it decreases exponentially. Then, the dynamics of the system for the time periods $t \in [t_0, +\infty)$ can be described by the following decomposable three-dimensional system of the differential equations.

i $\dot{\pi} = \varepsilon(\bar{y} - y) = \tilde{F}_1(y)$

ii $\dot{y} = \sigma\{(\beta_1 - 1)(\pi - \bar{\pi}) + (\varepsilon + \beta_2)(y - \bar{y})\} - \zeta = \tilde{F}_2(\pi, y, \zeta)$

iii $\dot{\zeta} = -\kappa\zeta; \kappa > 0, \zeta(t_0) = \text{given} \neq 0$ $\qquad\qquad$ (E4)

The Jacobian matrix of this system becomes

$$J^{**} = \begin{bmatrix} 0 & -\varepsilon & 0 \\ \sigma(\beta_1 - 1) & \sigma(\varepsilon + \beta_2) & -1 \\ 0 & 0 & -\kappa \end{bmatrix} \tag{E5}$$

and the characteristic equation becomes as follows.

$$\tilde{\Gamma}(\lambda) = |\lambda I - J^{**}| = |\lambda I - J^*|(\lambda + \kappa) = 0 \tag{E6}$$

where

$$J^* = \begin{bmatrix} 0 & -\varepsilon \\ \sigma(\beta_1 - 1) & \sigma(\varepsilon + \beta_2) \end{bmatrix}. \tag{E7}$$

The characteristic equation (E6) has the root $\lambda_3 = -\kappa < 0$ and the other two roots are determined by the equation

$$\Gamma(\lambda) = |\lambda I - J^*| = 0, \tag{E8}$$

which is the same as Eq. (69) in the text of this chapter.

For the purpose of illustration, let us consider the case of

$$1 < \beta_1 < 1 + \frac{\sigma(\varepsilon + \beta_2)^2}{4\varepsilon}. \tag{E9}$$

We know from **Proposition 4** in the text that Eq. (E8) has two positive real roots such that $\lambda_1 > \lambda_2 > 0$ in this case.

The general solution of a system of linear differential equations (E4) for the time periods $t \geq t_0$ becomes as follows (see Gandolfo 2009, chap. 18).

$$\begin{bmatrix} \pi(t) \\ y(t) \\ \zeta(t) \end{bmatrix} = \sum_{j=1}^{3} \begin{bmatrix} A_j \\ B_j \\ C_j \end{bmatrix} e^{\lambda_j(t-t_0)} + \begin{bmatrix} \bar{\pi} \\ \bar{y} \\ 0 \end{bmatrix} \tag{E10}$$

where $\lambda_1 > \lambda_2 > 0$, $\lambda_3 = -\kappa < 0$, and we have the relationships

$$\begin{bmatrix} \lambda_j & \varepsilon & 0 \\ -\sigma(\beta_1 - 1) & \lambda_j - \sigma(\varepsilon + \beta_2) & 1 \\ 0 & 0 & \lambda_j + \kappa \end{bmatrix} \begin{bmatrix} A_j \\ B_j \\ C_j \end{bmatrix} = \begin{bmatrix} 0 \\ 0 \\ 0 \end{bmatrix} \quad (j = 1, 2, 3). \tag{E11}$$

By using the relationships (E11), we can rewrite Eq. (E10) as follows.

$$\begin{bmatrix} \pi(t) \\ y(t) \\ \zeta(t) \end{bmatrix} = \begin{bmatrix} 1 \\ -\lambda_1/\varepsilon \\ 0 \end{bmatrix} A_1 e^{\lambda_1(t-t_0)} + \begin{bmatrix} 1 \\ -\lambda_2/\varepsilon \\ 0 \end{bmatrix} A_2 e^{\lambda_2(t-t_0)} +$$

$$\begin{bmatrix} \varepsilon/[\varepsilon\sigma(\beta_1 - 1) + \kappa\{\kappa + \sigma(\varepsilon + \beta_2)\}] \\ \kappa/[\varepsilon\sigma(\beta_1 - 1) + \kappa\{\kappa + \sigma(\varepsilon + \beta_2)\}] \\ 1 \end{bmatrix} C_3 e^{-\kappa(t-t_0)} + \begin{bmatrix} \bar{\pi} \\ \bar{y} \\ 0 \end{bmatrix} \tag{E12}$$

The constants A_1, A_2, and C_3 in this equation depend on the initial conditions $(\pi(t_0), y(t_0), \zeta(t_0))$. In fact, we have the following relationships from this equation.

i $\pi(t_0) = A_1 + A_2 + \dfrac{\varepsilon}{\varepsilon\sigma(\beta_1 - 1) + \kappa\{\kappa + \sigma(\varepsilon + \beta_2)\}} \zeta(t_0) + \bar{\pi}$

ii $y(t_0) = -\dfrac{\lambda_1}{\varepsilon} A_1 - \dfrac{\lambda_2}{\varepsilon} A_2 + \dfrac{\kappa}{\varepsilon\sigma(\beta_1 - 1) + \kappa\{\kappa + \sigma(\varepsilon + \beta_2)\}} \zeta(t_0) + \bar{y}$

iii $\zeta(t_0) = C_3$ (E13)

If all of the initial conditions $(\pi(t_0), y(t_0),$ and $\zeta(t_0))$ are pre-determined, we can determine A_1, A_2 and C_3 by solving Eq. (E13). However, in the 'New Keynesian' setting, only $\zeta(t_0)$ is treated as the pre-determined variable, but $\pi(t_0)$ and $y(t_0)$ are treated as not-pre-determined 'jump variables'. Furthermore, in the 'New Keynesian' setting, it is supposed that only the initial conditions of the 'jump variables' that ensure the convergence to the equilibrium point $(\bar{\pi}, \bar{y})$ are 'chosen' by the economic agents. This requires a set of conditions

$$A_1 = A_2 = 0. \tag{E14}$$

Substituting Eq. (E14) into (E13), we can see that the following initial conditions of the 'jump variables' must be 'chosen' by the economic agents.

i $$\pi(t_0) = \frac{\varepsilon}{\varepsilon\sigma(\beta_1 - 1) + \kappa\{\kappa + \sigma(\varepsilon + \beta_2)\}}\zeta(t_0) + \bar{\pi}$$

ii $$y(t_0) = \frac{\kappa}{\varepsilon\sigma(\beta_1 - 1) + \kappa\{\kappa + \sigma(\varepsilon + \beta_2)\}}\zeta(t_0) + \bar{y} \tag{E15}$$

In this case, we have

$$\text{sign}\{\pi(t_0) - \bar{\pi}\} = \text{sign}\{y(t_0) - \bar{y}\} = \text{sign}\,\zeta(t_0) \tag{E16}$$

because of the assumption $\beta_1 > 1$, and Eq. (E12) becomes as follows.

i $$\pi(t) - \bar{\pi} = \frac{\varepsilon}{\varepsilon\sigma(\beta_1 - 1) + \kappa\{\kappa + \sigma(\varepsilon + \beta_2)\}}\zeta(t_0)e^{-\kappa(t-t_0)}$$

ii $$y(t) - \bar{y} = \frac{\kappa}{\varepsilon\sigma(\beta_1 - 1) + \kappa\{\kappa + \sigma(\varepsilon + \beta_2)\}}\zeta(t_0)e^{-\kappa(t-t_0)}$$

iii $$\zeta(t) = \zeta(t_0)e^{-\kappa(t-t_0)} \tag{E17}$$

Figure E1 illustrates the so-called 'impulse response functions' of the particular solution (E17) in the case of $\zeta(t_0) < 0$. In this case, the paradoxical behaviors of the main variables are concealed by means of the convenient 'jump variables' technique.

However, it is not clear why the economic agents can instantaneously 'choose' the special initial conditions that are expressed by Eq. (E15) in response to the sudden exogenous disturbance. What occurs if another set of initial conditions is 'mistakenly chosen' by the economic agents or initial conditions are pre-determined like the traditional model? Suppose, as a thought experiment, that the initial condition cannot 'jump' so that we have

$$\pi(t_0) = \bar{\pi}, \ y(t_0) = \bar{y} \tag{E18}$$

even if $\zeta(t_0) \neq 0$. Substituting (E18) into (E13), we have the following equation with respect to A_1 and A_2.

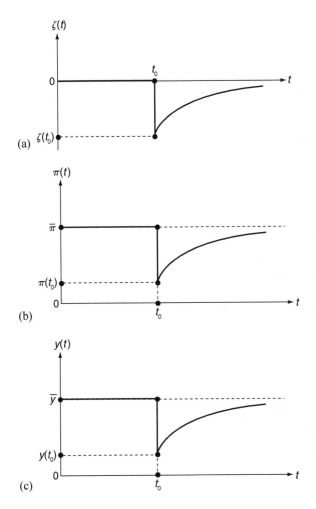

Figure E1 Impulse response functions of the special solution (E17) in case of $\zeta(t_0) < 0$.

$$\begin{bmatrix} 1 & 1 \\ -\lambda_1/\varepsilon & -\lambda_2/\varepsilon \end{bmatrix} \begin{bmatrix} A_1 \\ A_2 \end{bmatrix} = \begin{bmatrix} -\varepsilon\zeta(t_0)/[\varepsilon\sigma(\beta_1-1)+\kappa\{\kappa+\sigma(\varepsilon+\beta_2)\}] \\ -\kappa\zeta(t_0)/[\varepsilon\sigma(\beta_1-1)+\kappa\{\kappa+\sigma(\varepsilon+\beta_2)\}] \end{bmatrix}$$ (E19)

Solving this equation, we obtain the following expression.

i $A_1 = \dfrac{\varepsilon(\kappa+\lambda_2)}{(\lambda_1-\lambda_2)[\varepsilon\sigma(\beta_1-1)+\kappa\{\kappa+\sigma(\varepsilon+\beta_2)\}]}\zeta(t_0)$

ii $A_2 = \dfrac{-\varepsilon(\kappa+\lambda_1)}{(\lambda_1-\lambda_2)[\varepsilon\sigma(\beta_1-1)+\kappa\{\kappa+\sigma(\varepsilon+\beta_2)\}]}\zeta(t_0)$ (E20)

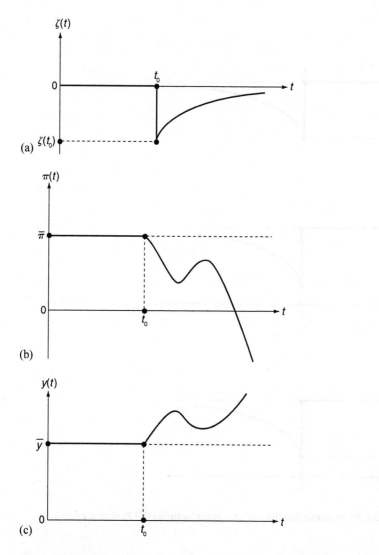

Figure E2 Impulse response functions of the solution (E12) in case of $\zeta(t_0)<0$, $\pi(t_0)=\bar{\pi}$, $y(t_0)=\bar{y}$.

Substituting (E20) and $C_3=\zeta(t_0)$ into Eq. (E12), we obtain the solution of this system in the case of (E18). It follows from the inequalities $\beta_1>1$ and $\lambda_1>\lambda_2>0$ that we have

$$\text{sign } A_1 = -\text{sign } A_2 = \text{sign } \zeta(t_0) \tag{E21}$$

in this case.

The process of the propagation of the exogenous disturbance in this case becomes as follows. We consider the case of $\zeta(t_0)<0$ for the purpose of illustration. It follows from Eq. (E4) that $\zeta(t_0)<0$ implies $\dot{y}(t_0)>0$ if the condition (E18) is satisfied. This will cause the *increase* of y and the *decrease* of π. Furthermore, we have $A_1<0$ and $A_2>0$. However, the effect of the first term in (E12) dominates the second term because λ_1 is the dominant root $(\lambda_1>\lambda_2>0)$. This means that the induced unstable dynamic process entails the continuous *decrease* of π and the continuous *increase* of y ultimately. In this case, the *deflationary prosperity* rather than the deflationary depression is caused by this disturbance. Figure E2 illustrates this unconvincing process.

Notes

1 For the empirical and theoretical analyses of the deflationary depression in Japan, see, for example, Asada (2006a, 2010, 2011), Broda and Weinstein (2004), Hamada (2004), Hamada and Okada (2009), Hosen (2009), Ito, Patrick and Weinstein (eds.) (2005), Iwata (2001), Iwata (ed.) (2004), Kataoka (2010), Krugman (1998), Kuttner and Posen (2001) and Noguchi (ed.) (2007).

2 Unlike B_N in Figure 6.1, which is measured by gross terms, B is measured by net terms. Needless to say, B is smaller than B_N. Theoretically, the net national debt is more appropriate than the gross national debt as a measure of the government's financial condition.

3 Hayashi and Prescott (2002) and Hayashi (2003) are the typical examples of the misleading mainstream preconception that the economic stagnation in such a long period of ten years must have nothing to do with the Keynesian 'effective demand'. But, the Great Depression in the 1930s and the deflationary depression in Japan in the 1990s and the 2000s reveal that the 'short run' disequilibrium situation in the traditional sense due to the shortage of the effective demand can last for such a long period of 10–20 years. Hayashi (2003) presented the data that the 'capital–output ratio' (K/Y) in Japan was relatively low and stable in the prosperous 1980s, but it continued to increase in the depression period of the 1990s, and asserted that this is the evidence that the cause of the 'lost ten years' in the 1990s in Japan is not the shortage of the effective demand but the deterioration of the rather ambiguously defined 'structure' of the Japanese economy. He writes that 'there may exist the model that entails the increase of the capital–output ratio under demand shortage, but I have not yet seen such a model' (Hayashi 2003, p. 5) This is a quite surprising description. In fact, it is usual that the capital–output ratio *increases* under demand shortage. In the simplest version of the conventional Keynesian (as well as neoclassical) model, the equilibrium condition of the goods market is $I=S=sY$, where I=real investment expenditure, S=real saving, and s=average propensity to save $(0<s<1)$. Then, we have the expression $g_K=I/K=s(Y/K)$, which is reduced to $K/Y=s/g_K$. This means that in the standard Keynesian system it is quite natural that the depression process that is accompanied by the *decrease* of the rate of investment (g_K) induces the *increase* of the capital–output ratio (K/Y) (reflecting the *decrease* of the rate of capacity utilization of the capital stock) contrary to Hayashi's (2003) assertion. Incidentally, we have Hayashi's (2003) formula $K/Y=s/n$ in case of the full employment long run equilibrium position, where n='natural' rate of growth=growth rate of labor supply+rate of technical progress. Although Hayashi (2003) derived this formula by using Solow's neoclassical growth model with neoclassical production function, we have just shown that we can derive this formula only from the simple effective demand condition $I=S=sY$ without referring to the neoclassical production function.

4　In the formulation in this chapter, the 'natural' rate of growth (the growth rate of population plus the rate of technical progress) is an endogenous variable that depends on the rate of (un)employment. This is the simplest procedure to introduce the variable natural rate of growth. However, Kaldor (1957) introduced in such an early period of the 1950s the 'technical progress function', which relates the rate of technical progress to the rate of capital accumulation (the investment expenditure of the firms), which makes the 'natural' rate of growth an endogenous variable that depends on the effective demand, because the investment expenditure is an important element of the effective demand. Needless to say, this 'Kaldorian' approach is more appropriate for the 'Keynesian' formulation of the endogenous growth theory. See Asada and Ouchi (2009) for the high-dimensional 'Keynesian model of endogenous growth cycle' that incorporates Kaldor (1957)'s idea of technical progress function.

5　This model, which explicitly considers the budget constraint of the consolidated government, including the central bank, belongs to a class of dynamic Keynesian models that are referred to as 'traditional macrodynamics' in Turnovsky (2000). Unlike Turnovsky's (2000) formulation, however, this model is not a 'short run' model in the sense of Keynes (1936) but a 'long run' dynamic model. That is to say, in this model the capital accumulation effect of investment, technical progress and population growth as well as the dynamics of money stock and public debt are explicitly incorporated.

6　As already noted in section 1, this does not represent the gross debt but it represents the *net* debt of the consolidated government to the private sector, net of government bonds held by governmental organizations and the central bank.

7　In this formulation, the international trade is abstracted from for simplicity, and it is supposed that $\dot{K}=I$, which implies that the capital depreciation and the capital accumulation effect of government expenditure are ignored. If a part of government expenditure contributes to capital accumulation, we must write $\dot{K}=I+\sigma G$; $0<\sigma<1$, but in this chapter we abstract from this kind of complication for simplicity of the analysis. Incidentally, we can interpret the output–capital ratio (y) as a surrogate variable of the rate of capital utilization (u), because we have the relationship $y=uy^f$; $0<u<1$, where y^f is the output–capital ratio in case of full capital utilization, which is assumed to be a positive constant in our model.

8　Money multiplier (m) is a decreasing function of the reserve ratio of the private bank (re) and the currency–deposit ratio of the public (cu), while re and cu are considered to be decreasing functions of r, which means that m becomes an increasing function of r (see Asada 2005).

9　From Eq. (1), we have $G=Y-C-I=Y-C-\dot{K}$. Substituting this relationship into Eq. (6), we obtain the relationship $\dot{K}+\dot{B}/p+\dot{H}/p=Y+rB/p-T-C\equiv S$, which is the flow consistency condition of the asset accumulation, where $S\equiv Y+rB/p-T-C$ is the real saving of the private sector.

10　In this formulation, we allow for the possibility that the 'natural rate of growth' (n) becomes an endogenous variable that has positive correlation with the rate of employment. That is to say, the decrease of the rate of employment may induce the decrease of the 'natural rate of growth' through the adverse effect on the labor supply and labor efficiency. This hypothesis is supported by the empirical analysis by Leon-Ledesma and Thirlwall (2007).

11　The original literature on the 'Taylor rule' is Taylor (1993). For the theoretical and empirical analyses of inflation targeting, see, for example, Asada (2006a, 2006b), Bernanke, Laubach, Mishkin and Posen (1999), Bernanke and Woodford (2005), Eggertsson and Woodford (2003), Ito and Hayashi (2006) and Krugman (1998), as well as the textbooks of the 'New Keynesian' dynamic theory, such as Galí (2008) and Woodford (2003).

12 It follows from Eq. (16) that $\{\bar{\pi}+n(\bar{e})\}\psi(\rho^*+\bar{\pi})=\{\bar{\pi}+n(\bar{e})\}H/(pY)$. On the other hand, we shall see later that at the equilibrium point we have $\bar{\pi}+n(\bar{e})=\dot{H}/H$ (see Eq. (30)). Therefore, we have $\{\bar{\pi}+n(\bar{e})\}\psi(\rho^*+\bar{\pi})=\dot{H}/(pY)$ at the equilibrium point.

13 See Gandolfo (2009, chap. 16).

14 It is worth noting that **Assumptions 1–4** do not play any role in the proof of **Proposition 1**, but they play some roles in the proof of **Proposition 2**.

15 For the Hopf bifurcation theorem, see Gandolfo (2009, chap. 24) and the mathematical appendices of Asada *et al.* (2003, 2010).

16 Totally differentiating the equation $F_2(g, b)=0$ with respect to g and b, we have
$$(db/dg)\big|_{F_2=0} = -(F_{21}/F_{22})<0$$
$$\quad\quad\quad\quad\quad\; (+) \;\; (+)$$
in case of instability.

17 See Woodford (2003), Galí (2008), Romer (2006), Asada *et al.* (2007), Flaschel *et al.* (2008) and Asada *et al.* (2010). This is the simplest version in the sense that the government expenditure, the budget constraint of the consolidated government and money do not play any explicit role, unlike the model of the previous sections in this chapter.

18 This implies that the aggregate demand becomes a decreasing function of the expected real rate of interest even if the firms' investment expenditure is ignored in this model.

19 We do not consider the nonnegative constraint of the nominal rate of interest here.

20 Usually, this procedure is rationalized because of the reason that the 'rational' agent with rational expectation will choose the true 'optimal' path that satisfies the 'transversality conditions' which ensure the convergence to the equilibrium point.

21 **Appendix D** of this chapter provides the detailed exposition of the 'jump variables' technique and the related concepts of stability, instability, determinacy and indeterminacy.

22 **Appendix E** provides an analysis of the motion that is caused by the exogenous disturbances in the 'New Keynesian' setting.

23 See Akerlof and Shiller (2009) for some related topics on the macroeconomic consequence of the 'bounded rational' behaviors which are driven by the human psychology that is called 'animal spirits'.

24 We should use the equation such as $x_{t+1}=Ax_t+b$ if we adopt the formulation by means of a system of difference equations.

25 Needless to say, we must modify this definition if we adopt a system of difference equations rather than differential equations.

26 The concepts of 'stability', 'instability', 'determinacy' and 'indeterminacy' are global concepts if the system is linear like Eq. (D1). However, these concepts become local concepts at the vicinity of the equilibrium point if the system is nonlinear.

References

Akerlof, G. A. and R. J. Shiller (2009) *Animal Spirits: How Human Psychology Drives the Economy, and Why It Matters for Global Capitalism*, Princeton: Princeton University Press.

Asada, T. (2005) *Makuro Keizaigaku Kiso Kougi (Introductory Lectures on Macroeconomics)*, Tokyo: Chuo Keizai-sha (in Japanese).

Asada, T. (2006a) 'Inflation targeting policy in a dynamic Keynesian model with debt accumulation: A Japanese perspective', in C. Chiarella, R. Franke, P. Flaschel and W. Semmler (eds.) *Quantitative and Empirical Analysis of Nonlinear Dynamic Macromodels*, Amsterdam: Elsevier, pp. 517–544.

Asada, T. (2006b) 'Stabilization policy in a Keynes-Goodwin model with debt accumulation', *Structural Change and Economic Dynamics*, 17: 466–485.

Asada, T. (2010) 'Central banking and deflationary depression: A Japanese perspective', in M. Cappelo and C. Rizzo (eds.) *Central Banking and Globalization*, New York: Nova Science Publishers, pp. 91–114.

Asada, T. (2011) 'Kokusai ruiseki to zaisei kinyu seisaku no makuro dogaku: Futekisetsu na porisii mikkusu ni tsuite' (National debt accumulation and macrodynamics of fiscal and monetary policies: On inappropriate policy mix), in K. Watanabe (ed.) *Kinyu to Shotoku Bunpai (Finance and Income Distribution)*, Tokyo: Nihon Keizai Hyoron-sha, pp. 3–30 (in Japanese).

Asada, T. and M. Ouchi (2009) 'A Keynesian model of endogenous growth cycle', in R. O. Bailly (ed.) *Emerging Topics in Macroeconomics*, New York: Nova Science Publishers, pp. 219–249.

Asada, T., C. Chiarella, P. Flaschel and R. Franke (2003) *Open Economy Macrodynamics*, Berlin: Springer.

Asada, T., C. Chiarella, P. Flaschel and C. R. Proaño (2007) 'Keynesian AD-AS, quo vadis?' University of Technology Sydney, Discussion Paper (reprinted in Flaschel 2009).

Asada, T., C. Chiarella, P. Flaschel and R. Franke (2010) *Monetary Macrodynamics*. London: Routledge.

Asada, T., P. Flaschel, T. Mouakil and C. Proaño (2011) *Asset Markets, Portfolio Choice and Macroeconomic Activity: A Keynesian Perspective*, Basingstoke, UK: Palgrave Macmillan.

Barro, R. and X. Sala-i-Martin (2004) *Economic Growth* (Second Edition), Cambridge, Massachusetts: MIT Press.

Bernanke, B. and M. Woodford (eds.) (2005) *The Inflation-Targeting Debate*, Chicago: The University of Chicago Press.

Bernanke, B., T. Laubach, F. Mishkin and A. Posen (1999) *Inflation Targeting: Lessons from the International Experience*, Princeton: Princeton University Press.

Blanchard, O. and C. Kahn (1980) 'The solution of linear difference equations under rational expectations', *Econometrica*, 48: 1305–1311.

Broda, C. and D. Weinstein (2004) 'Happy news from the dismal science: Reassessing Japanese fiscal policy and sustainability', NBER Working Paper 10988 (reprinted in Ito *et al.* eds. 2005).

Domar, E. (1957) *Essays in the Theory of Economic Growth*, Oxford: Oxford University Press.

Dockner, E., S. Jørgensen, N. Van Long and G. Sorger (2000) *Differential Games in Economics and Management Science*. Cambridge: Cambridge University Press.

Eggertsson, G. S. and M. Woodford (2003) 'The zero bound on interest rates and optimal monetary policy', *Brookings Papers on Economic Activity*, 1: 139–233.

Flaschel, P. (2009) *The Macrodynamics of Capitalism: A Synthesis of Marx, Keynes and Schumpeter*, Berlin: Springer.

Flaschel, P. and E. Schlicit (2006) 'New Keynesian theory and the new Phillips curves: A competing approach', in C. Chiarella, R. Franke, P. Flaschel and W. Semmler (eds.) *Quantitative and Empirical Analysis of Nonlinear Dynamic Macromodels*, Amsterdam: Elsevier, pp. 113–145).

Flaschel, P., R. Franke and C. R. Proaño (2008) 'On equilibrium determinacy in New Keynesian models with staggered wage and price setting', *B. E. Journal of Macroeconomics*, 8: Article 31 (10 pages).

Franke, R. (2007) 'A sophisticatedly simple alternative to the New Keynesian Phillips curve', in T. Asada and T. Ishikawa (eds.) *Time and Space in Economics*, Tokyo: Springer, pp. 3–28.

Fuhler, C. (1997) 'The (un)importance of forward-looking behavior in price specifications', *Journal of Money, Credit, and Banking*, 29: 338–350.

Galí, J. (2008) *Monetary Policy, Inflation, and Business Cycle: An Introduction to the New Keynesian Framework*, Princeton: Princeton University Press.

Gandolfo, G. (2009) *Economic Dynamics* (Fourth Edition), Berlin: Springer.

Hamada, K. (2004) 'Policy making in deflationary depression', *Japanese Economic Review*, 55: 221–239.

Hamada, K. and Y. Okada (2009) 'Monetary and international factors behind Japan's lost decade', *Journal of the Japanese and International Economics*, 23: 200–219.

Hayashi, F. (2003) 'Kozo kaikaku nakushite seicho nashi' (No structural reform, no growth), in K. Iwata and T. Miyagawa (eds.) *Ushinawareta 10 nen no Shin'in wa Nanika (What is the True Cause of the Lost Decade?)*, Tokyo: Toyo Keizai Shinposha, pp. 1–16 (in Japanese).

Hayashi, F. and E. Prescott (2002) 'The 1990s in Japan: A lost decade', *Review of Economic Dynamics*, 5: 206–235.

Hosen, M. (2009) *Defure to Infure no Keizaigaku (Economics of Deflation and Inflation)*, Tokyo: Nihon Hyoron-sha (in Japanese).

Ito, T. and T. Hayashi (2006) *Infure Mokuhyo to Kinyu Seisaku (Inflation Targeting and Monetary Policy)*, Tokyo: Toyo Keizai Shinpo-sha (in Japanese).

Ito, T., H. T. Patrick and D. E. Weinstein (eds.) (2005) *Reviving Japan's Economy: Problems and Prescriptions*, Cambridge, Massachusetts: MIT Press.

Iwata, K. (2001) *Defure no Keizaigaku (Economics of Deflation)*, Tokyo: Toyo Keizai Shinpo-sha (in Japanese).

Iwata, K. (ed.) (2004) *Showa Kyoko no Kenkyu (Studies of the Showa Crisis)*, Tokyo: Toyo Keizai Shinpo-sha (in Japanese).

Kaldor, N. (1957) 'A model of economic growth', *Economic Journal*, 67: 591–624.

Kataoka, G. (2010) *Nihon no Ushinawareta 20 Nen: Defure wo Koeru Keizai Seisaku ni Mukete (Lost Twenty Years in Japan: Toward the Economic Policy against Deflation)*, Tokyo: Fujiwara Shoten (in Japanese).

Keynes, J. M. (1936) *The General Theory of Employment, Interest and Money*, London: Macmillan.

Kirman, A. P. (1992) 'Whom or what does the representative individual represent?', *Journal of Economic Perspectives*, 6–2: 117–136.

Krugman, P. (1998) 'It's baaack: Japan's slump and return of the liquidity trap', *Brookings Papers on Economic Activity*, 2: 11–114.

Kuttner, K. N. and A. Posen (2001) 'The great recession: Lessons for macroeconomic policy from Japan', *Brookings Papers on Economic Activity*, 2: 93–185.

Leon-Ledesma, M. and A. P. Thirlwall (2007) 'Is the natural exogenous?' in P. Arestis, M. Badderly and S. L. McCombie (eds.) *Economic Growth: New Directions in Theory and Policy*, Cheltenham, UK: Edward Elgar, pp. 32–43.

Mankiw, G. (2001) 'The inexorable and mysterious tradeoff between inflation and unemployment', *Economic Journal*, 111: C45–C61.

Mitsuhashi, N., S. Uchida and Y. Ikeda (2010) *Zeminaru Nihon Keizai Nyumon (Introductory Seminar on Japanese Economy)*, Tokyo: Nihon Keizai Shinbun Publisher (in Japanese).

Miwa, R. and A. Hara (2010) *Kingendai Nihon Keizaishi Yoran, Zoteiban (Handbook of Modern Japanese Economic History, Revised Edition)*, Tokyo: University of Tokyo Press (in Japanese).

Noguchi, A. (ed.) (2007) *Keizai Seisaku Keisei no Kenkyu: Kitoku Kannen to Keizaigaku no Sokoku (Studies in Economic Policy Making: Preconceived Ideas versus Economics)*, Kyoto: Nakanishiya Publisher (in Japanese).

Romer, D. (2006) *Advanced Macroeconomics* (Third Edition), New York: McGraw-Hill.

Takahashi, Y. (2010) *Nihon Keizai no Uso (Fallacy on Japanese Economy)*, Tokyo: Chikuma Shobo (in Japanese).

Taylor, J. B. (1993) 'Discretion versus policy rules in practice', *Carnegie-Rochester Conference Series on Public Policy*, 39: 195–214.

Tobin, J. (1994) 'Price flexibility and output stability: An old Keynesian view', in W. Semmler (ed.) *Business Cycles: Theory and Empirical Methods*, Boston: Kluwer Academic Publishers, pp. 165–195.

Turnovsky, S. (2000) *Methods of Macroeconomic Dynamics* (Second Edition), Cambridge, Massachusetts: MIT Press.

Woodford, M. (2003) *Interest and Prices: Foundations of a Theory of Monetary Policy*, Princeton: Princeton University Press.

Index

Page numbers in *italics* denote tables, those in **bold** denote figures.

For Product Safety Concerns and Information please contact our
EU representative GPSR@taylorandfrancis.com Taylor & Francis
Verlag GmbH, Kaufingerstraße 24, 80331 München, Germany